W9-AMZ-860

The comic and satiric literature of the period from the 1670s to
is characterized by the allusive and elusive word play of Aug
The arguments of Augustan wit reveal preoccupations
metaphorical dimension of language so distrusted by Locke and
saw it as fundamentally opposed to the rational mode of judg
Sitter makes a challenging claim for the importance of wit in t
of Dryden, Rochester, Prior, Berkeley, Gay, Pope, and S
analytic mode as well as one of stylistic sophistication. He arg
– often regarded by modern critics as a quaint category
cleverness – in fact offers to current literary theory a legacy
Romantic and neo-Romantic idealizations of imagination.

This study works at once to emphasize the historical s
Augustan writing and to bring its arguments into dialogue wit
time. Shared preoccupations of the two eras include the com
of the quests for "universal" truths and the pursuit of cultu
and regional) particularity. By urging a reconsideration o
modern criticism has given to post-Augustan values and assi
book offers a new map of deceptively familiar territory,
eighteenth century and in our own.

Arguments of Augustan wit

CAMBRIDGE STUDIES IN EIGHTEENTH-CENTURY
ENGLISH LITERATURE AND THOUGHT

General Editors: Dr HOWARD ERSKINE-HILL, Litt.D., FBA, *Pembroke College, Cambridge*
and Professor JOHN RICHETTI, *University of Pennsylvania*

Editorial Board: Morris Brownell, *University of Nevada*
Leopold Damrosch, *Harvard University*
J. Paul Hunter, *University of Chicago*
Isobel Grundy, *University of Alberta*
Lawrence Lipking, *Northwestern University*
Harold Love, *Monash University*
Claude Rawson, *Yale University*
Pat Rogers, *University of South Florida*
James Sambrook, *University of Southampton*

Arguments of Augustan wit

JOHN SITTER
Professor of English, Emory University

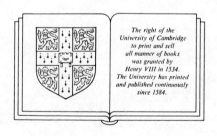

The right of the
University of Cambridge
to print and sell
all manner of books
was granted by
Henry VIII in 1534.
The University has printed
and published continuously
since 1584.

CAMBRIDGE UNIVERSITY PRESS

CAMBRIDGE   NEW YORK   PORT CHESTER

MELBOURNE   SYDNEY

Published by the Press Syndicate of the University of Cambridge
The Pitt Building, Trumpington Street, Cambridge CB2 1RP
40 West 20th Street, New York, NY 10011–4211, USA
10 Stamford Road, Oakleigh, Melbourne 3166, Australia

First published 1991

Printed in Great Britain at the University Press, Cambridge

British Library cataloguing in publication data
Sitter, John, 1944–
  Arguments of Augustan wit.
  1. English literature. History, 1702–1745
  I. Title II. (Cambridge studies in eighteenth-century
  English literature and thought. 11)
  820.9005

Library of Congress cataloguing in publication data
Sitter, John E.
  Arguments of Augustan wit/John Sitter.
     p.   cm. – (Cambridge studies in eighteenth-century English
  literature and thought)
  Includes bibliographical references and index.
  ISBN 0-521-41120-3 (hardcover)
  1. English wit and humour–History and criticism. 2. English
  literature–18th century–History and criticism. 3. English
  literature–Early modern. 1500–1700–History and criticism.
  4. English literature–Roman influences. I. Title. II. Series.
  PR935.S58 1991
  827'.409–dc20 90–28116 CIP

ISBN 0 521 41120 3 hardback

To Deborah, Zak, Amelia, and Ben, for encouraging,
enabling, enduring

Contents

Acknowledgments

It is a pleasure to thank several institutions and individuals for the intellectual and material support that has made this book possible.

I am grateful to the former Dean of Emory College, David Minter, to the Emory University Research Council, and to Walter Reed, chair of the English Department, for sabbatical leaves that enabled me to begin and conclude. An invitation near the outset to speak at Princeton University helped begin the long progress of chapter 1. The opportunity to deliver the Thomas Copeland Lecture at the University of Massachusetts at Amherst gave more order to chapter 5 than it might otherwise have. In colloquia and seminars, colleagues and students at Emory have listened and responded to much of what is here and (to the reader's benefit) much that is not. To them and to the members of two Summer Seminars for School Teachers on Swift and Twain, sponsored by the National Endowment for the Humanities, I am very grateful for both patience and provocation.

My greatest individual debt is to David B. Morris, who not only read and carefully corrected the entire manuscript but endured some of it in very rough draft; without his encouragement and direction, this work would have taken longer and fallen even shorter. Walter Reed and Jerome Beaty read parts of the manuscript and made helpful suggestions. Since this is a book that emphasizes the materialism of Augustan writing, it is particularly appropriate to thank Lee Ann Lloyd, without whose skillful word processing of several drafts none of these helpful readings could have occurred.

I owe less directly relevant but significant intellectual debts to the members of Emory's Luce Faculty Seminar and its humane director, James M. Gustafson, and to my friend and colleague Ulric Neisser. From Professor Neisser I have learned such cognitive psychology as I know. By introducing me to the work of James J. Gibson he led me unexpectedly to a more careful reading of Bishop Berkeley; but that is only the most identifiable of his encouragements.

A portion of chapter 2 appeared in earlier form in *Rhetorics of Order/Ordering Rhetorics in English Neoclassical Literature*, edited by J. Douglas Canfield and J. Paul Hunter; I am grateful to the University of Delaware Press for permission to use this material.

Abbreviations

References to frequently cited editions use the following shortened forms:

Characteristics   Anthony, Earl of Shaftesbury, *Characteristics of Men, Manners, Opinions, Times*, ed. John M. Robertson, 2 vols. in one (Indianapolis: Bobbs-Merrill, 1964)

Gay   *John Gay: Poetry and Prose*, ed. Vinton A. Dearing and Charles Beckwith, 2 vols. (Oxford: Clarendon Press, 1974)

Poems   *Jonathan Swift: The Complete Poems*, ed. Pat Rogers (New Haven: Yale University Press, 1983)

Prior   *The Literary Works of Matthew Prior*, ed. H. Bunker Wright and Monroe K. Spears, 2nd edn., 2 vols. (Oxford: Clarendon Press, 1971)

PW   *The Prose Writings of Jonathan Swift*, ed. Herbert Davis *et al.*, 16 vols. (Oxford: Basil Blackwell, 1939–68)

Tale   *A Tale of a Tub &c*, ed. A.C. Guthkelch and D. Nicol Smith, 2nd edn. (Oxford: Clarendon Press, 1958; corr. repr. 1973) (for citations from *A Tale of a Tub*, *The Battel of the Books*, and *The Mechanical Operation of the Spirit*)

TE   *The Twickenham Edition of the Poems of Alexander Pope*, ed. John Butt *et al.*, 11 vols. (London: Methuen; New Haven: Yale University Press, 1939–69)

Introduction

This book attempts to make collective sense of some of the major English texts of the late seventeenth and early eighteenth century, the period I have commuted to most regularly over the past two decades. Thinking about this special part of my literary education in and out of the classroom has often brought to mind two of the reasons Henry Adams gives for resigning his professorship at Harvard, reasons which may sound familiar to teachers in many other fields. Adams believed he lacked an adequate theory of his subject, and he felt that he was educating himself at the expense of his students.[1] To the extent that the second feeling of uneasiness is independent of the first, one is likely to learn to live with it, perhaps even finding in it a productive humility and tension. Failures of knowledge or tact can be corrected, after all, day by day; and besides, "learning together" can be justified as Socratic pedagogy or simply accepted as a fact of academic life. But if one's classroom incoherencies begin to seem coherent – the result, in other words, of conceptual problems in the field as well as local shortages of information – then one may become desperate enough to write a book.

This book is not, however, what for a time I naively imagined, a "theory of Augustan literature." As the work progressed it became clearer that I did not have much to say about the drama and the novel that has not been said by others and that, even apart from these large limitations, my discussion of texts and authors would be too selective to support a "unified field theory" of the period. For the omission of the drama I can only apologize; the omission of the novel (aside from Fielding and some general remarks in the first chapter) can be explained at least partly in more deliberate terms. Whether or not one still believes that the novel "rose" in the eighteenth century, the early

---

[1] *The Education of Henry Adams*, ed. Ernest Samuels (Boston: Houghton Mifflin, 1973), ch. 20, esp. pp. 300–01, 306.

novel has clearly risen in recent criticism. The reasons for its elevation include our greater interest generally in narrative forms and theory, canon reformation, rethinking the traditional boundaries between "high" and "low" culture, and historical issues of class and gender. All these developments seem to me to be genuinely progressive. Any progress, however, raises the possibility that some things of value may be left behind. There is some risk of the novel's recent promotion from poor relation to privileged landowner leading to a view in which other forms of writing are devalued as regressive or valued chiefly as evolutionary anticipations. This teleological bias, which I return to at the end of the first chapter, is a strong force in modern culture; it operates not only in eighteenth-century studies but within the work of a theorist as voraciously encyclopedic as Mikhail Bakhtin. It has seemed important, therefore, to lean the other way by emphasizing non-novelistic works and by considering them as alternatives rather than tributaries to the novel.

By focusing on authors who come to mind readily when we think of "wit" – such as Dryden, Rochester, Swift, Pope, Prior and Gay – rather than those associated with spiritual autobiography and individualism – such as Bunyan, Defoe, and Richardson – I do not mean to revive the quarrel of Ancients and Moderns or to resurrect the opposition of "high" and "low" cultural forms by claiming that poetry and intellectual prose are inherently more rigorous than novels. What I try to describe instead is how a number of texts usually regarded as "traditional" rather than "progressive" within the canon seem to me more contemporary – that is, capable of radically challenging our thought – than most accounts have recognized. "Wit" and "satire," for example, are often felt to be somewhat quaint categories, but it is possible that they may take us further toward genuine demystifications and deconstructions of authority than overly congenial neo-Romantic categories such as transcendent "imagination" or disembodied "textuality." In trying to put Augustan literature and late twentieth-century criticism into fuller dialogue, therefore, I have been less conscious of applying current "methods" to older texts than of bringing Augustan works to bear on contemporary literary theory. I do not imagine that I have done so purely (no contemporary critic has unfiltered access to an Augustan text "itself"), but the point of trying to let the traffic run in both directions is to find how our own thinking about literature needs to be refined, enlarged, more deeply historicized.

One of the hallmarks of modern Augustan studies is the requirement to defend or attack the use of "Augustan." My defense is simply pragmatic. I have chosen it not because I disagree with thoughtful scholars of the period who argue that the term is politically misleading but because I could not think of a better one.[2] Had the older writers discussed in this book been obliging enough to postpone their careers until 1700, as the later ones were sufficiently thoughtful to end theirs in the 1740s, "early eighteenth-century" might have replaced "Augustan." But "late seventeenth-century and early eighteenth-century" is not a modifier that bears much repetition.

The inadequacies of the "Age of Reason" (even if it could be readily converted to adjectival currency) and of "Enlightenment" have long been obvious; the first is condescending and inaccurate, the second essentially French and deistic. "Neoclassical" has been proposed, however, as a more accurate term, and it does have the advantage of not suggesting that English writers from the Restoration to the middle of the eighteenth century idealized Augustan Rome. This advantage does not seem, finally, to outweigh its disadvantages. These include the lingering suggestions (despite informed work to the contrary) of fastidiousness regarding "rules," slavishness about "unities" and decorum, obsession with Roman precedent. More broadly, unless "neoclassical" is applied to three centuries instead of one, or unless its "classical" half is arbitrarily limited in meaning, the term creates the illusion that Renaissance and nineteenth-century writers were less conscious of Greek and Roman literature than writers of the Restoration and eighteenth century.

So I find myself stuck with "Augustan," while not trying to reinterpret the relation of late seventeenth- and early eighteenth-century writers to the Rome of Augustus Caesar or their use of political analogies. None of this would matter beyond the level of stylistic annoyance if this book did not argue for a "logic" of the period: that is, both for the sensibleness of viewing the late seventeenth and early eighteenth century as a period and for the existence within it of collective ways of making sense through writing. "Arguments of wit"

---

[2] The fullest argument against using "Augustan" as a label for the period has been made by Howard Weinbrot in *Augustus Caesar in "Augustan" England* (Princeton: Princeton University Press, 1978). Howard Erskine-Hill's *The Augustan Idea in English Literature* (London: Edward Arnold, 1983) is an extended argument for the term's historical usefulness. Erskine-Hill also provides a useful summary and bibliography of the arguments (pp. 235–36n). My own usage is more one of convenience, however, since allusions to Augustus and self-conscious historical parallels are not under discussion here.

is intended in a similarly double sense, to point to some of the period's arguments *about* wit and those made *through* it.

Arguments about wit in the late seventeenth and early eighteenth century are more numerous and varied than my discussion suggests. I concentrate on Locke's objections to it because they are the most representative, influential, and central. Locke's opposition of wit to "judgment" is not only a sign of the tension between philosophic and literary claims on truth but also, I think, a sign of strain at the center of Locke's own epistemology. My reading of Locke in the second chapter, therefore, ranges beyond his often quoted passage on wit as the facile assemblage and judgment as the scrupulous distinction of ideas to many other parts of *An Essay concerning Human Understanding*. Although, or perhaps because, I am not a professional philosopher, I believe this reading is new; I hope it is true. To some readers this account of Locke will probably seem overly hostile, but I want to suggest that Locke's opposition of wit and judgment and the period's concern with the topic should be taken seriously and not regarded as a curiosity in the museum of dead ideas. To call attention to the continuing attraction of dichotomies between the perception of similarities and differences I draw an analogy between Locke's opposition and the influential modern dichotomy of metaphor and metonymy.

At stake in the arguments over wit are competing versions of truth. Roughly speaking, I believe that the distrust of wit is symptomatic of a desire to extricate true judgment – or Locke's knowledge of "things as they are" – from the materiality of language. In contrast, the arguments *of* wit embrace language as the means rather than barrier to truth. Many of the writers, of course, join Locke in attacking "abuses" of language; affectation, self-importance, pedantry, and even violent cruelty are all often portrayed in Augustan works as fundamentally linguistic vices. The difference is between seeing language as something to be transcended, as Locke longs for a philosophic "algebra," or regarding it as a material gift to be improved by use. If characters in Augustan satires who use language badly are ridiculed, the most ridiculous of all are those who seek a refuge from it altogether, whether in the pure mathematics of Laputa, in the doomed flight "beyond material sense" of Rochester's reasoner, in the rejection of words in Lagado, or on the transcendent lap of Dulness.

As these examples suggest, to accept the play of language is to accept the body as normative, and sections of the first, third, and fourth chapters concern images of the body as correctives to "abstraction" in Augustan writing. But the acceptance of language is also an acceptance of human historicity. One of the troubling impurities of wit for Locke is its dependence on allusion. In the final chapters I argue that allusion is exploited by Augustan authors in the recognition that they enter language not as Adam did but as latecomers to an ongoing conversation. Not only their contemporary opponents but also many of our contemporary critics seem to long for a language of imagination and "universal" truth beyond historical implication. In this respect, the Augustan writers have less in common with Locke than with Berkeley, who saw *general* ideas as useful and *abstract* ideas as delusions. That the great critic of Locke who called his own doctrine "immaterialism" should be enlisted to help in understanding the materialism and historical particularity of Augustan literature is an irony I did not anticipate in setting out, but one which might not have surprised some of his admirers, including Pope, Gay, Prior, and Swift.

Finally, it is only fair to warn the reader who may have picked this volume up by its title that this is not a witty book; I hope it is not entirely witless.

1

The character progress as an Augustan phenomenon

In spite of substantial and at some levels decisive continuities in grammar and vocabulary, no generation speaks quite the same language as its predecessors …What really changes is something quite general, over a wide range, and the description that often fits the change best is the literary term "style"…For what we are defining is a particular quality of social experience and relationship, historically distinct from other particular qualities, which gives the sense of a generation or of a period.

Raymond Williams, on "structures of feeling"[1]

If a significant structure of feeling connects English Augustan authors, the best evidence of it should perhaps rest less in shared thematic preoccupations than in common stylistic and formal expressions of a mode of perception and analysis. Looking for a period style, in other words, an observer may hope to fasten on features not primarily decorative and to find a style of experiential construction as well as reconstruction, a style of knowing as well as a manner of speaking. One way of beginning is to study a mode of presenting character that seems peculiar to the period from roughly the 1670s to the 1740s, a kind of character sketch I will call the character progress. The most immediately memorable examples are Hogarth's *Harlot's Progress* and *Rake's Progress* and the brilliant series *Marriage à la Mode*. Literary counterparts to (and possible influences on) these visual progresses are brief narratives, generally in poetic satire where they range from about twenty to over a hundred lines, that portray a character by giving his or her ill-fated career, a career that may run from birth or early adulthood to death, disaster, or an ironic success.

These sketches differ from the "characters" of Theophrastus and those popular throughout the seventeenth century in being linear and

---

[1] For Williams's discussion of "structures of feeling" see *Marxism and Literature* (Oxford: Oxford University Press, 1977), 128–35; the quoted passage is on p. 131.

6

dynamic. In the character progress, sequence is essential to the story; and the character progress differs from the static character in being a story, in having a plot rather than a list of ingredients.[2] The character progress is usually Hogarthian – to use a kind of shorthand – in giving a sequence of scenes or stages, visualized and emblematic in their temporal order. In the earlier characters of Overbury or Hall or Butler, on the other hand, sequence is rarely significant. The organization is often rhetorically climactic but atemporal and basically paratactic. An "Amorist," for example, sighs, cries, writes verses, dotes, daydreams, and so on – all at once. Even when such sketches occasionally end with the character's death, that event serves more as a punch line than as the end of a narrative line. Thus John Earle's Attorney dies unafraid of the Last Judgment because, like a good lawyer, he assumes he can always appeal.[3]

The character progress does not supplant these relatively static portraits in the late seventeenth and early eighteenth centuries; many of the best character sketches (such as Dryden's Coram or Pope's Atticus and Sporus) are intensifications of the older models. But the *progress* of character becomes a new comic possibility, able to exist side by side with paratactic portraits. We can see the two modes juxtaposed in the section of the *Epistle to Bathurst* where Pope first portrays the miser Cotta atemporally (lines 179–98) and then changes manner to portray Cotta's son through narrative stages (lines 199–218). These two sketches are exactly the same length, equally brilliant, but fundamentally different. The elder Cotta is characterized through the cumulative description of his house – an absurdly inhospitable "char-treux" where the "gaunt mastiff growling at the gate, / Affrights the beggar whom he longs to eat" – and a single flash of indirect discourse: "To cram the Rich was prodigal expence, / And who would take the Poor from Providence?" The heir, however, marches through a career of prodigality and mindless "patriotism":

> What slaughter'd hecatombs, what floods of wine,
> Fill the capacious Squire, and deep Divine!
> Yet no mean motive this profession draws,

[2] In his authoritative work, *The Character-Sketches in Pope's Poems* (Durham: Duke University Press, 1962) Benjamin Boyce does not differentiate dynamic from static sketches. He would categorize what I take to be Pope's major character progress, that of Sir Balaam in the *Epistle to Bathurst*, as a "tale ... rather than a character-sketch" (p. 98).

[3] John Earle's collection of characters, *Microcosmographie*, first appeared in 1628. The standard study of the character sketch in the English Renaissance is Benjamin Boyce's *The Theophrastan Character in England to 1642* (Cambridge, MA: Harvard University Press, 1947); a more recent – and longer and broader – survey is provided by J.W. Smeed, *The Theophrastan "Character": The History of a Literary Genre* (Oxford: Clarendon Press, 1985).

His oxen perish in his country's cause;
Tis GEORGE and LIBERTY that crowns the cup,
And Zeal for that great House which eats him up.
The woods recede around the naked seat,
The Sylvans groan – no matter – for the Fleet:
Next goes his Wool – to clothe our valiant bands,
Last, for his Country's love, he sells his Lands.
To town he comes, completes the nation's hope,
And heads the bold Train-bands and Spurns a Pope.
And shall not Britain now reward his toils,
Britain, that pays her Patriots with her Spoils?
In vain at Court the Bankrupt pleads his cause,
His thankless Country leaves him to her Laws.

                                    (*Epistle to Bathurst*, lines 203–18)

I will discuss these lines in connection with other character progresses by Pope later in this chapter, but for now the passage may illustrate the difference between a pattern of reinforcing emblematic details (as in the father's portrait) and a linear sequence of *stages*, marked here by the son's successive spending of his oxen, timber, wool, lands, and remaining capital.

It seems worthwhile to differentiate the character progress from the static sketch in studying Augustan literature because It Is There – and apparently not somewhere else. Exclusive claims are always hazardous, but the character progress does seem to be a genuine period phenomenon, emerging into sight in the Restoration and fading at the middle of the eighteenth century. While the character progress remains a relatively minor mode in itself, tracing the career of its careers may help us understand the historical specificity of Augustan literature. The progress becomes merely one of many modes of characterization in Augustan literature, but it includes some of the period's most "characteristic" perceptions of character.

A spectrum of examples

Since the character progress is not a conventional category, and thus not one for which all the pertinent works or parts of works will be in the disinterested memory, a survey of some examples may suggest both the variety of possible analyses and their common structural perception. These range from such generalized progresses as that of modern philosophical man in Rochester's *Satyr against Reason and Mankind* or the representative Grand Tourist of the final *Dunciad* to more particularized individuals like Dryden's Shimei in *Absalom and Achitophel*, or Shaftesbury "himself" in *The Medall*, to Pope's apparently idiosyncratic Atossa in the *Epistle to a Lady*.

Sometimes we encounter a dual or parallel progress, as in *Marriage à la Mode* or Prior's "Epitaph" for "Saunt'ring Jack and Idle Joan," an inoffensive couple who for sixty-one years found, like Pope's Cloe, "Virtue too painful an endeavour, / Content to dwell in Decencies forever." Of them Prior concludes,

> Nor Good, nor Bad, nor Fools, nor Wise;
> They wou'd not learn, nor cou'd advise:
> Without Love, Hatred, Joy, or Fear,
> They led – a kind of – as it were:
> Nor Wish'd, nor Car'd, nor Laugh'd, nor Cry'd:
> And so They liv'd; and so They dy'd.
>
> ("An Epitaph," Prior, i. 461–62)

In addition to poems already mentioned and to Swift's *Phyllis, or the Progress of Love* and *The Progress of Marriage* (to which I will turn in a moment), other character progresses include Rochester's sketch of Corinna in *Artemisia to Chloe*, Gay's "Eclogue, The Birth of the Squire," and, from elsewhere in Pope, Wharton in the *Epistle to Cobham*, Villiers, Cutler, and Balaam in the *Epistle to Bathurst*. To these may be added some exemplary prose narratives, such as some chapters of *The Memoirs of Martinus Scriblerus*, the stories of Mr. Wilson in *Joseph Andrews* and the Man of the Hill in *Tom Jones*, and much of *Jonathan Wild* – although the longer the story the more complex the perspective. I will also try to suggest how *Gulliver's Travels*, if not simply a character progress, is understood more fully in this company.

The character progress is the reduction of identity to career. Of Dryden's Shimei or, more explicitly, of Shaftesbury in *The Medall*, the sequential career appears to be all there is to know. In both cases, and in both senses, the career *becomes* the man. Before allowing Shaftesbury to speak Dryden gives us a close approximation to the modern curriculum vitae:

> A Martial Heroe first, with early care,
> Blown, like a Pigmee by the Winds, to war.
> A beardless Chief, a Rebel, e'r a Man:
> (So young his hatred to his Prince began.)
> Next this, (How wildly will Ambition steer!)
> A Vermin, wriggling in th'Usurper's Ear.
> Bart'ring his venal wit for sums of gold

He cast himself into the Saint-like mould;
Groan'd, sigh'd and pray'd, while Godliness was gain;
The lowdest Bagpipe of the squeaking Train. . .
Pow'r was his aym: but, Thrown from that pretence,
The Wretch turn'd loyal in his own defence;
And Malice reconcil'd him to his Prince.[4]

A considerably more generalized "vita" sums up Rochester's modern reasoner. The full title of *A Satyr against Reason and Mankind* is important because it suggests Rochester's concentration on humanity in a particular aspect, through the progress of "that vain animal / Who is so proud of being rational." Such a man begins his doomed career by abandoning "sense" in favor of the "*ignis fatuus* in the mind" that leads through fens and thickets,

Whilst the misguided follower climbs with pain
Mountains of whimseys, heaped in his own brain;
Stumbling from thought to thought, falls headlong down
Into doubt's boundless sea, where, like to drown,
Books bear him up awhile, and make him try
To swim with bladders of philosophy;
In hopes still to o'ertake th'escaping light,
The vapor dances in his dazzling sight
Till, spent, it leaves him to eternal night.
Then old age and experience, hand in hand,
Lead him to death, and make him understand,
After a search so painful and so long,
That all his life he has been in the wrong.
Huddled in dirt the reasoning engine lies,
Who was so proud, so witty, and so wise.[5]

Although this is the most general of the character progresses, it is still more socially particularized than Jacques's speech on the Seven Ages of Man. The subject is not "the human condition" but the course of one historically situated class of proud humans, a contemporary social cliché as it were, from which the speaker recommends escape through the mingled epicurean-empiricist counsels later in the poem. The sketch is of course reductive, the man-as-cliché reduced yet further in the startling last couplet to the matter he sought to ignore, a broken and half-buried machine.

[4] "The Medall," lines 26–35, 50–52, in *The Works of John Dryden*, ed. Edward Niles Hooker, H.T. Swedenberg, *et al.* (Berkeley and Los Angeles: University of California Press, 1956 –), ii. 44.

[5] *A Satyr against Reason and Mankind*, lines 6–30, in *The Complete Poems of John Wilmot, Earl of Rochester*, ed. David M. Vieth (New Haven: Yale University Press, 1968), 94–95.

The disdain of the climactic lines is worth pondering because Rochester's sketch is the most abstract and *nearly* tragic of the character progresses. But even in it, the protagonist's fate is inevitable only within his scheme of things, not presumably the reader's. If there is inevitability – and the character progresses give the pleasure of a prediction coming true – it is comic fatality, the inevitability of comic history. Comic history is the framework that Hogarth as well as Fielding invokes for his narratives, and the material determinism of the progresses needs further thought. It is "inevitable" that Hogarth's Moll Hackabout will, given a particular historical starting point – early eighteenth-century London – and her particular class, education, and social infatuations, run the headlong career she runs. But the "givens," historical rather than transcendental, are all important to remember.

Swift's progresses

Although the character progress portrays an individual agent, or occasionally a pair of agents, the individuals are not private selves. The title of Swift's "Phyllis, or the Progress of Love" suggests immediately the institutionalization of sexuality and Phyllis's near interchangeability with the cultural commodities defining her or, in this limited sense at least, determining her. The respective places of determination and freedom are brought forward for analysis in the progresses and constitute an especially complex conflict in Swift. In this section I will try to describe two things at once: the typical movement of the character progress as "typified" in two poems of Swift, and the way in which the possibilities of human freedom preoccupy Swift. The attempt rests on the premise that while this preoccupation is perhaps more vivid in Swift than in most of his contemporaries, the difference is finally of intensity rather than kind.

The first section of Swift's "Phyllis, or the Progress of Love" establishes the educational constituents of her character. If these lines were the whole sketch we would have an interesting but static portrait of the prudish coquette:

> Desponding Phyllis was endued
> With every talent of a prude:
> She trembled when a man drew near;
> Salute her, and she turned her ear:
> If o'er against her you were placed
> She durst not look above your waist:
> She'd rather take you to her bed,

> Than let you see her dress her head;
> In church you heard her, through the crowd
> Repeat the absolution loud;
> In church, secure behind her fan
> She durst behold that monster, man ...

This scene is actually the first scene in a series of roughly eight stages. *Roughly* because the translation of the narrative progress into visual moments is necessarily imperfect; but something like the following sequence will be apparent:

– A second scene, lightly drawn in lines 19–24, in which Phyllis's marriage is contracted, "the writings drawn, the lawyer fee'd."
– The wedding morning, lines 25–32, upon which "the bride was missing":

> The mother screamed, the father chid;
> Where can this idle wretch be hid?
> No news of Phyl! The bridegroom came,
> And thought his bride had skulked for shame,
> Because her father used to say
> The girl had such a bashful way.

The last line is the first of several wonderful clichés situating the family.

– A fourth scene, lines 33–38, in which the butler is summoned to search out Phyllis but is found to have done so the night before:

> Now John, the butler, must be sent
> To learn the road that Phyllis went;
> The groom was wished to saddle crop;
> For John must neither light nor stop;
> But find her whereso'er she fled,
> And bring her back, alive or dead.

The last phrase is a piece of operatic rigidity, another cliché. But a nicer one occurs in line 35, "The groom was wisht to saddle crop." Swift glossed the idiom "was wisht to" in his copy of an early printing as "a tradesman's phrase."

– At almost the same moment, lines 43–72, the mother goes upstairs and finds Phyllis's elopement letter, full of clichés – "the choicest commonplaces," Swift calls them, "By others used in the like cases" – and *itself* a cliché.[6] "'Tis always done, romances

---

[6] Pat Rogers discusses the relation of the catchphrases of "polite conversation" and Swift's poetry in "Swift and the Revival of Cliché," in Claude Rawson (ed.), *The Character of Swift's Satire* (Newark: University of Delaware Press, 1983), 203–26. Rogers does not discuss the "progress" poems and is more concerned with Swift's use of stale phrases than with his

tell us, / When daughters run away with fellows." I will return to this document in a moment.

– A sixth scene, lines 73–84, portrays Phyllis and John muddy, hungry, and quarrelling on their journey.

– A seventh scene, lines 85–94, pictures Phyllis in prostitution and disease, and the eighth brings the couple to the present in an un-Ovidian metamorphosis:

> When food and raiment now grew scarce,
> Fate put a period to the farce,
> And with exact poetic justice;
> For John is landlord, Phyllis hostess:
> They keep, at Staines, the Old Blue Boar,
> Are cat and dog, and rogue and whore.

As Swift himself puts a period to the farce in these last lines one is reminded of his remark to Pope that the farce of life is a "ridiculous tragedy" – the "worst kind of composition."[7] The phrase "with exact poetic justice" underscores the staged familiarity of the stages and what appears, is made to appear, as their logical inevitability – a sequence turned to consequence.

Perhaps all narrative works out such transformations – of parataxis to hypotaxis, of "then" in the sense of "and next" to "then" in the sense of "and thus." In the progress, however, the element of predictability is stronger than usual, the recognition of cause and effect apparently inescapable. We would not in fact be able to predict everything that follows had we only the first section of Swift's poem, or the first engraving of Hogarth's Harlot. But we are led to feel that we could have done so, perhaps should have. Much of the game is to make the story fresh in close-up while persuading the viewer or reader that in outline it is, to use a favorite adjective of Swift's, the "tritest" thing in the world. In a later poem, "The Furniture of a Woman's Mind," Swift inventories as the first item "a set of phrases learned by rote." As we will see, the minds of most of Swift's men are similarly furnished; for, like Pope, he often portrays in women the strongest versions of restricted and restrictive behavior common to both sexes.

Phyllis's letter (lines 51ff) is composed almost entirely of such phrases, several of them long proverbial and so identified in Pat Rogers'

portrayal of predictable actions; but his contention that "Swift always works with the grain of popular speech" (p. 220) is very helpful for these poems as well.

[7] Swift to Pope, April 20, 1731: "The common saying of life being a Farce is true in every sense but the most important one, for it is a ridiculous tragedy, which is the worst kind of composition." I quote from *The Correspondence of Alexander Pope*, ed. George Sherburn (Oxford: Clarendon Press, 1956), iii. 190.

recent edition of Swift's poems: for example, line 56, that marriages are made in heaven, or line 68, that things done cannot be undone. Others are unmistakably formulaic, like the alliterative "neither shame nor sin" (line 59), or the all-inclusive pairs "rich and poor" (line 61: "Love never thinks of rich and poor") or maid and wife, in line 65: "She never before in all her life / Once disobeyed him, maid nor wife." From Romance comes the fortuneteller and "serving man of low degree" at the beginning of Phyllis's letter and at the end her protestation that "She valued not what others thought her" – and of course the whole letter.

It is not the commonplaces but their places that are ludicrous and reductive. For all the reader knows, marriages may be made in heaven (though, as Swift reminded himself elsewhere, they are not made between heaven's inhabitants).[8] But the maxim can mean different things to different minds. One suspects that for Swift all it *safely* means is that, once made, marriages are not to be put asunder *on earth*. To Phyllis, however, it means that she has, in the person of John, an irresistible fate, a special providence.

Tragic and romantic characters have *fates*; comic and satiric characters have *parts*, social parts. The irony surrounding Phyllis is that her declaration of autonomous individualism – "She valued not what others thought her" – is clearly the exchange of one part for another: the career of the tradesman's daughter progressing to a viable marriage traded instead for a part gleaned from romances, a role learned by rote and played out with mechanical decorum. The act of individual rebellion is an act of illusory freedom.

Swift puts the problem in something like these terms from the beginning of his life as a writer to the end. It is the characters most persuaded of their unique destinies and who depart most from the common forms whose actions are the most common and whose spirits operate most mechanically. Henry the Great, Alexander the Great, Louis XIV, Jack of Leyden, and "Monsieur Des Cartes" are all individuals among whom the "sole point of individuation" is the precise angle at which their vapors have overtaken their understandings. "For the brain, in its natural position and state of serenity, disposeth its owner to pass his life in the common forms…"

The phrases are from *A Tale of a Tub*, shortly before we find Jack claiming guidance by personal providence:

---

[8] "What they *do* in Heaven we are ignorant of; what they do *not* we are told expressly; that they neither marry, nor are given in Marriage." From "Thoughts on Various Occasions" (published in 1711, dated 1706), *PW* i. 244.

He would shut his eyes as he walked along the streets, and if he happened to bounce his head against a post, or fall into a kennel (as he seldom missed to do one or both) he would tell the gibing prentices who looked on that he submitted with entire resignation as to a trip, or a blow of fate. "It was ordained," said he, "some few days before the creation, that my nose and this very post should have a rencounter and therefore nature thought of it to send us both into the world in the same age, and to make us countrymen and fellow citizens. Now, had my eyes been open, it is very likely the business might have been a great deal worse…"

The claim to a special providence is a claim to inspiration. In his treatise on that topic, "The Mechanical Operation of the Spirit," Swift's speaker says,

I think it is in *life* as in *tragedy*, where it is held … a great defect … to interpose to assistance of preternatural power without an absolute and last necessity. However, it is a sketch of human vanity for every individual to imagine the whole universe is interested in his meanest concern. If he hath got clearly over a kennel, some angel unseen descended on purpose to help him by the hand; if he hath knocked his head against a post, it was the devil, for his sins, let loose from hell on purpose to *buffet* him.

The dismissal of these pretensions concludes in a sentence that anticipates the perspective of the king of Brobdingnag: "Who that sees a little paltry mortal, droning and dreaming, and drivelling to a multitude, can think it agreeable to common good sense that either Heaven or Hell should be put to the trouble of influence or inspection upon what he is about."

Clearly the observer is meant to smile at Phyllis's pretensions of predestination, a secular version of Jack's theological self-importance. With more humility and more mindful education, she should have recognized that she was not in the hands of fate. But the observer, having recognized what Phyllis does not, is left with a paradox. If the protagonist's claims to fate are absurd, the *feeling* of fatality is real for the reader. Phyllis does indeed seem to *have* a fate, though not the one she imagines, and the progress offers the pleasure of predictability. Where, if not in heaven, *was* Phyllis's marriage made?

It is hard to know just what weight to give the word Fate the second time it occurs, not in Phyllis's phrases but in the commentary of the speaker, who says "Fate put a period to the farce." One would like not to be a *grave* interpreter – Swift almost always uses that adjective laughingly – but it does seem that the role of fate is more than a bit of polite conversation, that movement follows movement with something of the regularity of Newtonian mechanics, and that the whole career has the certainty of gravity.[9] For a fundamental question posed by this progress is "What is a free act?" Much has been written about Swift and national liberty, perhaps not enough about Swift and personal freedom. The reason is probably plain. "Fair LIBERTY was all his cry," he advertised in *Verses on the Death of Dr. Swift*, and one is certainly on safer ground in sorting out Swift's position on the rights of the Church or of Ireland than in trying to piece together his sense of individualism.[10] This is especially true because Swift tends to respond skeptically and ironically to protestations of self-reliance and self-expression.

Before returning to the issue of freedom in Swift generally, I would like to turn, more briefly, to *The Progress of Marriage*. At this point we might simply add one more question to the reading of Phyllis's progress. If to depart from the common forms leads inexorably to a triter fate, how would one, ideally, become ethically *un*common, that is, *good*? Or, more explicitly from the spectator's point of view, at what level of meaning are the recognition and analysis of predictability reconciled?

The *Progress of Marriage* was not published in Swift's lifetime. It is not a finished poem in tone, but visually it is very rich. Like Hogarth's *Marriage à la Mode*, it is a dual progress, with the husband and wife progressively separated, occupying different scenes or alien spaces within the same painting. Swift's speaker notes as much, at line 31: "Both from the goal together start; / Scarce run a step before they part."

I count ten stages in this progress, though again several divisions are arbitrary. The first scene is the wedding day, in mock-mythological style. Next comes the night, in homelier comedy (line 21):

> The bridegroom dressed to make a figure,
> Assumes an artificial vigour;
> A flourished nightcap on, to grace
> His ruddy, wrinkled, smirking face,
> Like the faint red upon a pippin
> Half withered by a winter's keeping.

Through the remaining 140 lines Swift actually follows two structural models. One is a day-in-the-life of this January-May couple, the "times of day" from morning to night (in this case from noon to near dawn).

---

[9] Ironic uses of the word "gravity" and of the idea are discussed in ch. 4, pp. 125–29.

[10] Swift's views of political freedom are surveyed in Irvin Ehrenpreis, "Swift on Liberty," *Journal of the History of Ideas*, 13 (1952), 131–46. In addition to Oliver Ferguson's authoritative *Jonathan Swift and Ireland* (Urbana: University of Illinois Press, 1962), see Carole Fabricant, *Swift's Landscape* (Baltimore: Johns Hopkins University Press, 1982), esp. pp. 210–35, for discussion of the psychology of Swift's Irish patriotism.

The other is the course of the year that the marriage was to last. The times of day dominate up to line 98, with several scenes well defined:
  – lines 38 ff, the bride at her dressing table, Betty buzzing in her ear about her husband, perhaps pointing as he exits;
  – lines 56–70, dinner at four, the wife preoccupied with plans for the evening, the husband with his poor appetite and economic worries.
Then three brief jostling scenes beginning at line 77:
  – in the coach, the wife on her way to the theater, dropping her husband at church;
  – from line 83, the husband returning as his wife is "hasting to the ball" and as "her chairmen push him from the wall";
  – and then, lines 91–98, the wife returning at five in the morning from a masquerade, the husband waking to hear her complaints at being kept out late, in another fine series of clichés:

> The masquerade began at two
> She stole away with much ado,
> And shall be chid this afternoon
> For leaving company so soon;
> She'll say, and she may truly say it,
> She can't abide to stay out late.

There are two more actual scenes and a hypothetical one closing the progress. Having persuaded her rapidly aging spouse to take her to Bath, the wife – lines 131ff – frequents the prolific Cross Bath while the Dean skulks in the gallery, "Till banished by some coxcomb's raillery." His role ends (lines 151ff) with a second wedding night:

> The Dean with all his best endeavour
> Gets not an heir, but gets a fever;
> A victim to the last essays
> Of vigor in declining days.
> He dies, and leaves his mourning mate
> (What could he less?) his whole estate.

The final verse paragraph creates an imaginary future scene to sweep the widow from the stage as well:

> Oh, may I see her soon dispensing
> Her favours to some broken ensign!
> Him let her marry for his face,
> And only coat of tarnished lace;
> To turn her naked out of doors,
> And spend her jointure on his whores:
> But for a parting present leave her
> A rooted pox to last forever.

This last scene is where the tone most obviously falters, ironic detachment collapsing into a sort of visual invective. One might guess that Swift held the poem back sensing that the resolution was unsatisfactory. The "Dean" is too simply the fool, the wife too entirely the knave at the end for "exact poetic justice" to conclude the progress appropriately. Although the speaker addresses the clergyman scornfully along the way, by the end he has lost sight somewhat of the "rich divine's" pride and dynastic ambitions, just as he seems to recede from the recognition that the "young imperious girl" of line 3, empty enough to be filled by the remarks of her maid early in the marriage, is *still* only a year away from being the young girl who seems not to have sought the match originally. Readers will account for Swift's vehemence variously, some attributing it to misogyny, some to biographical event (Benjamin Pratt, who seems to have been a model for the clergyman, had been a friend),[11] and some with reference to Swift's undeniable anxieties concerning marriages, especially such asymmetrical marriages.

But it may be more useful to consider what the crudity of this last scene reveals about the character progress as a structure of apprehension. In its lack of finish this final scene may show more clearly the narrative desire of the progress; for the final scenes of *all* the progresses are of course imaginary, hypothetical, willed. The logical progression revealed is organic, namely that of progressive disease. The future pox that Swift's speaker calls down here is merely a more openly "fated" version of the diseased fatality attending most of the progress characters.

There is nothing new in the use of medical metaphors (a staple of Renaissance satire) or in the identification of the passions with disease (a common topic in the seventeenth-century moralists). The new emphases are two: the perception of disease as something which defines itself over time, in stages, and the perception of these stages as steps of economic and social entanglement. (To use today's phrase, we can say that the character's diseases are "social diseases.") The characters of the progresses become increasingly enmeshed in their environments, revealing themselves most fully as they grow not more but less recognizable as distinct selves.

The progress of character for Swift is usually a fall into society. The three brothers in *A Tale of a Tub* spend their unconvincing childhood in a world of romance, where they "carefully observed their father's

---

[11] See *Poems*, pp. 719, 927–28.

will, and kept their coats in very good order ... travelled through
several countries, encountered a reasonable quantity of giants, and slew
certain dragons." Then Swift brings them at once to adulthood and
London, where they "quickly began to improve in the good qualities
of the town":

They Writ, and Raillyed, and Rhymed, and Sung, and Said, and said
Nothing; They Drank, and Fought, and Whored, and Slept, and Swore, and
took Snuff: They went to new Plays on the first Night, haunted the *Chocolate-
Houses*, beat the Watch, lay on Bulks, and got Claps ... they kill'd Bailiffs,
kick'd Fidlers down Stairs, eat [ate] at *Locket's*, loytered at *Will's* ... The three
Brothers had acquired forty other Qualifications of the like Stamp, too tedious
to recount, and by consequence were justly reckoned the most accomplish'd
Persons in Town.   (*Tale*, p. 74 [section 2])

   A Tale of a Tub is not a character sketch, but the underlying
mechanism is the same: one tumbles into town, sets off in pursuit of an
imaginary selfhood, seeking position, wealth, power, and romantic
recognition, and the result is polite conversation, a set of rote phrases,
a fate of the "tritest" sort, a series of adventures "too tedious to
recount."
   Or so it seems ninety-nine times out of a hundred. Since it is arguable
that Swift never directly gives us that hundredth character, what place
can individual freedom have in Swift's writing? Or if, as I have been
maintaining, Swift is not a brooding eccentric but in the mainstream
– *is* much of the mainstream – of High Augustanism, what place can
the question of individual freedom have in Augustan literature? The
obvious answer may be the best one, so long as we recognize that its
implications are complex. That is, that in presenting characters whose
progress is mechanical, degenerative, and fatal, and in providing the
real pleasure of predictability, the character progress automatically
posits a higher ground, inhabited by author and viewer, where
movement is less blind and more vital.
   But the implications are complex because we do not, automatically,
share the Augustan vocabulary of experience. While we would tend to
locate "real" human freedom in the realm of private experience, the
character progress minimizes personal existence, in fact questions the
existence of such a category as the private. Its narrative structure
questions private autonomy and authority at the same time that
autobiography, fictional autobiography, and the epistolary novel are
indeed rising and beginning to show that, whatever its political
validity, private experience has a phenomenal literary future.
   Progress characters have choices to make, and get them wrong, but

since we do not see them debate or struggle over their choices, these seem – almost – to have been made for them. We cannot imagine any of the characters writing an autobiography, even keeping a diary (Mr. Wilson's extract from his London journals in *Joseph Andrews* [book III, ch. 3] functions like Falstaff's bill of fare), or writing exploratory epistles (Phyllis's letter is a string of commonplaces).

The witlessness of Swift's characters becomes more meaningful, in relation to Swift's reflections on individual choice in his sermon "On the Testimony of Conscience." The point of this sermon, as in all of Swift's, is deliberately plain: the only sure basis of virtue is a "conscience founded on religion"; principles of morality without religion and codes of honor are insufficient. But the terms and emphases of Swift's argument are intriguing. Swift begins by defining conscience primarily in the sense of consciousness, as "properly" signifying "that knowledge which a man hath within himself of his own thoughts and actions." If conscience is correctly understood, then we can avoid "those mistakes about what is usually called Liberty of Conscience; which properly speaking is no more than a liberty of knowing our own thoughts, which liberty no one can take from us" (*PW* ix. 150–51).

But the liberty of knowing their own thoughts is precisely what the characters of the progresses do not possess. If no one can take it from another, it is not the case that one will necessarily have it. The notion of conscience as an intuitive "guide and director" is a mistake, Swift says, that "hath been the occasion of more evils under the sun than almost all other causes put together." "For, as conscience is nothing else but the knowledge we have of what we are thinking and doing, so it can guide us no farther than that knowledge reacheth." Lacking sufficient knowledge, individuals will claim conscientious objection (or personal necessity) in things not properly matters of conscience for them. Ask Dissenters, Swift claims, why they do not come to church and "They will say they dislike the ceremonies, the prayers, the habits, and the like, and therefore it goes against their conscience. But they are mistaken, their teacher hath put those words into their mouth…" More important here than Swift's categorical conclusion is the intermediate analysis on which it rests: that is, that the individual claiming personal direction is the victim of phrases learned by rote.

Reading this sermon on what might have been the most private of topics – the testimony of the voice within – one is struck by Swift's utilitarian and communitarian norms. "Private Ends" are steadily contrasted with "Service of the Publick" (*PW* ix. 157). Individuals lacking a conscience founded on religion are not dramatized as sinners bound for perdition but as a wholly private person weakening the commonweal: "they can give no Security that they will be either good Subjects, faithful Servants of the Publick, or honest in their mutual Dealings" (*PW* ix. 158). Swift goes so far as to suggest that the civic education of the ancient heathens was an even stronger security than modern Christianity. They "far exceed[ed] us in all manner of Virtue," for "those heathens did in a particular manner instil the Principle into their Children of loving their Country; which is so far otherwise now-a-days, that, of the several Parties among us, there is none of them that seem to have so much as heard, whether there be such a Virtue in the World" (ix. 155–56).

Swift describes the present state of society as one where "so little truth or justice" exists "because there are so very few, who either in the Service of the Publick, or in common Dealings with each other, do ever look farther than their own Advantage, and how to guard themselves against the Laws of their Country." In pointing out that one may serve one's self and stay out of legal trouble "by Favour, by Secresy, or by Cunning, although he breaketh almost every Law of God," Swift comes close to defining God politically as the Common Good (*PW* ix. 157).

Swift remarked that he was always "preaching pamphlets," that is, politics.[12] This sermon at any rate is on what we might call *political conscience*, or, keeping in mind Swift's definition, *political consciousness*. Putting it this way is not to separate artificially Swift's theology and politics, either in church or in the fictions. Certainly it is significant that the characters in the progresses are secular, essentially unreligious individuals – including Lemuel Gulliver, who, although uncomfortable at the prospect of actually trampling on a crucifix, never mentions God or prayer. But we seem to be likelier at present to misunderstand or underestimate Swift's social analysis than his religious doctrines.

His character progresses construct individuals who are political liabilities, in both senses of the word. They are political casualties and they threaten the body politic. They lack any understanding of the "public," of history, of social and economic relations, and are in this way "fated" to embody the failed individualism of private ends. From the other perspective, as *merely* private agents they can have no commitment to, no role in, the common good. The progresses invite the

---

[12] The remark is quoted by both Laetitia Pilkington and Lord Orrery; see *PW* ix. 98.

viewer to adopt both of these perspectives toward the case studies the characters quickly become. But whether one feels more keenly the characters' trite tawdriness or their selfishness, the sense of fatality remains strong. Made up of rote phrases, class fantasies, unapprehended decorums, they move, in Swift's works, without consciences and without liberty. If they claim unique destinies and spontaneous liberty of conscience, such talk is for Swift part of what makes them ideological puppets. "But they are mistaken, their teacher hath put those words into their mouth."

Pleasures of predictability: Pope's character progresses and the problem of free will

Twice in less than a year, at the close of *An Essay on Man* and the *Epistle to Arbuthnot*, Pope suggests a "progress" of sorts for his own career, in which he has turned "From sounds to things, from fancy to the heart," leaving the "Description" of his youth for a poetry now more rigorously "moraliz'd" (*An Essay on Man*, IV. 392; *Epistle to Arbuthnot*, lines 148, 340–41). It is not coincidental that Pope's most studied analyses of character occur in the "ethic epistles" written at the same time as these two poems and framed by them in the collected *Works* Pope published in 1735. While it has been common practice for the last century to separate Pope's poetic achievement in his *Epistles to Several Persons* (1731–35) from his philosophical ambitions, it is useful to remember that most of his character sketches were composed or completed while Pope was attempting to synthesize a satisfactory human science, a science especially of people in relation to the order of providence. Perhaps the simplest name for this relation is the problem of free will.

   That is not the only problem animating *An Essay on Man* and the related epistles, but it is the biggest. Clearly it is relevant as well to the character progresses we have already surveyed, where characters seem "determined" to their "fates," despite their authors' orthodoxy (only Rochester's is questionable) and despite the premises of individual responsibility that make satire possible. While in the strictest terms any claim to know another person entirely may veer toward heterodoxy, since only God reads the soul, the character progress raises the potential conflict more openly by pretending to know how all has ended or will end. Because the problem is so central in Pope his poetry offers the best "prospect" from which to see its personal and communal contours.

After surveying some of his character progresses and the debate within his poetry that surrounds them, I will turn to Locke and then to Prior to suggest that free will was a more difficult issue for Augustan writers than modern accounts tend to allow.

"Prospect" is the term Pope uses in his poem "On the Knowledge of the Characters of Men" (the *Epistle to Cobham*) for the psychological vista opened when one discovers the "ruling passion" of an otherwise illegible character. "This clue once found, unravels all the rest, / The prospect clear, and Wharton stands confest" (lines 178–79). The poem's one extended portrait immediately follows:

> Wharton, the scorn and wonder of our days,
> Whose ruling Passion was the Lust of Praise;
> Born with whate'er could win it from the Wise,
> Women and Fools must like him or he dies;
> Tho' wond'ring Senates hung on all he spoke,
> The Club must hail him master of the joke.
> Shall parts so various aim at nothing new?
> He'll shine a Tully and a Wilmot too.
> Then turns repentant, and his God adores
> With the same spirit that he drinks and whores;
> Enough if all around him but admire,
> And now the Punk applaud, and now the Fryer.
> Thus with each gift of nature and of art,
> And wanting nothing but an honest heart;
> Grown all to all, from no one vice exempt,
> And most contemptible, to shun contempt;
> His Passion still, to covet gen'ral praise,
> His Life, to forfeit it a thousand ways;
> A constant Bounty which no friend has made;
> An angel Tongue, which no man can persuade;
> A Fool, with more of Wit than half mankind,
> Too quick for Thought, for Action too refin'd;
> A Tyrant to the wife his heart approves;
> A Rebel to the very king he loves;
> He dies, sad out-cast of each church and state,
> And (harder still) flagitious, yet not great!
> Ask you why Wharton broke thro' ev'ry rule?
> 'Twas all for fear the Knaves should call him Fool.
>
> (178–207)

It is plausible to object that the fascination of the portrait owes little to the "theory" of a ruling passion, that the "lust of praise" is either not a passion in any elemental sense or is so general as to include multitudes of characters less individualized than the Wharton of these lines. (Edward Young, for example, had recently published a series of seven satires intended to show that the "Universal Passion" is the "Love of Fame.") But reduction has its uses. While many of Swift's most enjoyable characters are fools as well as knaves, some of Pope's are extraordinarily intelligent, and of these Wharton is perhaps the most "gifted" (line 192). The natural question is how such a brilliant man should come to look so foolish. Pope in fact suggests several conventional answers as the portrait and career progress. Wharton is indiscriminately hungry for approval, in a word, undiscriminating (lines 182–85). Wharton is too fond of novelty (line 186). He is dishonest (line 193); too inconstant (line 194), too irresolute (lines 196–97), too clever (lines 200–01). All of these are partial truths, but they remain parts. What they do not quite catch is the personal style that marks Wharton through his several stages, that "same spirit" with which he *adores* and then *whores* (lines 188–89). Listening for applause, Wharton himself presumably never heard the rhyme.

The ruling passion and the "same spirit" are not exactly the same thing. The former is a description of motivation and the latter a description of behavior. The equation is sufficient here, however, because the functional imprecision of Pope's summary (Wharton's "passion" for "praise") allows him to reduce "parts so various" to an unvarying movement. Unlike Swift's puppetlike characters, Pope's most intelligent actors tend to appear initially as too "spiritual" rather than too mechanical. Flavia has "too much Spirit to be e'er at ease" and, like Wharton, "too much Quickness" and "too much Thinking" for "common Thought." Even the more physical Calypso is a creature of "strange graces" and "stranger flights," and Atossa, storming from "loveless youth to unrespected age," is all the while "by Spirit robb'd of Pow'r" (*Epistle to a Lady*, lines 41, 96–98, 125, 144).

As any reader of the poetry will also recall, however, not all of Pope's characters suffer from an excess of mind. Even without taking into account the hero or herds of the dunces, several Popean figures are dull plodders who lumber on from stage to stage. What the "slow" and the "quick" have in common is their participation in a narrative they do not understand. (Ironically, the *Dunciad*'s chief dunces come closest to knowing what they are about and to enjoying their compulsions. But whether people working for the destruction of the world can be said in any usual sense to have either hindsight or foresight remains an open

question, more literal and urgent for us than for the Augustans.) The
more representative or typical a character's role, the more conspicuous
the absence of insight. Thus the one individual character progress in
the fourth book of the *Dunciad*, that of the Grand Tourist (lines
282–330), presents the career of a young aristocrat so inarticulate at the
end of his travels that his tutor must tell his history to Dulness:

> "The Sire saw, one by one, his Virtues wake:
> The mother begg'd the blessing of a Rake.
> Thou gav'st that Ripeness, which so soon began,
> And ceas'd so soon, he ne'er was Boy, nor Man.
> Thro' School and College, thy kind cloud o'ercast,
> Safe and unseen the young Æneas past.
> Thence bursting glorious, all at once let down,
> Stunn'd with his giddy Larum half the town.
> Intrepid then, o'er seas and lands he flew:
> Europe he saw, and Europe saw him too.
>
>   .   .   .
>
> With nothing but a Solo in his head;
> As much Estate, and Principle, and Wit,
> As Jansen, Fleetwood, Cibber shall think fit;
> Stol'n from a Duel, follow'd by a Nun,
> And, if a Borough chuse him, not undone . . ."
>   (IV. 285–94, 324–28)

Framing the subject twice, within the tutor's narration and his own
poetic narrative, Pope reduces the traveler's subjectivity to the
vanishing point. In a turn that describes the implied careers of most of
the dunces, subject becomes object: "Europe he saw...Europe saw
him."

In the *Epistle to a Lady*, where the average intelligence of the major
characters is the highest of any of Pope's satires, the interplay between
individual and categorical "fates" is more delicate. The career of
Atossa did not enter the poem until 1744 (in the "deathbed edition"
of the *Epistles to Several Persons*), but it is a good example of Pope's
shrewdness in structural as well as stylistic revision. For the peculiarities
of her character complicate but finally conform to the collective
progress (lines 219–48) of a set of women Pope calls "queens," that is,
women who relentlessly seek "sway" as sexual objects by making
sexual subjects. Their thirty-line progress moves three times from youth

to death. The first movement plays primarily on the military metaphors
concentrated in "conquests":

> Yet mark the fate of a whole Sex of Queens!
> Pow'r all their end, but Beauty all the means.
> In Youth they conquer, with so wild a rage,
> As leaves them scarce a Subject in their Age:
> For foreign glory, foreign joy, they roam;
> No thought of Peace or Happiness at home.
> But Wisdom's Triumph is well-tim'd Retreat,
> As hard a science to the Fair as Great!
> Beauties, like Tyrants, old and friendless grown,
> Yet hate to rest, and dread to be alone,
> Worn out in public, weary ev'ry eye.
> Nor leave one sigh behind them when they die.

The second survey builds on the pathos lurking in the fear of being
alone, a "dread" both realistic and self-fulfilling:

> Pleasures the sex, as Children Birds, pursue,
> Still out of reach, yet never out of view,
> Sure, if they catch, to spoil the Toy at most,
> To covet flying, and regret when lost:
> At last, to follies Youth could scarce depend,
> 'Tis half their Age's prudence to pretend;
> Asham'd to own they gave delight before,
> Reduc'd to feign it, when they give no more:
> As Hags hold Sabbaths, less for joy than spight,
> So these their merry, miserable Night;
> Still round and round the Ghosts of Beauty glide,
> And haunt the places where their Honour dy'd.

The final review is the most compressed, fusing under great pressure
the initial military conceit ("Veterans"), poignancy, and disdain – the
last complicated by the prudential reminder that the judgment is
rendered by the "World" rather than the poet:

> See how the World its Veterans rewards!
> A Youth of frolicks, an old Age of Cards,
> Fair to no purpose, artful to no end,
> Young without Lovers, old without a Friend,
> A Fop their Passion, but their Prize a Sot,
> Alive, ridiculous, and dead, forgot!

Less sarcasm saturates the word "fate" in Pope's introduction of this

group of sexual queens than in Swift's parodies of personal provi-
dentialism. Yet it is equally clear here that such fates are not divine
whispers or individual destinies but social scripts.

The character progress is of course no more Pope's only mode of
characterization than it is the period's. At the beginning of this chapter
I contrasted the portraits in the *Epistle to Bathurst* of Cotta and Cotta's
son, only the second of which moves chronologically, hoping to indicate
at once the difference between the narrative and non-narrative modes
and their peaceful coexistence. But Pope's interest in showing the life-
through-death careers of his characters emerges persistently in these
poems of the early 1730s. Roughly a hundred lines after the sketch of
Cotta's son Pope returns to the life of the elder Cotta, identified
outright on his second entrance as the historical Sir John Cutler and
traced through four emblematic stages of miserly madness:

> Cutler saw tenants break, and houses fall,
> For very want; he could not build a wall.
> His only daughter in a stranger's pow'r,
> For very want; he could not pay a dow'r.
> A few grey hairs his rev'rend temples crown'd,
> 'Twas very want that sold them for two pound.
> What ev'n deny'd a cordial at his end,
> Banish'd the doctor, and expell'd the friend?
> What but a want, which you perhaps think mad,
> Yet numbers feel, the want of what he had.
>
> (323–32)

This time the sketch ends with a comic death scene obviously
intended to be read as logical rather than historical: "Cutler and
Brutus, dying both exclaim, / 'Virtue! and Wealth! what are ye but a
name!'" (lines 333–34). The sketch creates a structural transition
between the famous deathbed portrait of Villiers, whose profligate
career is hinted in flashback, to the most elaborate of Pope's character
progresses, the "tale" of Balaam (lines 339–402) that concludes the
poem.

Balaam's career is, as perceptive readings by Earl Wasserman and
others have helped show, much more than "his" story, encompassing
the epistle's biblically resonant critique of "blest paper credit" and
new capitalist notions of "worth." For our purposes it will help to look
primarily at the individual progress and the providential question that
"causes" the story's telling. In the stages Pope envisions for him,
Balaam (1) begins as a "sober" Citizen with a respectable credit rating

("Religious, punctual, frugal, and so forth; / His word would pass for
more than he was worth"); (2) inherits his father's knighthood and
estate and becomes the beneficiary of two dubious Cornish shipwrecks;
(3) spends more, steals a diamond (only one but large: possibly the Pitt
diamond), and satisfies his conscience ("'Where once I went to church,
I'll now go twice – / And am so clear too of all other vice'"); (4) invests
in stocks that "pour" an "abundant show'r of Cent. per Cent." and
swells to a corporation director; (5) appears as a "man of spirit" too
busy for church or (Pope's reticence implies) to notice his wife's death;
(6) marries "quality," "bows at Court, and grows polite"; (7) buys a
commission for his son (who in his own capsule progress "drinks,
whores, fights, and in a duel dies") and marries his daughter to a
viscount; (8) gains a seat in Parliament and becomes a pensioner; (9)
takes a bribe and (remarkably, Pope's later satires would suggest)
hangs for it; (10) evades self-recognition to his last breath: "The Devil
and the King divide the prize, / And sad Sir Balaam curses God and
dies."

While this summary may help to emphasize the narrative kinship of
Balaam's progress with Swift or Hogarth, it does not give the devil his
due. Pope's Satan frames the progress almost from the beginning:

> The Dev'l was piqu'd such saintship to behold,
> And long'd to tempt him like good Job of old:
> But Satan now is wiser than of yore,
> And tempts by making rich, not making poor.

(349–52)

One is likely to read these lines first as mock-heroic jesting. Balaam
is no Job. His virtues have already been registered as perfunctory
("...and so forth") in the preceding paragraph, his "worth" as less
than his "word," his morality dubious ("constant at Church, and
Change"), his generosity invisible ("save farthings to the poor"). From
one perspective Balaam has already "framed" himself. But the lines
deepen as Satan makes another half dozen appearances in Pope's
account, most decisively as Balaam's "demon":

> The Tempter saw his time; the work he ply'd;
> Stocks and Subscriptions pour on ev'ry side,
> 'Till all the Daemon makes his full descent,
> In one abundant show'r of Cent. per Cent.,
> Sinks deep within him, and possesses whole,
> Then dubs Director, and secures his soul.

(369–74)

If the persistence of Balaam's tempter takes the reader back more thoughtfully to his initial appearance, one is likely to go back – or up – two more steps as well. The first is to the providential question to which the tale turns out to be a response:

> Say, for such worth are other worlds prepar'd?
> Or are they both, in this their own reward?
> A knotty point! to which we now proceed.
> But you are tir'd – I'll tell a tale. "Agreed."

(335–38)

This question of whether supernatural ends await the worthless leads in turn all the way back to the opening of the poem, where the mixture of eschatology and epistolary self-mockery is similar. There Pope attributes to Bathurst an amused Epicureanism –

> You hold the word, from Jove to Momus giv'n.
> That Man was made the standing jest of Heav'n;
> And Gold but sent to keep the fools in play,
> For some to heap, and some to throw away –

while playfully but pointedly advancing his own view that God is more "careful" than the gods:

> But I, who think more highly of our kind,
> (And surely, Heav'n and I are of a mind)
> Opine, that Nature, as in duty bound,
> Deep hid the shining mischief under ground:
> But when by Man's audacious labour won,
> Flam'd forth this rival to, its Sire, the Sun,
> Then careful Heav'n supply'd two sorts of Man,
> To squander these, and those to hide agen.

(3–6, 7–14)

One way of grasping the differences is to hear these as competing readings of the description of humans at the beginning of the second epistle of *An Essay on Man*. Pope's Bathurst seems likely to hear "The glory, *jest*, and riddle of the world," while I think Pope has written (and surely Pope and I are of a mind) "The glory, jest, and *riddle* of the world." The *Epistle to Bathurst* is filled with worldly riddles that seem to require supernatural explanation. Since the avaricious are so unhappy they "Must act on motives pow'rful, tho' unknown / ...Some Revelation hid from you and me" (lines 114–116).

The "ruling passion" is an explanation of sorts, of the different sorts of people in the world and of the consistent spirit that sorts out the

apparently contradictory actions of an individual. The latter emphasis
dominates in the *Epistle to Cobham*, where we have seen it offered as the
"clue" to interpreting character, and in the *Epistle to a Lady*; the former
presides over *An Essay on Man*, where the variety of ruling passions
ensures a kind of vocational plenitude:

> A mightier Pow'r the strong direction sends,
> And sev'ral Men impels to sev'ral ends.
> Like varying winds, by other passions tost,
> This drives them constant to a certain coast.
> Let pow'r or knowledge, gold or glory, please,
> Or (oft more strong than all) the love of ease;
> Thro' life 'tis followed, ev'n at life's expense...
>
> (II. 165–71)

But whether serving as a psychological clue or part of an explanation
of social ecology, the idea of the ruling passion does not sit easily with
the doctrine of free will, as Samuel Johnson pointed out.[13] The verb
impels is crucial; one senses Pope carefully avoiding *compels* here, as in
the *Epistle to Cobham* (cf. "The same adust complexion has impell'd /
Charles to the Convent, Philip to the Field" [lines 59–60]), but the
verbal distinction was possibly even finer in Pope's day than ours. It
should be said at once that Pope seems to have anticipated the problem
of determinism here (as he did not in other parts of *An Essay on Man*),
stressing that the ruling passion can be turned to good or ill, "And
Nero reigns a Titus, if he will" (II. 198), a line where the final accent
is unmistakable. It also needs to be remembered that Pope seems to
have thought of the ruling passion as a "hypothesis" rather than as a
doctrine; it is introduced in *An Essay on Man* (II. 133) with "perhaps,"
a word underscored in the manuscript and used again when Pope
develops the closely related idea that motives are as elusive as the logic
of dreams: "Something as dim to our internal view, / Is thus, perhaps,
the cause of most we do" (*Epistle to Cobham*, lines 49–50). Finally and
most obviously, there is no making sense of Pope's ethical and political
satires if we assume that he was committed to a position leaving no
room for individual choice or responsibility.

But when all of these things have been recalled, one may well feel
that the problem of free will has been elevated rather than eliminated.
That it is not "solved" in Pope's poems is scarcely surprising. What is

---

[13] Johnson, "Life of Pope," in *The Lives of the English Poets*, 3 vols., ed. George Birkbeck Hill
(Oxford: Clarendon Press, 1905), iii. 174.

interesting is that for all his impatience with theological controversy
Pope did not feel "impelled" to leave it alone. A few years later he
returns to the problem in one of the *Imitations of Horace*, this time
referring it more explicitly to a higher authority. Why one man should
be "driven" by insatiable greed and another by insatiable benevolence

> Is known alone to that Directing Pow'r,
> Who forms the Genius in the natal Hour;
> That God of Nature, who, within us still,
> Inclines our Action, not constrains our Will;
> Various of Temper, as of Face or Frame,
> Each Individual: His great End the same.
>
> (*Epistle II.ii*, 278–83)

William Warburton, who had so eagerly defended Pope from the
charges of determinism lodged against *An Essay on Man*, took the first
occasion to comment on this passage as well. "Here our Poet has an
opportunity of illustrating his own Philosophy; and thereby giving a
much better sense to his Original; and correcting both the *naturalism*
and the *fate* of Horace, which are covertly conveyed in these words, Scit
Genius, natale comes qui temperat astrum / NATURAE DEUS HUMANAE."
(The Genius alone knows [why we do things], that companion who
rules our star of birth, that god of human nature.)[14]
Whether Warburton is right about Pope's intention is always a fair
question. I think that in this case he probably is. But it is interesting
that even if the lines are read with all the eighteenth-century orthodoxy
he finds in them, the possibilities of individual control still seem
dramatically limited and precarious. If Nero could have been a Titus,
certainly Balaam could have been something better than "sad Sir
Balaam." But where, exactly, in his progress might he have begun to
be driven or impelled by a different spirit? And if he had somehow
steered his passion to a different "end," would "careful Heav'n" have
required another in his place?
Both questions are too crude for comedy, human or divine; nor does
either speak very precisely to individual consciousness. I raise them,
however, not to show that the character progresses tend to cancel
traditional doctrine but that they suggest its strain by being structures
of foresight – that is, of providence. In one of the several exchanges
Boswell prompted on the subject, Johnson remarked, "All theory is

---

[14] *Epistle II. ii.* 187 in Horace, *Satires, Epistles and Ars Poetica*, trans. H. R. Fairclough, Loeb
Classical Library (Cambridge, MA: Harvard University Press, 1929).

against the freedom of the will; all experience for it."[15] The character progresses are, in this sense, "theoretical" narratives.

Booth's passion, Locke's will, Prior's *Predestination*

The role of the will is a greater theoretical problem and literary preoccupation in the Augustan period than modern accounts emphasizing its pragmatic energies may suggest. One way to sense the problem's shadow is to consider the riddle of Fielding's *Amelia*, published in 1751 and set in the 1730s. The intellectual knot dissolved near the novel's end, and then mysteriously, is the belief of Amelia's husband, Booth, in the power of one's "uppermost passion," a sort of random determinism: "he did not believe Men were under any blind Impulse or Direction of Fate; but that every man acted merely from the Force of that Passion which was uppermost in his Mind, and could do no otherwise." Booth's position leads to essentially the same view of the "Necessity of human Actions" as the fatalist's and to ethical relativism. The "chief Doubt" he eventually repudiates "was founded on this, that as Men appeared to me to act entirely from their Passions, their Actions could have neither Merit nor Demerit."[16]

It has been argued that Booth's error flows from Mandeville (who speaks of humanity as a "compound" of passions, governed by those that come "uppermost") and, more recently, that it is even close to Hume's discussion of natural religion and necessity in his *Philosophical Essays concerning Human Understanding* (1748).[17] But whatever Fielding's polemical engagements or immediate stimuli may have been, we do not need to turn to these heterodox writers to find the broad basis of Booth's intellectual difficulties. Much of his skepticism concerning free will could easily have been derived from a philosopher widely regarded as much more moderate in the period and certainly more influential, John Locke.

The discussion of the will seems to have given Locke himself more difficulty than any other part of *An Essay concerning Human Understanding*. The first sign of strain is its location, in a chapter entitled "Of Power" (II. xxi), amid the treatment of "modes" and complex ideas. (The second may be the stylistic stress of the opening sentence, interrupted

---

[15] James Boswell, *Life of Johnson*, account of Apr. 15, 1778, in Oxford Standard Authors Edition (London: Oxford University Press, rev. edn. 1953), 947.

[16] *Amelia*, ed. Martin C. Battestin (Middletown, CT: Wesleyan University Press, 1984), 32, 511.

[17] Martin C. Battestin, "The Problem of *Amelia*: Hume, Barrow, and the Conversion of Captain Booth," *ELH* 41 (1974), 613–48.

immediately by a parenthesis five times longer than this one.) The chapter held its peculiar place, but Locke revised it in each of the five editions until it had become by far the longest chapter of the *Essay*. The most radical revision was undertaken almost at once and appears in the second edition, in 1694. The essential change in this "stricter examination" is from a description of the will choosing the apparent greater good to a view in which the will avoids "uneasiness."[18] Roughly speaking, Locke changes from a rationalistic to a psychological account of the will. Here is how Locke puts it:

> To return, then, to the Enquiry, *what is it that determines the Will in regard to our Actions*? And that upon second thoughts I am apt to imagine is not, as is generally supposed, the greater good in view: But some (and for the most part the most pressing) *uneasiness* a Man is at present under. This is that which successively determines the *Will*, and sets us upon those Actions, we perform. This *Uneasiness* we may call, as it is, *Desire*; which is an *uneasiness* of the Mind for want of some absent good. All pain of the body ... and disquiet of the mind, is *uneasiness*: And with this is always join'd Desire, equal to the pain or *uneasiness* felt; and is scarce distinguished from it.
>
> (II. xxi. 31)

The rest of the chapter is Locke's argument "that it is this *uneasiness* that determines the *Will* to the successive voluntary actions, whereof the greatest part of our Lives is made up, and by which we are conducted through different courses to different ends" (II. xxi. 33). We will come in a moment to Locke's own will to avoid the uneasiness of fatalism; but the passive voice and submerged metaphor of the last phrase (the discrete careers through which people are conducted) suggest the greater burden accompanying this severer review of passions and conduct.

Within a few paragraphs the successive voluntary actions – "unavoidably voluntary," Locke had called them (II.xxi. 24) – that comprise a life become a Hobbesian "train" of actions, each of them "for the most part" determined by the "greatest present *uneasiness*." When we reflect on how frequently we act to relieve the pressure of natural or "fantastical" pains, "we shall find that a very little part of our life is so vacant from these uneasinesses as to leave us free to the

---

[18] Locke explains his revised view of the will in terms of a "closer inspection into the working of Men's Minds, and a stricter examination of those motives and views, they are turn'd by" in "The Epistle to the Reader." See *An Essay concerning Human Understanding*, ed. Peter H. Nidditch (Oxford: Clarendon Press, 1975; corr. repr. 1987), 11. For convenience, subsequent parenthetical references to the *Essay* proper will give book, chapter, and section numbers rather than pages.

attraction of remoter absent good." As one desire is "jostled" by the
next, "we are seldom at ease and free enough... but a constant
succession of uneasinesses take the will in their turns" (II. xxi. 40–45).

Despite the skeptical implications of his psychology, Locke would no
more have welcomed Fielding's Booth as a disciple than he would have
Pope's Balaam or Swift's Phyllis. Locke takes pains to show that we
have responsibility for our actions because we have the ability to pause
long enough to act upon consideration rather than on the uppermost
uneasiness of the moment. But the course through which one is
conducted by Locke to this conclusion makes some abrupt turns. The
italics for "natural" and "so all" in the following passage are mine.

> There being in us a great many *uneasinesses* always solliciting and ready to
> determine the *will*, it is *natural*, as I have said, that the greatest and most
> pressing should determine the *will* to the next action; and so it does for the
> most part, but not always. For the mind, having in most cases, as is evident
> in Experience, a power to *suspend* the execution and satisfaction of any of its
> desires, and *so all*, one after another, is at liberty to consider the objects of
> them, examine them on all sides, and weigh them with others ... This seems
> to me the source of all liberty; in this seems to consist that which is (as I think
> improperly) called *Free will* ...and 'tis not a fault, but a perfection of our
> nature to desire, will, and act according to the last result of a fair *Examination*.
> (II. xxi. 47)

An irreverent but considered summary might come to this: Although
it is natural to act quickly and although experience confirms that most
people most of the time do just that, most people most of the time are
shown by experience to be entirely free to act otherwise and are natural
when they do so.

Locke is not the first or last philosopher to appeal to nature or
experience in competing senses. "Nature" is such a perennially elastic
term, and especially in the Augustan period, that it is not surprising to
find it meaning something like "common" or "normal" at the
beginning of this section and by the end occupying the space today
marked by the word "potential." It is perfectly natural for
contradictions to be resolved by a *natura ex machina*. But the equivocal
use of "experience" pertains more directly to literary characterization
in general and to the character progress in particular. Locke's first
reference to experience is made in the phrase "and so it does," where
it appeals to one's perception of others; the second ("as is evident in
Experience") is an appeal to introspection. If the former suggests the
generalized "Observation" presiding over the *Vanity of Human Wishes*,

the latter approaches Johnson's conversational remark, "Sir, we *know* our will's free, and *there's* an end on't."[19] Both are calls for collective agreement, but it is primarily to the former collectivity – the recognition of experienced perceivers of others – that the character progresses make their appeal.

Yet one may be more struck, finally, by the limitations of Locke's end than by the course's turnings, and here, too, Johnson helps dramatize how much might be felt to be at stake. Locke's conclusion that whatever liberty we have consists in the ability to defer our desires while we examine the matter on all sides rings rather hollowly against his almost physiological account of "uneasiness," as it does against his forceful protestation elsewhere that the "greatest part of Mankind, who are given up to Labour and enslaved to the Necessity of their mean condition" are "by the natural and unalterable State of Things ...unavoidably given over to invincible ignorance of those Proofs on which others build" (IV. xx. 2). Locke's assurances that, because we are all "short-sighted Creatures" living in a "state of Ignorance," divine benevolence has endowed us with the power of "*standing still*" (II. xxi. 50) could not be of much pertinence to Pope's characterological world of "quick whirls" and "shifting eddies" and of even less to Johnson's landscape of mists and restless motion.

Both Pope and Johnson knew Locke's *Essay* well and often refer to it approvingly.[20] Locke's emphasis conforms in general to the limited role Pope assigns to reason, and his account of "uneasiness" may have contributed to Pope's description of "love of ease" as often the strongest motive (*An Essay on Man*, II. 170). But it is possible, too, that Locke's uneasy location of free will in the "*suspension* of any desire" (II. xxi. 47) lies behind at least one of the questions near the close of *The Vanity of Human Wishes*:

> Where then shall Hope and Fear their objects find?
> Must dull Suspense corrupt the stagnant mind?
> Must helpless man, in ignorance sedate,
> Roll darkling down the torrent of his fate?

With Johnson's poem, however, we enter another world. The many tales that point the moral of *The Vanity of Human Wishes* take the form

---

[19] *Life of Johnson*, 411 (Oct. 10, 1769).
[20] In addition to Kenneth Maclean's *Locke and English Literature of the Eighteenth Century* (New Haven: Yale University Press, 1936) see Christopher Fox's very helpful *Locke and the Scriblerians: Identity and Consciousness in Early Eighteenth-Century Britain* (Berkeley and Los Angeles: University of California Press, 1988).

of progresses; but despite the successive invocations of Observation, History, and Democritus, detachment repeatedly gives way to identification and pathos. For Johnson there are no comedies that end in death.

Locke's account of the will is in one way close to the orthodox view and in another perhaps bleaker. His emphasis on human haste, myopia, and impulsiveness agrees finally with the "Augustinian" vision that Donald Greene persuasively identifies as the English theological mainstream through the eighteenth century, in which the will is fallen, blind, and confused.[21] This more than occasional conformity to established doctrine is no doubt part of what made Locke as comfortably acceptable as he was. (I do not mean to undervalue Locke's rigor or overestimate his acceptance. Pope wryly notes his exclusion from the Oxford curriculum as well as from Timon's library.)[22] But even those eager to find faith confirmed by the newer philosophy might find it disquieting that an inquiry beginning with the spirited rejection of innate ideas and innate principles should lead to an affirmation of innate weakness. Locke's new psychology, and more generally much of the increasingly sophisticated writing about the passions on both sides of the Channel during the seventeenth century, begins to look like an internalization of predestination. Instead of the view in which an individual performs an act "because" God's story includes – has always included – his or her damnation or salvation, we enter a theory in which a particular kind of individual will act in generally predictable ways "because" of his or her internal constitution and situation.

This second view differs in some important ways from the first, providing a stronger impetus, for instance, for reform movements to improve the external situation and quickening interest in the question of how education might best alter or guide the internal constitution. But unless the newer view were secularized altogether (and only Hume was prepared systematically to exclude questions of origin as pertaining to the "religious hypothesis" rather than to philosophy), it leads logically enough either to the elevation of chance or to the question of whence these different constitutions and circumstances. Despite the atmosphere of fresh starts that accompanies the new psychology, and despite the assurance of Article XVII of the Church of England that

[21] For Donald Greene's discussion of "Augustinianism" see *The Age of Exuberance* (New York: Random House, 1970), 92–100.

[22] See *Epistle to Burlington*, line 139; *Dunciad*, IV. 196 and Pope's note.

predestination should be a pleasant and sweet thought to the godly, one would not have to be unusually melancholy to feel that the question of predestination *or* free will was very much alive and perhaps not well. One place where we see both its old impasses and new intensity is in the last major poem of that most urbanely witty of Augustan arguers, Matthew Prior.

Predestination was written in the late summer of 1721, read shortly later by Pope, Robert Harley, and other friends of Prior, but not published until 1907. It has since been carefully re-edited from the several manuscript *brouillons* by H. Bunker Wright and Monroe K. Spears and appears substantially complete. Prior's outlook is pious but troubled; as the concluding prayer suggests, the question of whether one runs a free or "destined" course remains unresolved:

> O Soveraign! great Three One! O God and Man!
> Who set those Measures which I dare not Scan;
> If I have leave to chuse, I beg that choice
> Guided at least by thy Assistant Voice.
> If I must pursue a Destin'd way
> Direct my Footsteps for thou can'st not stray.
> From dangerous doubts my wandering Soul retrieve
> I cannot Argue, grant me to believe!
> Lifeless I lay, Thou wak'st me into Sense;
> Frailty is mine, and Thine Omnipotence.
>
> (267–76)

In Prior's end is his beginning, which is the premise that God made and maintains the speaker, who otherwise "must eternally have laid / In Nothings bosom" and would return to the "sad Negation" of pre-existence (lines 5–18). The personal dilemma is familiarly stated:

> Collected to my self I sadly find
> Ten thousand doubts divide my anxious mind.
> The potent biass of my crooked will
> If found averse to good, and prone to ill;
> Whence rises this depravity of thought
> Was it from mine or my forefathers fault?
> Shal I descend and say that Death and Sin
> Did from ill judging Adams crime begin
> Or tracing them from springs perhaps too high
> To good and Ill give Coeternity?
>
> (25–34)

While the poem does not strive for theological originality, Prior goes beyond mild summary. The doctrine of election (in "Austin's words transfer'd to Calvins school") leads to a view of man as "reasonable machine, / A puppet danc'd upon this Earthly Scene" and to the question of whether "destin'd Judas long before he fell" could "Avoid the terrors of a future Hell" or "Paul deny, resist or not embrace / Obtruded Heav'n, and efficacious Grace?" (lines 81–88). Paul's own text, that we are clay in the potter's hands (Romans ix. 21), unacceptably ignores the distinction between God's "senseless" and "rational" artifacts:

> If Both alike by primitive decree
> Are bound to act, and if what is must be;
> For Slain Goliah to young Davids Praise
> Can we in justice greater triumph raise,
> Than to the chosen Pebble, which he took
> Among the thousand from the Neighb'ring brook?
>
> (110–15)

Determinism is clearly unattractive, but the alternative seems to be indeterminism, with God having "left the Slacken'd Reins of Providence / To the mad guidance of our feeble Sense" (lines 152–53). The "Fatalist" who has the last and longest word in the debate (lines 231–263) is not a deist but a thoughtful believer: "Or trace your Steps thro the determin'd way / Or from the Christian Principles You stray . . ." On the other hand, those who argue for "spontaneous Liberty" by invoking the "inward Power" or "Nature" of the soul overlook its mutability and limitations:

> By time and Age its Notions are disrang'd
> By passions short and by temper chang'd
>
>   .   .   .
>
> Our operations by his Will were wrought
> And when he gave he Fixt the Pow'r of thought.
>
>   .   .   .
>
> 'Tis Sisyphys' stone returning stil
> If God who gave the freedom Form'd the Will
> To form it and incline it was the same
> You grant the thing while You dispute the Name.
>
> (166–67, 172–73, 188–91)

With the force of these conflicting arguments in mind, it seems that however Prior might have revised the poem the concluding note of supplication probably would have remained. Like Prospero, he speaks from a place where his "ending is despair, / Unless it be relieved by prayer."

The relation of Prior's *Predestination* to comic character progresses can be seen in three ways. First, the characters of the progresses (including Prior's Jack and Joan) *are* unrelieved by prayer, or any other form of introspection, and *do* end in despair or uncomprehending oblivion. They tend to be sketched from a perspective like that Prior extrapolates from Augustine and Calvin, as "reasonable Machines" (compare Rochester's "reas'ning engine") and as "puppets danc'd upon this Earthly Scene." The more predictable the progress is – or seems to have been – and the greater the illusion that the career has been read all at once, the more providential or godly the observer's assumed role becomes. But (secondly) suggestions are never far away that this role is ultimately more assumed than becoming. The character's compulsions, rationalizations, and rote responses amuse only by being more schematic than the imputed observer's train of uneasinesses and successive, hurried attempts at ease. In other words, the progresses are clearer than the observer's career, not alien to it. Finally, Pope's "hypothesis," Locke's quandary, and Prior's brooding all suggest that the character progress may have pleased as well by realizing in comic form some of the period's deepest fears of determinism and by wittily displacing the mechanical operations of "fate" onto the unwitting.

The larger relation, often antagonistic, between comic and pious "relief" will be part of the next chapter's study of wit. Before entering that province it may help to consider the more specific relation of the character progress to the different careers running through the new territory called the novel. I will begin with one of the more complexly unwitting characters of the period, Lemuel Gulliver.

Prose character progresses and the novel: Swift and Fielding

In discussing Swift's poetry I argued that he uses "phrases learned by rote" to portray his characters as cultural clichés and political liabilities, that is, as men and women whose delusions of autonomy and singular destinies make them socially vulnerable and dangerous. Clearly Swift recognizes, however, that a great distance separates being guilty of clichés and being a threat to the public security. Even in the

tortuous verbal pastoral of *A Tale of a Tub*, which like its Augustan
counterpart in difficulty, *The Dunciad*, makes a strenuous case for the
unity of dullness, even there Swift recalls that butchering the language
and butchering countries are sins of different sizes. But Swift's work
argues as powerfully as any for the relation of these two points on the
moral map. After Swift and his great contemporaries, one is likely to
think only of Orwell as a writer sensitive in the same way to the political
gravity of the cliché. That is so because for the Augustans the cliché is
not simply a boredom-bearing nuisance but the carrier of ideology – a
term I use here in the restricted sense of false consciousness.

The road from polite pettiness to political enormity is clearest in
Gulliver's Travels. That work is too encyclopedic to be read well as
simply the character progress of Gulliver, or, say, as the Progress of
Self-Reliance. But something like the structure I have tried to describe
seems to underlie it: that is, a series of emblematic scenes tending
toward the protagonist's reductive and predictable dead-end. Such a
model may prove useful if it helps mediate between the claims that
Gulliver's Travels is a novel (though an unusual one) and thus Gulliver
a novelistic character, and that it is not a novel at all but a rhetorical
satire and thus Gulliver a convenience. Reading the work as a
character progress would emphasize Gulliver's status as a political
liability, that is, as an ostensibly self-made man who is made of words
his teachers have put into his mouth and who is – *therefore*, not also –
a danger to others and himself.

Gulliver does not have the psychological consistency we have come
to expect of a novel's protagonist, but the *career* he runs is
circumstantially, ethically, and verbally predictable. His fate becomes
the more logical, almost tautological, the more carefully we are attuned
to his polite conversation. Becoming *sufficiently* attuned is not always
easy, because Gulliver is often a decent gentleman and we are often
gentle readers. A challenging point occurs in book I when Gulliver
comments on the Lilliputian decision to take him prisoner rather than
kill him in his sleep. It is an interesting moment because it helps
explain, as a matter of political conscience, how the basically amiable
Gulliver of book I is ready to try soon after to interest the
Brobdingnagian king in the attractions of gunpowder and absolute
power. And I have to confess that it interests me personally because I
managed to miss its ironic challenge through many readings. Of the
Lilliputian decision Gulliver says that while he is confident that it
would not be imitated by any prince in Europe, he is persuaded of its

wisdom. Had he awakened with the first volley of arrows he might have broken his bonds and killed the Lilliputians – "for, as they were not able to make Resistance, so they could expect no Mercy."[23]

I want partly to excuse my obtuseness by noting that several things are going on at once at this moment – including the glance at European princes – and that one does feel that a man attacked by an army has a right to defend himself, even if it is a very small army. But that is not what Gulliver claims; he instead argues ponderously that "as they were not able to make Resistance they could expect no Mercy." Mercy, of course, is *for* those who cannot make resistance – unless, that is, one is speaking a polite political language of honorable phrases, believing the words put into one's mouth by his teachers to be the testimony of conscience.

Gulliver's verbal rigidity surfaces at revealing points in his progress. These usually involve the assertion of his self-importance, ranging from the claim in Lilliput that "our" wine is better than what they drink in Blefuscu (I. v. 9) to the oratorical attempts at sublimity in describing English life to the king of Brobdingnag(II. vi-vii). The moments often recalled as primarily visual reductions – Gulliver trying to jump over a dung heap, for example, and falling short – usually turn as well on verbal stilts. Here is Gulliver's account of three "little unlucky Adventures" that occurred while he was on his own in Brobdingnag:

Once a Kite hovering over the Garden, made a Stoop at me, and if I had not resolutely drawn my Hanger, and run under a thick Espalier, he would certainly have carried me away in his Talons. Another time, walking to the Top of a fresh Mole-hill, I fell to my Neck in the Hole through which that Animal had cast up the Earth; and coined some Lye not worth remembering, to excuse my self for spoiling my Cloaths. I likewise broke my right Shin against the Shell of a Snail, which I happened to stumble over, as I was walking alone, and thinking on poor *England*.   (II. v. 4)

In the first encounter, drawing his sword "resolutely" is verbal cover for an effective but undignified retreat. In the third, "thinking on poor England" is sonorous nonsense for absent-mindedness or self-regard (thinking on poor Gulliver). In between, peeps out the vulnerable man's urge to misremember. A larger instance of Gulliver's inflation by rote phrasing occurs at the end of the second book. After returning from Lilliput Gulliver had explained that he went back to sea because of

---

[23] Passages from *Gulliver's Travels* are quoted from Herbert Davis's edition (1941, rev. 1959), which is vol. xi of *PW*. So that more commonly owned editions may be consulted, however, parenthetical references will be to part (when not evident), chapter, and paragraph.

"my insatiable Desire of seeing foreign Countries." But once home from Brobdingnag, he is drawn to travel again for the weightier reason that "my evil Destiny so ordered."

The self-importance and fondness for the fixed phrase that prompt Gulliver to convert desire to destiny also help define the impasse in Houyhnhnmland. Enough of the modern critical discussion of *Gulliver's Travels* concerns the fourth book to indicate that it is clearly more than the wholly predictable last stage of a progress.[24] But at least one simple reduction seems to "determine" Gulliver's end. Confronted progressively with the presence of the Yahoos, Gulliver sees the problem as a choice between opposing statements: (*a*) humans are Yahoos, or (*b*) humans are not Yahoos. Clinging wishfully to the second, he bitterly accepts the first. The third possibility that I take Swift to be posing is that humans are *like* Yahoos. In other words, Gulliver plucks an equation where Swift has planted a simile. To grasp the simile – a bitter enough reality for humankind – Gulliver would need a capacity for metaphor and linguistic playfulness that are beyond the frame of his progress.[25]

Fielding's *The Life of Mr. Jonathan Wild the Great* shows the difference between the character progress and the novel more clearly than any other work of the early eighteenth century. It is generally if not always comfortably read as a novel only because it contains the narrative of Wild's victims, the Heartfrees, in addition to Wild's own. Readers have long disagreed about the plausibility of the Heartfree plot itself and about whether the integration of two "co-plots" so different in atmosphere is successful, many even theorizing that they must have been composed separately. The issue here is not which of the two stories is more interesting or how cleanly they are fused but how to understand the basic difference between them.

Without the Heartfree plot, *Jonathan Wild* could easily be subtitled "The Progress of Greatness," or, more specifically, of what is commonly called greatness. In addition to Fielding's prefatory essay on the theme, the narrator frequently points to Wild's career as a pattern of the "many perils to which great men are daily subject while they are in their progress," one which proceeds unimpeded until enemies of "this

---

[24] Some of the controversies concerning the last book of *Gulliver's Travels* are reviewed in ch. 5.

[25] Martin Price observes of Gulliver among the Houyhnhnms that "he can respond to images but not to their metaphorical significance"; *Swift's Rhetorical Art* (New Haven: Yale University Press, 1953), 100.

kind of greatness" at last move to "put a stop to the future progress of our hero."[26]

Heartfree's story, however, is not a progress but an imprisonment of "sufferings" and "unmerited misfortunes" (book IV, ch. 15) that eventually requires a difficult "providential" extrication.[27] In other words, Wild's story demands a different reading than Heartfree's not only because of its topical allusions to Walpole but also because of its more axiomatic narrative predictability and simpler linearity. One of the work's running jokes is that Wild is safe from drowning (or any other fatality) because he was born to hang. On this level his career is the elaborate working out of proverbial wisdom, similar to the ironic fates of the miser's sons "born to be" spendthrifts in the *Epistle to Bathurst* or *The Rake's Progress*.

Despite Fielding's professional interest in the historical gangster, the Jonathan Wild he creates is immediately and exuberantly hyperbolic. "To confess the truth, my narrative is rather of such actions which he might have performed, or would, or should have performed, than what he really did ... Roguery, and not a rogue is my subject..." (Preface). If the pattern of predictability consists primarily of Wild's "large strides toward the summit of human glory" (that is, the gallows), much of the narrative's humor derives from his compulsively characteristic behavior between one step and the next (book III, ch.4). These intervals often suggest a comic *Inferno*, as in the card game Wild and the count undertake despite the fact that neither has any money:

a circumstance which I should not have mentioned but for the sake of observing the prodigious force of habit; for though the count knew if he won ever so much of Mr Wild he should not receive a shilling, yet could he not refrain from packing the cards; nor could Wild keep his hands out of his friend's pockets, though he knew there was nothing in them.

(book I, ch. 6)

This scene resonates at the end when Wild hangs just as he has picked the parson's pocket, the final instance of his "most admirable conservation of character" (book IV, ch. 13). Beyond their cartoon

---

[26] Henry Fielding, *Jonathan Wild*, ed. David Nokes (London: Penguin Books, 1982), book I, ch. 14; book IV, ch. 1).

[27] "Providence" and "heaven" are repeatedly invoked as the cause of Mrs. Heartfree's preservation, while the "good magistrate" who keeps Heartfree from the gallows takes on a role of authorial agency in the final chapters. In Wild's story, however, "Nature," "Fortune," and the "prodigious force of habit" are the controlling forces, while "providence" is associated with him only sarcastically. For the references to the Heartfrees see e.g. book IV, chs. 7–9, 11; for Wild see book I, ch. 6; book II, chs. 11–13; book IV, chs. 1, 14.

humor, such moments define a life of secrecy without privacy, reflex blocking out reflection. For Shaftesbury, a philosopher to whom Fielding often alludes, the incapacity for meditative self-correction marks both the bad author – "though they are often retired, they are never by themselves" – and the bad man; the ancient philosophers could fairly claim that they were "never less alone than when by themselves," while "a knave, they thought, could never be by himself."[28] Alone in a rowboat at sea, Fielding's modern philosopher "spent his time in contemplation, that is to say, in blaspheming, cursing, and sometimes singing and whistling," the same meditative acts that occupy his final hours in jail (book II, ch. 13).

Heartfree's imprisonment, meanwhile, sets in motion the plot that is fundamental to virtually all of the major novels of the early eighteenth century, a story of redemption. Heartfree does not need to be reformed, any more than Tom Jones really does, but he does need to be redeemed from captivity. If we attend to this basic structure we are reminded of the kinship of the turning points of *Robinson Crusoe, Moll Flanders, Tom Jones, Clarissa, The Female Quixote, Pamela, Amelia, The Vicar of Wakefield,* and, even, *Ferdinand Court Fathom* – the last a Wildian-Blifilian progress of roguery until Fathom's fifth-act reformation changes the narrative momentum. Undoubtedly, when we compare one novel with another it matters greatly whether the misunderstanding from which the protagonist is freed is his or her own construction or the fabrication of others, as will the question of whether the redemption seems earned or imposed. But these issues involve finer distinctions than the historically generic fact that these disparate early novels all turn, finally, on a mystery of redemption, while the character progresses run straight on to damnation. From this perspective, the early novels are progresses interrupted.

The story of Nightingale in *Tom Jones* may illustrate the point. Nightingale is "one of those young Gentlemen, who, in the last Age, were called Men of Wit and Pleasure about Town" (although less learned than his Restoration models since his reading is divided between love songs and Hoyle). He is the prospective heir of a tradesman father now turned capitalist, described later as "what they call a Man of the World, that is to say, a Man who directs his Conduct in this World, as one who being fully persuaded there is no other, is resolved to make the most of this." While young Nightingale has more generosity, being a "modern fine Gentleman ... only by Imitation, and

---

[28] *Soliloquy, or Advice to an Author,* in *Characteristics,* i. 109, 113.

meant by Nature for a much better Character," he is about to leave
Nancy Miller (the daughter of his and Tom's landlady) pregnant and
ruined in order to marry the wealthy bride his father has chosen.[29] He
is apparently destined, in other words, for a career somewhere between
The Rake's Progress and *Marriage à la Mode* – until Tom intercedes.
Releasing Nightingale simultaneously from his father's greed and his
own misunderstanding of honor, Tom's intervention converts an
otherwise predictable career into a miniature mirror of the novel's
eventual resolution in marriage. As well as any single instance could,
this point late in the novel, and late in the 1740s, at which Tom's
generic "nature" meets and overpowers Nightingale's modish "imitation" marks the end of the significant career of the character progress
itself.

From the gallows

Discussing a narrative mode that tends to conclude in bankruptcy,
disease, or stupefied death, one comes to the final critical stage with
heightened diffidence. But it is time to attempt some final generalizations concerning the character progress as an Augustan analysis and
concerning the need for a more historically sensitive "cultural poetics"
through which to view it.[30] To understand its particular social
materialism requires distinguishing it from both the "progress piece"
and the novel.[31]

   That most of the character progresses I have discussed are poems or
parts of poems is not accidental. Although prose progresses exist, the
character progress seems to be an essentially Augustan poetic mode,
depending for its effects on subtle variations within strong rhythms of
repetition, expectations of closure, and epigrammatic containment.
Because it focuses on a main character or pair of characters and moves,
him, her, or them through a temporal course, it might at first seem to

---

[29] *The History of Tom Jones*, ed. Martin C. Battestin and Fredson Bowers (Middletown, CT:
Wesleyan University Press, 1975), book xiii, ch. 5 and book xiv, ch. 8 (pp. 701, 706, 771).

[30] I borrow the phrase from Alvin B. Kernan's provocative discussion of the changing relation of
literature and society in *The Imaginary Library* (Princeton: Princeton University Press, 1982),
esp. pp. 3–36. Kernan means by "cultural poetics" (pp. 10–11) the study of the "complex
relations of literature and society," of "just how literature is immediately affected by and
responds to social change." He is particularly helpful in emphasizing the historical variability
of a "poetics" derived from the study of this changing relationship rather than from the "usual
abstractions of literary criticism, cultural history, and social theory."

[31] Perhaps it is necessary to emphasize that I am not considering many of the works included in
the standard catalogue of the progress piece, Reginald Harvey Griffith's "The Progress Pieces
of the Eighteenth Century," *Texas Review*, 5 (1920), 218–33. Griffith includes virtually all
works with "progress" in the title, making no distinction between the epochal careers of
abstractions and the brief careers of characters.

"lead to" the novel. But it is probably more accurate to think of the
character progress as an alternative to the novel than as its precursor.
Both modes of portraying character flourish, along with many others,
in the early eighteenth century. If our assumptions are evolutionary,
there is no doubt that the novel "won." If we adopt a less teleological
perspective, however, we may begin to see that those aspects of the
Augustan formation that have *not* turned out to be fittest to survive in
our era can offer the most useful entry to its historical specificity. The
progress tells, I have argued, a fundamentally different story than the
early novel and a necessarily shorter one. Too much detail, as Dryden
says of Juvenal's satires, "would make a journey of a progress, and turn
delight into fatigue," a fatigue we can imagine were Gulliver's progress
the only concern of *Gulliver's Travels* or Wild's of *Jonathan Wild*.[32]

The progress is, then, a conspicuous reduction. It modifies an
individual by an institutional idea, usually debased: thus Swift's Phyllis
is subsumed under the category "love" and Pope's Balaam under
"worth." At the same time, the general category is redefined by the
individual-as-instance, so that "honor," "reasoning," or marriage à la
mode are as tattered as the individuals constituting them. If we
compare Granville's *The Progress of Beauty* (1701), an etherial pageant
of famous lovelies culminating in present-day Hampton Court, with
Swift's poem of the same title, we descend abruptly to a world of
biological, economic, and social vulnerability. In this respect the
character progress is distant from the idealist narratives of the progress
of an abstraction, whether positive, like Thomson's *Liberty*, or negative,
like the *Dunciad*, where the individuals appear as immortals – heroic
spirits or comic proofs of the transmigration of souls. The character
progress's redefinition of transcendental categories by appeal to
biological–political instances is similar to Eliot's use of Sweeney to
"refute" philosophical Idealism:

> (The lengthened shadow of a man
> Is history, said Emerson
> Who had not seen the silhouette
> Of Sweeney straddled in the sun.)[33]

Like other forms of reduction, the character progress does not
encourage identification with the subject as individual, offering only

[32] Dryden, "A Discourse concerning the Original and Progress of Satire," in *Of Dramatic Poesy
and Other Critical Essays*, 2 vols., ed. George Watson (New York: Dutton, 1962), ii. 130.
[33] "Sweeney Erect," lines 25–28, in T.S. Eliot, *The Complete Poems and Plays, 1909–1950* (New
York: Harcourt, Brace and World, 1962), 26.

what Hans Robert Jauss would classify as "ironic identification." In its
particular selectivity, the progress tends to present character as
materially "determined" by class goals, economic relationships, and
physical conditions; as a specialized form of satire, the progress shares
the tendency Keith Fort identifies in satire generally to depict
characters as "subservient to the laws of nature, society, and type when
they pridefully think they are unique in their individual differences."[34]
Partly because of its cautionary morality and partly because when
viewed through the later moralistic traditions its typologies may appear
class-bound and unpsychological, the character progress can easily, too
easily, be seen as essentially reactionary. It is arguable, however, that
the progress offers a starker political analysis than many of the
autobiographies or novels commonly felt to be more congenially
"progressive." Jauss's general claim that "procedures of ironizing
identification and the destruction of illusion" pull the reader out of
"unreflected advertence to the aesthetic object" suggests how irony
and analysis can join in the character progress. Ironic identification
makes us more conscious of aesthetic conventions, but it may also lead
to a more fundamental "questioning of the aesthetic attitude as
such."[35] I would take this argument one step further to say that the
particular aesthetic attitude emerging along with the novel in the
eighteenth century – and tacitly challenged by the character progress
– is one that grows increasingly reverential toward individual consciousness as the anchor of realism. Catherine Belsey puts forth the
strong argument that "classic realism" – a category that includes most
of the canonical English novels – "does the work of ideology" by
investing so heavily in individual consciousness and thus reflecting the
bourgeois reader's assumptions. "Initially (and continuously) constructed in discourse, the subject finds in the discourse of the classic
realist text a confirmation of the position of autonomous subjectivity
represented in ideology as 'obvious.'"[36] The character progress, on

---

[34] Keith Fort, "Satire and Gnosticism," *Religion and Literature*, 20.2 (Summer 1988), 1–18; the
quotation is from p. 6.
[35] Hans Robert Jauss, *Aesthetic Experience and Literary Hermeneutics*, trans. Michael Shaw
(Minneapolis: University of Minnesota Press, 1982), 181–82.
[36] Catherine Belsey, *Critical Practice* (London and New York: Methuen, 1980), 72, 84. Belsey's
discussion of ideology is based primarily on Louis Althusser. Frank Kermode makes a related
point concerning the arbitrariness of "natural" psychology in the novel: "That character, in
the modern sense of the word, takes precedence over story (or 'agent' over 'fable') seems
natural enough after two and a half centuries of the novel, and after endless practice in reading
the narrative clues on which – with the help of our memories of other books, our knowledge of
character codes – we found our conventional notions of individuality. Yet there is nothing

the other hand, by limiting its sympathies toward the subjective individual, presents private experience as socially categorical, questioning the very reality of an autonomous realm of the private.[37]

As with Augustan satire generally, the political analysis of the character progress is misunderstood if labelled "conservative"; for a perspective which attends to class and social role is not intrinsically more conservative than one that relegates those realities to the supposed status of "accidentals." It is true that we can, in the old phrase, say of Hogarth's harlot or Swift's Phyllis that "she is no better than she should be." But the more radical diagnosis equally available is that she is no better than she could be.

It is important to understand that when we praise other fictions, especially later and longer narratives, for their three-dimensional characterization, organic development of character, transcendence of types, or psychological authenticity, we are usually speaking from within the perspective sometimes called the Whig Interpretation of History. That perspective is a teleological one in which the novel, like the middle class, has "risen" and in which premises of liberalism and historically conditioned ideas of the ultimate autonomy of the individual are taken as if they were forces of nature. Recognizing the partiality of this story helps us hear the Augustan story more fully.

natural about it; it is a cultural myth . . ." (*The Genesis of Secrecy: On the Interpretation of Narrative* [Cambridge, MA: Harvard University Press, 1979], 76–77).

[37] For a brief sketch of the political contentions surrounding "private" see Raymond Williams's entries on it and on "individual" in *Keywords: A Vocabulary of Culture and Society*, rev. edn. (London: Flamingo, 1983).

2

About wit: Locke, Jakobson, and
Augustan ideas

For thee explain a thing till all men doubt it,
And write about it, Goddess, and about it...

Dunciad, IV. 251–52

Sooner or later in any discussion of Augustan literature the word Wit, if not the spaniel, splashes its way back to the hunter's side. That major authors of the Restoration and early eighteenth century prized and practiced wit is perhaps the one thing every succeeding generation has agreed on, although with widely differing evaluations of that achievement. Each retrospective estimate of Dryden or Pope seems, interestingly, to approach Dryden's view of one of his predecessors: "if we are not so great wits as Donne, yet certainly we are better poets." As Dryden's usage and the work of many modern scholars remind us, the value and definition of wit have been complex all along. Wit is Nature in ambiguity dressed – and so is Nature.[1]

Despite the broad problems of historical semantics, readers continue to agree that Restoration repartee, *The Rape of the Lock*, Fielding's asides and prefaces, most of the poetry of Swift and Prior, and *The Beggar's Opera* are all witty. Whatever we take Augustan wit to be, we are likelier to seek it in Gay than Gray. We do not seek it everywhere in the period – rarely in Defoe, scarcely in Richardson, for example – but wherever we find it the impression is generally one of hearing a shared language of the age rather than a clever idiolect. The examples mentioned range greatly but call to mind a familiar mixture of

---

[1] Dryden, "A Discourse concerning the Original and Progress of Satire," in *Of Dramatic Poesy and Other Critical Essays*, 2 vols., ed. George Watson (New York, 1962: Dutton), ii. 144; additional references to this edition of Dryden's criticism will be given parenthetically. An eminently useful survey of the status of "wit," especially in relation to the opposition of wit and judgment, is in the Introduction by Aubrey L. Williams and Emile Audra to *TE*. i: *Pastoral Poetry and An Essay on Criticism*.

"common" sense, unconventional perspective, quickness, economy, and irreverence, to which no single writer (no Austen or Wilde, for example) has a unique claim in the period. We might attempt to focus this historical impression by looking for a moment at what might be called the epitaph of Augustan wit, the couplet John Gay wrote for his tomb, and at the reaction it provoked in a young writer of a later generation, Samuel Johnson. The lines Gay asked Pope to put on his grave and which duly appeared in Westminster Abbey are these:

> Life is a jest; and all things show it.
> I thought so once; but now I know it.
> ("My Own Epitaph," Gay, i. 253)

Writing for the *Gentleman's Magazine* in 1738, Johnson finds this "trifling distich" more proper for the "window of a brothel" than for a monument. All people, he argues, do or do not believe in a future state of rewards and punishment. "In one of these classes our poet must be ranked ... If he was of the latter opinion, he must think life more than a jest, unless he thought eternity a jest too; and if these were his sentiments, he is by this time most certainly undeceived. These lines, therefore, are impious in the mouth of a Christian, and nonsense in that of an atheist."[2] Nothing suggests that Gay saw any contradiction between making a good end and making a jest, or that friends such as Pope, Arbuthnot, and Swift found the epitaph trifling. Johnson's objections have their reason, but not the reason of his predecessors. The encounter reminds one again how often Augustan wit plays upon mortality and how often it laughs at the oppositional logic of either/or. The common language Gay counted on was quickly disappearing.

While this episode suggests wit's passage, the more closely we look for the common language the less explicit it seems to have been. Not only does "wit" itself have an array of meanings, as even the casual reader of *An Essay on Criticism* soon suspects, but it has its own oppositional story through the late seventeenth and early eighteenth centuries. The best-known version is that of True Wit versus False Wit in Addison's series of *Spectator* essays (nos. 58 to 63), but Addison builds on Locke's earlier opposition of Wit and Judgment. Locke in turn was probably influenced by Malebranche, almost surely by Hobbes, perhaps by Boyle, and possibly by Bacon. We may begin with Locke not only because his oppositions seem to have been the most influential but also

---

[2] "On Gay's Epitaph," in *Samuel Johnson*, ed. Donald Greene (New York: Oxford University Press, 1984), 51–53.

because a careful reading of *An Essay concerning Human Understanding* shows that behind the desire to derogate or dignify wit lie issues far distant from coffeehouse decorum. At stake are conflicting notions of intellectual coherence and competing versions of reality. After exploring Locke's dichotomy and its implications in his theory of knowledge, I will turn to its subversion, respectively genteel and raucous, by Addison and Prior. Less suspicious of language than Locke, both Addison and Prior are more deeply skeptical of individual aspirations to an unmediated agreement of thinking and things.

Wit and judgment in Locke

I shall imagine I have done some Service to Truth, Peace, and Learning, if, by any enlargement on this Subject, I can make Men reflect on their own Use of Language; and give them Reason to suspect, that since it is frequent for others, it may also be possible for them, to have sometimes very good and approved Words in their Mouths, and Writings, with very uncertain, little, or no signification. And therefore it is not unreasonable for them to be wary herein themselves, and not to be unwilling to have them examined by others.
An Essay concerning Human Understanding, book III
("OF WORDS"), CH. V

In a later chapter of the same book Locke would attend to wit under the rubric "Of the Abuse of Words," but he had in fact discussed it at some length before deciding to take language as his province. This earlier passage from book II ("Of Ideas") is the one Addison put into broad circulation the morning of May 11, 1711, by quoting most of it in the fifth of six *Spectators* on wit.

If in having our *Ideas* in the Memory ready at hand, consists quickness of parts; in this, of having them unconfused, and being able nicely to distinguish one thing from another, where there is but the least difference, consists, in a great measure, the exactness of Judgment, and clearness of Reason, which is to be observed in one Man above another. And hence, perhaps, may be given some Reason of that common Observation, That Men who have a great deal of Wit, and prompt Memories, have not always the clearest Judgment, or deepest Reason. For *Wit* lying most in the assemblage of *Ideas*, and putting those together with quickness and variety, wherein can be found any resemblance or congruity, thereby to make up pleasant Pictures, and agreeable Visions in the Fancy: *Judgment*, on the contrary, lies quite on the other side, in separating carefully, one from another, *Ideas* wherein can be found the least difference, thereby to avoid being misled by Similitude, and by affinity to take one thing for another. This is a way of proceeding quite contrary to Metaphor and Allusion, wherein, for the most part, lies that entertainment and pleasantry of Wit, which strikes so lively on the Fancy, and therefore [is] so acceptable to all People; because its Beauty appears at first sight, and there is required no labour of thought, to examine what Truth or Reason there is in it. The Mind, without looking further, rests satisfied with the agreeableness of the Picture, and the gayety of the Fancy: And it is a kind of affront to go about to examine it, by the severe Rules of Truth, and good Reason; whereby it appears, that it consists in something, that is not perfectly conformable to them.

(II. xi. 2)

This passage is worth considering more carefully than has been the modern habit. What is regrettably still the standard work on Locke and eighteenth-century literature points to the influence of the dichotomy but refers to it as a "detached bit of psychology" of "obviously little significance" in Locke's philosophy, a view more recent commentators seem to endorse by passing on in silence.[3] Even literary critics as alert to Locke's metaphorical valences as Paul de Man tend to proceed directly to book III and the explicit remarks on language. My view is that this piece of psychologizing is thoroughly attached to the tensions in Locke's argument throughout the *Essay* and that understanding those tensions can help us read several Augustan works of wit with something more of the spirit that their authors writ.

Since Locke's account is clearly on the side of judgment – itself finding differences rather than resemblances – it may help to underscore just what is "quite contrary" to what. One can make the following lists of constituents or qualities, although without complete symmetry:

Wit	*Judgment*
assemblage of ideas	discrimination of ideas
quickness	care
variety	clarity
entertainment and pleasantry	truth and reason
immediate picture	labor of thought
gaiety of fancy	severity of truth and good reason
metaphor	(distinction?)
allusion	(?)

Although Locke does not provide an opposing term to metaphor, it

---

[3] Kenneth MacLean, *John Locke and English Literature of the Eighteenth Century* (New Haven: Yale University Press, 1936), 63.

is clear that metaphor marks the appetite of wit for similarities, while judgment patiently seeks out differences. The place of allusion may seem less obvious, however, first because we do not necessarily associate it with wit in particular (as distinguished, for example, from scholarly writing or sermons), and secondly because Locke gives no plain counterpart to it other than judgment's "whole way of proceeding." But plainly allusion is still on Locke's mind when he discusses wit again in book III. This section, too, is long, but worth quoting whole in the interests of "care" rather than "quickness":

Since Wit and Fancy finds [*sic*] easier entertainment in the World, than dry Truth and real Knowledge, *figurative Speeches*, and allusion in Language, will hardly be admitted as *an* imperfection or *abuse* of it. I confess, in Discourses, where we seek rather Pleasure and Delight, than Information and Improvement, such Ornaments as are borrowed from them, can scarce pass for Faults. But yet, if we would speak of Things as they are, we must allow, that all the Art of Rhetorick, besides Order and Clearness, all the artificial and figurative application of Words Eloquence hath invented, are for nothing else but to insinuate wrong *Ideas*, move the Passions, and thereby mislead the Judgment; and so indeed are perfect cheat; and therefore however laudable or allowable Oratory may render them in Harangues and popular Addresses, they are certainly, in all Discourses, that pretend to inform or instruct, wholly to be avoided; and where Truth or Knowledge are concerned, cannot but be thought a great fault, either of the Language or Person that makes use of them. What, and how various they are, will be superfluous here to take notice; the Books of Rhetorick which abound in the world, will instruct those, who want to be informed: Only I cannot but observe, how little the preservation and improvement of Truth and Knowledge, is the Care and Concern of Mankind; since the Arts of Fallacy are endow'd and preferred. 'Tis evident how much Men love to deceive, and be deceived, since Rhetorick, that powerful instrument of Error and Deceit, has its established Professors, is publickly taught, and has always been in great Reputation: And I doubt not but it will be thought great boldness, if not brutality in me, to have said thus much against it. *Eloquence*, like the fair Sex, has too prevailing Beauties in it, to suffer it self ever to be spoken against. And 'tis in vain to find fault with those Arts of Deceiving, wherein Men find pleasure to be Deceived.

(III. x. 34)

The opposition of "truth" and "rhetoric," it has been frequently noted, has been essential to philosophy's self-definition since Plato's attack on the Sophists; philosophy is distinguished by not being rhetoric or poetry. Locke's particular "plain-style" aversion to the "arts of fallacy" is familiar. What the passage emphasizes most strongly are the values implicit in Locke's earlier distinction, since the quasi-psychological opposition of wit and judgment now becomes the openly ethical contest of wit and fancy on one side (the syntax of the first sentence merges them) against knowledge and truth on the other. Keeping the "sides" in the same order as before, we can extend the list of oppositions partially but significantly.

Wit and Fancy	Knowledge and Truth
pleasure and delight	information and instruction
rhetoric and eloquence	speech of "things as they are"
artificial and figurative ap- plication of words	(?)
allusion	(?)

Before trying to fill in the blanks we need to consider the dramatic entrance from the right of "things as they are." The phrase entails a claim to full knowledge of the world which contradicts countless reminders of epistemological limits in every major part of the *Essay*. Many of these are familiar and prudential (for example, "Our Business here is not to know all things, but those which concern our Conduct" [I. i. 6]); the point behind them is that we do not, generally speaking, have knowledge of things but knowledge of "things" as they appear in the mind, that is, knowledge of ideas. If we look back to the distinction between wit and judgment in book II, we find Locke attempting to be more careful in describing the operations of the mind that assemble and that separate as both being operations upon *ideas*. But we also find there a brief lapse important enough to suggest that the recurrence to "things as they are" in book III is unguarded but not exactly accidental.

The first sentence of the earlier passage associates wit with "having our *ideas* in the memory ready at hand" but judgment with "having them unconfused and being able nicely to distinguish one *thing* from another" (my emphasis). This silent slide from ideas to things is crucial to Locke's dichotomy and, as I will try to show, a clue to greater problems within the *Essay*. Attributing to wit the "artificial and figurative application of words" and "allusion" implies, of course, contrary ways of proceeding in the world of judgment, knowledge, and truth. What exactly are these contraries? Presumably the first would be the natural and literal application of words, and the second would be unallusive language.

In short, Locke's charged opposition of wit and judgment entails three major claims: (1) we can know and speak of things as they are; ·

(2) we can (and should) speak naturally and literally; (3) we can (and should) speak without allusion. The question is whether there is really any space in Locke's *Essay* for any of the three assumptions. Put another way, in light of Locke's rigorous contributions to epistemology, to the study of language, and to ethics, what are we to make of his supposition that we can and should seek an unartificial language free of allusion and illusion? The boundaries between the epistemological and linguistic-ethical claims Locke makes in attacking wit are less clear than my listing of them.may suggest, but I will try to consider them in the order enumerated above.

I have already suggested that the general difficulty behind Locke's claim that judgment distinguishes *things* or that it guides us in speaking of "things as they are" stems from the commitment of the *Essay* as a whole to the view that what we know are (only) our ideas. Since able readers of Locke from Thomas Reid to the present have commented on the tension between that commitment and Locke's equally strong belief that our senses give knowledge of the external world, we may concentrate selectively on a few of the *Essay*'s moments of attempted reconciliation in order to see the range of Locke's ideas about ideas. Seeing that range may help in understanding Locke's occasional vehemence, because it stretches, sometimes awkwardly, from ideas as "mental Draughts" or "Pictures of Things" (II. xxix. 8) to ideas as barely legible signs.

In his discussion of "clear and obscure, Distant and Confused Ideas," Locke launches at once into visual metaphor – "the Perception of the Mind, being most aptly explained by Words relating to the Sight" – in order to argue that "our *simple Ideas* are *clear*, when they are such as the objects from whence they were taken did or might in a well-ordered sensation or perception, present them" (II. xxix. 2). This painstakingly worded statement seems to offer more certainty than it provides. It sounds as if clear ideas are visual copies ("taken") of objects viewed in the way a normal person perceives them. But if in place of the words Locke italicizes we attend to *as* and *might*, we find that what seemed a generic or casual account of the origin of clear ideas is a conditional description of them based on a simile: Ideas are clear when they are kinds of mental images *like* those that normal viewers *might* have registered had they been there.

The fate of *simple* ideas is noteworthy because while Locke is habitually ready to grant that *complex* ideas are things we make up to think and talk with ("fictions of the mind") rather than direct perceptions, he is understandably less willing to sever the mimetic link between simple ideas and the external world. At his most scrupulous, however, he does sever most of it. Not only is "likeness" to things in the world restricted to simple ideas, it is narrowed still further to simple ideas of "primary qualities" of body (solidity, extension, figure, motion, and number as opposed to colors, sounds, tastes, and so on). It would seem that only Newton spent most of his time having ideas "like" the world. Such ideas "*are resemblances*" of bodies and "these patterns do really exist." The rest "*have no resemblance* of them at all. There is nothing like our *Ideas* existing in the bodies themselves" (II. viii. 15). It is in this chapter that Locke's "idea" becomes more like the response to a sign than like a picture. Most simple ideas of sensation are "no more the likeness of something existing without us than the names that stand for them are the likeness of our *ideas*, which yet upon hearing they are apt to excite in us" (II. viii. 7).

Our experience, in other words, is closer to reading or listening to speech than to looking at things. We have, with the exception of primary qualities, access not to objects but to signifiers. Had Locke pursued this model of experience consistently, rather than the complex of visual metaphors noted earlier, the *Essay* would be a very different book; as it is, the linguistic analogy surfaces at several revealing points, often in negative terms, as in the remarks on wit or rhetoric. Before going further it is necessary to underscore the significance of the analogy here by recalling that Locke is perhaps the first major analyst of language to stress that the relation of signifier to signified is not divinely instituted or mimetic but "perfectly arbitrary" (III. ii. 8). What the linguistic analogy implies, then, is a functional, convenient, but wholly ungrounded relation of idea and world.

At this point we can begin to see Locke's denigration of figurative expressions and allusions in the context of his uneasiness about language in general. There are moments in Locke, as we will see, where words alone are certain truth, but many more, and more explicit ones, of linguistic skepticism: "For he that shall well consider the *Errors* and Obscurity, the Mistakes and Confusion, that is *spread in the World by an ill use of Words*, will find some reason to doubt whether Language, as it has been employ'd, has contributed more to the improvement or hindrance of Knowledge amongst Mankind" (III. xi. 4). Locke's suspicion of what he terms the "cover of wit and good language" runs deeper than the currents of plain-style "Puritanism" or scientific polemic. The tension between Locke's thinking of ideas as pictures or as interpretations of signs (or correspondingly of objects available to us as things or as signifiers) is played out at large in the *Essay* as a tension between truth as residing in perceptions or in propositions. The explanation I want to try to illustrate is this: having reached the uncomfortable insight that our experience of "things" is in fact the experience of signifiers, Locke seeks to manage the radical implications of the linguistic analogy by reverting to the model of perceptions and pictures and by stipulating impossibly strict standards for proper language. If experience may be just a language, then language itself had best be kept determinate. It should, against all odds, speak of things as they are.

Locke's treatment of language in book III of the *Essay* strikes readers as remarkably free of theories of origin and (perhaps therefore) surprisingly consistent on the arbitrariness of the relation between signified and signifier. Hans Aarsleff's *From Locke to Saussure* claims more than chronological priority for Locke. To be sure, language is God's gift to humanity, but the terms remain general: language is defined as the totality of all natural languages and as their use by the totality of speakers. Unlike vast numbers of his contemporaries and many later writers, Locke nowhere in the *Essay*'s chapters on language speculates about Adam and Eve, the Tower of Babel, or, except dismissively, mysterious or mystical connections between names and things named. However pious his intentions at large (the "main end of these inquiries" being "knowledge and veneration" of the "Sovereign Disposer of all things" [II. vii. 6]i), for purposes of philosophic discussion there is no linguistic paradise lost.[4] But where an Adamic myth surfaces instead is in Locke's notion of a language of judgment that names things as they are, without figure and, as only Adam could, without allusion.

Locke's contradictions on the subject of figurative language in book III have been brilliantly illustrated by de Man,[5] and the issue of metaphor in the *Essay* as a whole can be best considered in connection with the responses to Locke of Addison and Prior. For now at least a partial answer emerges to the question of what allusion has to do with

---

[4] Cf. Hans Aarsleff, *From Locke to Saussure* (Minneapolis: University of Minnesota Press, 1982), 25: "Looking toward the past, Locke's argument was aimed at the most widely held seventeenth-century view of the nature of language, a doctrine that can best be called by the umbrella term the Adamic language ... In the Adamic doctrine the relation between signifier and signified is not arbitrary; the linguistic sign is not double but unitary."

[5] Paul de Man, "The Epistemology of Metaphor," *Critical Inquiry* (1978), 13–30; repr. in Sheldon Sacks (ed.), *On Metaphor* (Chicago: University of Chicago Press, 1979), 11–28.

figurative speech in Locke's opposition of wit and judgment. Like
"eloquence" and other "artificial" uses of language, allusions lack
original innocence, are in fact the most emphatic figure of this lack, of
having fallen into time. Let us return briefly, then, to the question of
how an idea of an *un*allusive language fits so uneasily with Locke's
arguments elsewhere in the *Essay*.

The two arguments that run counter to the unallusive norm are
linguistic and epistemological, although again the boundaries are not
always distinct. The linguistic argument is relatively simple. When
discussing language directly Locke argues, consistently, that since
words have "naturally no signification" the "*Idea* which each stands
for, must be learned and retained by those, who would exchange
Thoughts and hold intelligible Discourse with others" (III. ix. 5). What
such learning and retention of common usage amounts to is a continual
series of allusions, to the usage of past and present speakers. Most of
these allusions are of course non-conscious, and any conventional
notion of language implies our ability to make them, even our inability
not to make them most of the time. But Locke goes further to
recommend conscious allusions. If we would seek "propriety of
speech," as indeed we should since words are "no man's private
possession but the common measure of commerce and communication," we will find propriety by studying and imitating the usage of
our linguistic predecessors: "The proper signification and use of Terms
is best to be learned from those, who in their Writings and Discourses,
appear to have had the clearest Notions, and apply'd to them their
Terms with the exactest choice and fitness" (III. xi. 11).

Let me acknowledge at once that my use of "allusion" may well be
broader than Locke intended and that he might have been thinking not
of the shared use of words but of distinctive phrases and sentences –
something closer to quotation. But it is also clear that in the attacks on
wit in books II and III he is not criticizing the citation of authorities,
something he does attack elsewhere, although even then as characteristic of scholasticism rather than of wit, fancy, or eloquence. It may
be that he means something close to what allusion usually means in
modern literary discussion, that is, intentional reference to previously
used phrases or verbally established contexts for the complication of
present meaning. And if we add that allusion often complicates by
suggesting at least a fleeting parallel, we may see why Locke repeats the
word in the same breath with "figurative speeches" and "similitude."
But when we have granted all of this, it remains true that Locke's

notion of a wholly direct and unallusive discourse belongs to a less sophisticated theory of language "quite contrary" to allusion. In view of Locke's account of language as the sum of common conventions, a speech that is the opposite of allusive speech would seem to belong to a world of neither wit nor judgment but desire.

If the allusiveness Locke denigrates is in fact central to his theory of language, is it also central to his theory of knowledge? Much of the *Essay* can be read as a succession of attempts to answer no to this question, to put the knower and the known in a direct relation, unmediated by community or language. Before considering a few of the efforts to find extralinguistic certainties in book IV, I want to turn to a final episode in the discussion of language which seems already an epistemological episode as well. Locke is discussing the names of "mixed Modes," that is several ideas of "sorts or Species of Things" (III. v. 1), and arrives at the interesting observation that, unlike simple ideas, these complex ideas usually become known to us *after* we have learned the words for them.

I confess, that in the beginning of Languages, it was necessary to have the *Idea*, before one gave it the Name: And so it is still, where making a new complex *Idea*, one also, by giving it a new Name, makes a new Word. But this concerns not Languages made, which have generally pretty well provided for *Ideas*, which Men have frequent Occasion to have, and communicate: And in such, I ask, whether it be not the ordinary Method, that Children learn the Names of mixed Modes, before they have their *Ideas*? What one of a thousand ever frames the abstract *Idea* of *Glory* and *Ambition*, before he has heard the Names of them?

(III. v. 15)

With the rare exceptions, then, of new coinages, the large range of ideas that make converse of any complexity possible are learned by a process of allusion. The vocabulary of these ideas exists first as a vocabulary.

I have been arguing that Locke's criticism of the figures and allusions of wit is part of an uneasiness about language at large and that his criticism was sharpened by the suspicion that knowledge and language are inseparable. Locke would not concede their inseparability. What he says instead, explaining how he came to write book III, is that he found that knowledge and words had "so near a connexion" that "very little" could be "said clearly or pertinently" about knowledge without first observing the "face and manner of signification" of words.

Because knowledge is, in Locke's suggestive phrase, "conversant about truth," it has "constantly to do with propositions." While it ends "in things," it arrives there "so much by the intervention of words" that they seem "scarce separable" from general knowledge. "At least they interpose themselves so much between our Understandings, and the Truth, which it would contemplate and apprehend, that like the *Medium* through which visible Objects pass, their Obscurity and Disorder does not seldom cast a mist before our Eyes, and impose upon our Understandings" (III. ix. 21). The progress of actions attributed to words is striking: words intervene, then interpose, and finally impose.

In a landscape so populated or where, to take a later metaphor, so many have wandered "lost in the great Wood of Words," mathematics often looks like the safest way out of allusion and illusion. By "abstracting their Thoughts from Names, and accustoming themselves to set before their Minds the *Ideas* themselves ... and not sounds instead of them," mathematicians have escaped most of the "perplexity, puddering, and confusion" of other fields (IV. iii. 30). If we would "but separate the *Idea* under consideration from the Sign that stands for it" moral knowledge would be "as *capable of real Certainty*, as Mathematics" (IV. iv. 7, 9). I will return to Locke's admiration for mathematical method in discussing Prior's response to the *Essay*, but the general point is simply that the main appeal of mathematics for Locke seems to be that it offers not a world of symmetry unencumbered by matter, or (as one might expect) more direct access to primary qualities, but an escape from words.

Locke's desire for extralinguistic certainty shows forth even when he argues more fully the point that truth resides in propositions. The chapter in which he does so, "Of Truth in General" (IV. v), is one of the most curious in the *Essay*, and it is so because of Locke's insistence on a distinction between mental and verbal propositions, "truth of thought" and "truth of words." For it turns out that when he begins by defining truth as "nothing but *the joining or separating of Signs, as the Things signified by them, do agree or disagree one with another*" (IV. v. 2), Locke is not at all making the same definitional move that Hobbes has made in declaring that "*True* and *False* are attributes of Speech, not of Things. And where Speech is not, there is neither Truth nor Falsehood.... *Truth* consisteth in the right ordering of names in our affirmations."[6] On the contrary, for Locke the "signs" we join or separate to make propositions can be either words *or* ideas: "So that

---

[6] Thomas Hobbes, *Leviathan*, ed. C.B. Macpherson (London: Penguin, 1968), 104 (i.iv).

Truth properly belongs only to Propositions: whereof there are two sorts, viz. Mental and Verbal; as there are two sorts of Signs commonly made use of, *viz. Ideas* and Words" (IV. v. 2). This is a most unusual definition of "idea," I believe unprecedented in the *Essay* to this point. (Although I have argued that some of Locke's descriptions of ideas imply that they are like our responses to signs, the synonyms he himself normally uses are phantasms, motions, perceptions, pictures, and so on.) This odd twist allows Locke, however, to go on to assert the necessity of considering truth of thought and truth of words "distinctly one from another" (IV. v. 2–3).

Necessary as it is, there are two difficulties conceded. The first is that as soon as we begin to describe mental propositions in words they become verbal propositions (a problem analogous to trying to observe oneself without being self-conscious, say, which does not usually lessen the belief that one has periods of unselfconsciousness). The second, much greater difficulty Locke poses to his own distinction appears to undo it entirely: "And that which makes it *harder to treat of mental* and verbal *Propositions separately*, is That most Men, *if not all* [my emphasis], in their Thinking and Reasonings within themselves, make use of Words instead of *Ideas*, at least when the subject of their meditation contains in it complex *Ideas*" (IV. v. 4; cf. IV. vi. 2). Having opened the possibility that all propositions of much complexity are verbal rather than purely mental, Locke vacillates between extremes in the rest of this brief chapter "Of Truth in General." He wishes at one point that those who speak on subjects like religion, power, or melancholy (all of them remarkably complex ideas) would "think only of the Things themselves" (IV. v. 4) rather than their words, while at another point he restricts his definition of truth further to only verbal propositions: "*Truth* is the marking down in Words, the agreement or disagreement of *Ideas* as it is" (IV. v. 9).

The following passage encapsulates the difficulties in Locke's view of the relation of thought and language that he seems alternately to admit and expel from serious discussion:

Every one's Experience will satisfie him, that the Mind, either by perceiving or supposing the Agreement or disagreement of any of its *Ideas*, does tacitly within it self put them into a kind of Proposition affirmative or negative, which I have endeavoured to express by the terms *Putting together* and *Separating*. But this Action of the Mind, which is so familiar to every thinking and reasoning Man, is easier to be conceived by reflecting on what passes in us, when we affirm or deny, than to be explained by Words.

(IV. v. 6)

Locke's meaning seems to be that our habit of making non-verbal propositions can be better imagined non-verbally than explained verbally. In other words, the proposition that we habitually make tacit propositions is most clear as a tacit proposition.

Addison, Prior, and Locke's dichotomy

If Locke's opposition of wit and judgment involves as many problems as the previous section claims (and a few more will be suggested here), it is material to ask why it ever attracted Joseph Addison. That we cannot know Addison's motivation as he sat to the pages that would become *Spectator* 62 does not preclude some guesses. There is the general prestige of the *Essay*, and there is Addison's particular interest in bringing philosophy from the closet to the coffeehouse. Moreover, Locke's opposition has the appeal of familiar wisdom (so-and-so is "clever" but not thoughtful, or "steady" but not quick) suddenly bolstered by modern analysis ("and hence perhaps may be given some reason ... "), all looking for the moment like it might offer an exhaustive characterological dichotomy. The recurrent fantasy of such a dichotomy is neatly satirized in the quip that there are two kinds of people: those who divide things into two and those who don't. Neither eighteenth- nor twentieth-century intellectuals are immune to the charms of such a prospect. But it is probably safer to modify the question about Addison to *how* he found Locke's dichotomy attractive. How much of it does he accept, how does he use it, and how does it look when he has finished?

Like the rest of the series (nos. 58–63), *Spectator* 62 contrasts "true" wit and "false" wit.[7] Addison begins it by referring to Locke's "admirable Reflection upon the Difference of Wit and Judgment, whereby he endeavours to shew the Reason why they are not always the Talents of the same Person." He then quotes all of the passage from II. xi. 2 quoted earlier in this chapter (see p. 51), except the first sentence, replaced by his summary, and the last sentence and a half, thus ending with Locke's observation that through metaphor and allusion wit "strikes so lively on the Fancy, and is therefore acceptable to all People." The passage, then, that Addison commends as the "best and most philosophical Account that I have ever met with of Wit" has

---

[7] My quotations from *Spectator* 62 are from *The Spectator*, 5 vols., ed. Donald F. Bond (Oxford: Oxford University Press, 1965), i. 263–70; for convenience, parenthetical references indicate paragraphs rather than pages.

already changed clothes for the meeting. His introduction neutralizes Locke's explanation of why men of wit are often not good judges (Locke says nothing of wit being beyond the reach of men of judgment) to a distinction of talents. And in silently ignoring the latter part of Locke's section he suppresses Locke's *regret* that wit is so "acceptable to all people," a fact due to its requiring "no labour of thought" and not being up to the rigor of "truth or reason." Similarly, Addison makes no mention of Locke's attack on wit, figurative language, and allusion in book III (quoted above on p. 53).

To what he does quote Addison adds and qualifies. Locke's is the best (previous) explanation of wit, "which generally, tho' not always consists in such a Resemblance and Congruity of Ideas as this Author mentions. I shall only add to it, by way of Explanation, That every Resemblance of Ideas is not that which we call Wit, unless it be such an one that gives *Delight* and *Surprize* to the Reader: These two Properties seem essential to Wit, more particularly the last of them." The reserve clause ("generally, tho' not always") we can hold, with Addison, until the conclusion of his consideration of Locke. Before going there it is worth noting, first, that Addison's "Resemblance and Congruity of Ideas" replaces Locke's assertion that wit is an "assemblage of ideas" based on "any resemblance or congruity" the assembler can find, and, second, that Addison's emphasis on the *surprize* of wit suggests pleasure from the discovery of real resemblance in place of Locke's "beauty ... at first sight." Both alterations are important for Addison's later propositions (para. 8) "That the Basis of all Wit is Truth" and that a beautiful thought has "its Foundation in the Nature of Things."

The essential claim of most of the rest of Addison's essay, where he appropriates Locke's dichotomy between wit and judgment into his own between two kinds of wit, is that true wit is true. The point is explicit but sometimes lost sight of because "true" wit can be taken to mean something like "genuine" or "pure" wit and because Addison also uses contrasts like "Gothic" versus "natural" (para. 9); but the starker terms are "Falsehood" and "Truth" (para. 6). The phrase probably quoted most often in summarizing Addison's position is "true Wit consists in the resemblance of Ideas, and false Wit in the Resemblance of Words" (para. 4). What he actually says is that this description covers the examples he has just cited ("according to the foregoing Instances"), among which figure prominently the familiar targets, such as shaped verses, acrostics, quibbles, and puns. The attack on puns (which false wit might call an argument *ad homonym*) is usually best remembered because it fits so readily the distinction between resemblances of words and resemblances of ideas. But *similarity* of ideas is not the basis of all true wit, as Addison's conclusion makes clear:

I must not dismiss this Subject without observing, that as Mr. *Locke* in the Passage above-mentioned has discovered the most fruitful Source of Wit, so there is another of a quite contrary Nature to it, which does likewise branch it self out into several Kinds. For not only the *Resemblance* but the *Opposition* of Ideas does very often produce Wit; as I could shew in several little Points, Turns, and Antitheses, that I may possibly enlarge upon in some future Speculation.

Perhaps if Addison had returned to the opposition of ideas in a later essay this passage would by now have attracted more notice. Standing almost as an afterthought, its casual tone is as disarming as the suave appearance of agreement with Locke earlier in the essay.[8] Here Addison does much more than shift Locke's emphasis. If it is true that wit discerns differences as well as similarities, then the dichotomy between wit and judgment collapses. Having enlisted it in an argument for the truth of wit, Addison leaves Locke's distinction, so to speak, without judgment.

It may be coincidence that Addison characterized the wit of opposition as "quite contrary" to the more familiar sort Locke had described. Accident or allusion, the phrase suggests their distance since it is the one Locke used to oppose not one kind of wit to another but the ways of difference and similitude. My brief discussion of *Spectator* 62 no doubt reveals the judgment that Addison knew exactly what he was doing. But judgment, as Locke eventually argues in some passages to which it is now time to turn, should be distinguished from knowledge.

The fourth book of Locke's *Essay*, "Of Knowledge and Opinion," begins with the proposition that because the mind's only immediate object is its own ideas, knowledge is "nothing but *the perception of the connexion and agreement, or disagreement and repugnancy of any of our Ideas.* In this alone it consists. Where this Perception is, there is Knowledge, and where it is not, there, though we may fancy, guess, or believe, yet we

---

[8] As on many other topics, Addison seems to me here to be agreeable rather than in agreement, and I believe E.N. Hooker is wrong in asserting that "Addison accepted Locke's definition of wit, thereby splitting off wit from judgment and demoting wit to the role of a mild spice serviceable in making morality pleasing to the palate"; see "Pope on Wit: The *Essay on Criticism*," in R.F. Jones *et al.*, *The Seventeenth Century: Studies in the History of English Thought and Literature from Bacon to Pope* (Stanford: Stanford University Press, 1951), 242.

always come short of Knowledge" (IV. i. 1–2). In fact, as Locke everywhere emphasizes, we usually do come short of knowledge. Fancying, as we have seen, has nothing to do with knowledge, yet we must often guess or believe in order to "know" how to live. "He that in the ordinary Affairs of Life, would admit of nothing but direct plain Demonstration, would be sure of nothing, in this World, but of perishing quickly" (IV. xi. 10). Rarely in the presence of certainty, our guesses and beliefs in this "twilight" of probability are guided by judgment, the subject of a late chapter (IV. xiv).

To understand Locke's account it is necessary to see what is at stake. The starting point of book IV makes clear that knowledge – like truth, its expression in propositions – is conversant about similarities of ideas ("agreement") as well as about differences. The difference between wit and knowledge in this respect seems to be that wit *makes* similarities and knowledge *perceives* them. The question, which Addison helps indirectly to focus, is whether the same is true of judgment, that is, whether judgment really traffics primarily in similarities. And if so, is judgment closer to knowledge or to wit?

Locke does what he can to close the gap between judgment and knowledge by associating them with each other as much as possible, and, as I have argued, the attacks on wit and eloquence in books II and III provide occasion to use judgment, truth, reason, and knowledge as near synonyms. Whatever the discriminations to be made elsewhere among the four terms, Locke seems to fuse them to compose whatever it is that is "quite contrary" to wit. Judgment ("being able nicely to distinguish") and knowledge ("perception" of agreement or dis- agreement) are closely associated elsewhere by Locke's tendency to speak of perceiving and distinguishing as the same thing: the mind recognizes separate ideas "at first view," for example, "by its natural power of Perception and Distinction" (IV. i. 4).

A broader association of judgment with knowledge by virtue of what "it" is opposed to operates in the chapter "Of the Reality of Knowledge," where Locke contrasts the knowledge of a "sober" man and a man of the "most extravagant Fancy in the world" (IV. iv. 1). How do these two differ, Locke imagines his reader asking, if knowledge is only the internal agreement or disagreement of one's own ideas? Like the original contrast of judgment and wit, this opposition of sobriety and fancy signals a great deal of strain. Locke's official answer to the question is that our knowledge is limited but consists of "two sorts of *Ideas*, that, we may be assured, agree with things," simple ideas and all complex ideas except those of substances. What he in fact argues is much narrower: simple ideas "*are not fictions* of our Fancies" because they represent things to the extent "ordained" by the "wisdom and will of our Maker," in the way we are "fitted" to perceive them; complex ideas have all the "*conformity necessary to real knowledge*" because they are "*Archetypes* of the mind's own making" and were never "intended to be the Copies of anything" (IV. iv. 3–5). When, after several paragraphs on the desirability of separating ideas from words, Locke concludes that we have "certain real knowledge" whenever "we are sure those ideas agree with the reality of things," the words come uncomfortably close to his later dismissal of enthusiasts: "They are sure because they are sure" (IV. xix. 9). The chapter ends in a tone weirdly reminiscent of *A Tale of a Tub*:

Of which agreement of our *Ideas* with the reality of things having here given sufficient marks, I think I have shown wherein it is, that *Certainty, real Certainty*, consists. Which, whatever it was to others, was, I confess, to me heretofore, one of those *Desiderata* which I found great want of.

(IV. iv. 18)

When Locke finally comes to write of the judgment directly rather than by way of "contraries," it is still on the side of truth, but the fundamental association with knowledge no longer holds. The brief chapter (IV. xiv) concludes with a new refinement.

Thus the Mind has two Faculties conversant about Truth and Falsehood.
    First, Knowledge, whereby it certainly perceives and is undoubtedly satisfied of the Agreement or Disagreement of any *Ideas*.
    Secondly, Judgment, which is the putting *Ideas* together, or separating them one from another in the Mind, when their certain Agreement or Disagreement is not perceived, but *presumed* …And if it so unites or separates them as in Reality Things are, it is *right Judgment*.

(IV. xiv. 4; cf. IV. xvii. 17)

In this scheme knowledge perceives but judgment puts together and separates. At least half (and if Addison is right, all) of judgment's operations, then, are less contrary than kindred to the "assemblage of ideas, and putting those together" previously assigned to wit. The function of the original dichotomy (II. xi. 2) seems in retrospect to have been to protect the "good" assemblages (complex ideas, for example) from the taint of fiction and thus make a firmer claim on "things as they are" than the Lockean way of ideas can consistently justify. Having in this chapter momentarily opened the possibility that judgment may after all proceed rather like wit, Locke attempts to close it in the last sentence with the sudden introduction of "*right Judgment.*" It might fairly be objected that if we can have right and wrong judgment we can have right and wrong – or true or false – wit as well. In that case, wit and judgment are not distinct actions but different manners: one "quick," the other "careful." To Matthew Prior, at least, Locke's judgment would seem a name for slow wit.

Prior's *A Dialogue between Mr: John Locke and Seigneur de Montaigne* was not published until this century. By far most of the best of its roughly 10,000 words are given to Montaigne, whose urbanity and ranging observation are plainly more sympathetic to Prior than is Locke's earnest introspection. When Locke objects that as the "loosest of writers" Montaigne naturally undervalues "my close way of Reasoning," Montaigne replies: "All the while you wrote you were only thinking that you thought; You and Your understanding are the *Personae Dramatis*, and the whole amounts to no more than a Dialogue between John and Lock" (Prior, i. 620). And the shortcomings of monodrama are as plain as the maxim that "he that does not talk with a Wiser Man than himself may happen to Dye Ignorant." "Really who ever writes in Folio should convince people that he knows something besides himself, else few would read his Book, except his very particular Friends" (i. 623). When Locke again criticizes Montaigne's lack of method, this time enlisting Chanet, Scaliger, and Malebranche for support, Montaigne says: "I have observed that there is Abcedarian Ignorance that precedes Knowledge, and a Doctoral Ignorance that comes after it... Method! our Life is too short for it" (i. 629–30).

Despite the breezy antipathy of these exchanges, references to arguments and examples from all four books of the *Essay* make clear that Prior read it with care if not respect. He is particularly attentive to Locke's suspicion of figurative language and allusions. Prior approaches allusion by having Locke boast that while Montaigne's writing is a collection of stolen goods, "I spin my Work out of my own thoughts." The claim predictably leads Montaigne to "allude" to *The Battel of the Books* and play Swift's bee to Locke's spider, with an additional shake of the metaphor: "But to come nearer to you, Mr: Lock, You like many other writers, Deceive your Self in this Point, and as much a Spider as you fancy your Self, You may often cast your Webb upon other Mens Textures." Locke answers that if he has been anticipated in some points without knowing it, "what I write is as much my own Invention as if no Man had thought the Same thing before me," while Montaigne simply copied materials from his commonplace book. To this Montaigne replies laconically: "Why the best One can do is but compose, I hope you do not pretend to Create." Finding Locke undaunted, Montaigne charges him with unwitting allusion:

Your Ideas, as you call them ... were so mixed and Blended, long before You began to write, in the great Variety of things that fall under their Cognizance that it was impossible for You to Distinguish what you Invented from what You Remembered ... [W]hen you Seem to have least regard to Orators and Poets you have recourse to both for your very turn of Style and manner of Expression. Parblew Mr. Lock, when you had writ half your book in favor of your own Dear Understanding you quote Cicero to prove the very Existence of a God.

(i. 632–33)

In another part of this long speech Montaigne asserts that Malebranche, like Locke, warned against misleading the judgment with figurative language but was wise to ignore his own advice: "the Strength of his Argument consists in the beauty of his Figures" (p. 633). This claim, that figurative language discovers rather than covers an author's judgment, conveys the radical difference between Prior and Locke. It emerges more resonantly in a passage that gains point when we recall that Locke's suspicion of language had led to celebrations of mathematics;[9] on at least four occasions he had paused in particular to hope that philosophy would attain an "instrument" of "sagacity" approaching algebra (IV. III. 18, 20; IV. xii. 15; IV. xvii. 11). In this exchange Montaigne has just attacked Locke with a series of analogies, the last taken from the *Essay* itself:[10]

LOCK. Simile upon Simile, no Consequential Proof, right Montaigne by my
    Troth. Why, Sir, you catch at Similes as a Swallow does at Flies.
MONTAIGNE. And you make Similes while you blame them. But be that
    as it will, Mr Lock, arguing by Simile is not so absurd as some of You dry
    Reasoners would make People believe. If your Simile be proper and good,
    it is at once a full proof, and a lively Illustration of Your matter, and

[9] In "The Invention of the Ethical Calculus," Louis I. Bredvold puts Locke in the line of philosophers from Descartes to Godwin who hoped for a "universal science with a universal method, applicable to human nature as well as to physical nature"; see R.F. Jones *et al.*, *The Seventeenth Century: Studies in the History of English Thought and Literature from Bacon to Pope*, pp. 165–80. My concern here is with Locke's mathematical longings in relation to his theory of language rather than to ethics as such.

[10] Prior's reference to one of Locke's optical analogies (a kind of painting that appears confused until seen in a cylindrical mirror) is noted by Wright and Spears; see *Essay*, II. xxix. 8 and Prior, ii. 1015.

where it does not hold the very disproportion gives You Occasion to reconsider it, and You set it in all it's lights, if it be only to find at least how unlike it is. Egad Simile is the very Algebra of Discourse. (p. 625)

This simile (or "metasimile") falls so neatly that it may seem, as Locke would say (the actual Locke: *Essay*, II. xi. 2), a "kind of affront to go about to examine it by the severe Rules of Truth, and good Reason." Locke's point is that the obvious inappropriateness of such an examination is itself an admission that wit is not "conformable" to the way of judgment. Prior's is quite different; he invites the reader to apply the test of truth, maintaining in fact that all similes issue such invitations. If a simile succeeds in being at once "full proof" and "lively illustration" it conveys knowledge (as Locke's agreement of ideas); if it does not, it calls judgment into action ("gives ... occasion to reconsider") and will still lead to knowledge (as Locke's disagreement of ideas). Bad similes may lower our estimate of a work; but for the reader a simile "works" whether it succeeds or fails.

Prior clearly assumes a less vulnerable reader than Locke's, one whose judgment will be quickened rather than outdistanced by wit's quickness. Exactly how much more he assumes in the passage is difficult to determine, but it seems likely that he might expect the reader who would examine the comparison of algebra and simile to be thinking of algebra as more than a shorthand notation. Considering algebra generally as the study of functions rather than fixed quantities (and the word seems to have had at least this currency), "the algebra of discourse" suggests the working out of relationships within language. This is another way of claiming, with Addison, that wit has verity as well as brevity; in other words, it not only paints pictures but contemplates general relations. If the philosopher's desire is ultimately the Hobbesian one that words be used as the wise man's "counters" rather than as the fool's "money" (*Leviathan*, I. iv), to seek an extralinguistic discovery procedure for moral philosophy is simply to turn one's back on the higher mathematics already at hand in the liveliest uses of language.

With different emphases but complementary doubts, Addison and Prior both question Locke's devaluation of wit and the opposition of wit to judgment. Challenging the claim that discrimination is peculiar to judgment, Addison points politely to the collapse of the dichotomy. Prior more explicitly raises the problem of any such dichotomy (regardless of which side is "privileged") by questioning whether making similitudes and making distinctions are really separable acts of mind. This is the fundamental question at the level of common sense, and I think common sense (like Pope) houses with Locke one moment and with Prior's Montaigne the next: yes, we sometimes "distinguish," sometimes "assemble," and can "distinguish" between the operations; no, we cannot differentiate without comparing and vice versa.[11] But behind this armchair antinomy the problem dividing Locke from Addison and Prior can be seen as a question with particular pertinence to our own era and criticism: does it make more sense to think of "things as they are" as represented (perhaps badly) by language or as constituted by language?

The preceding commentary suggests at several points that Locke's accounts of language in general and of figurative language in particular are efforts to reclaim indirectly an access to pre- or extralinguistic "things" that other parts of his *Essay* seal off. In suggesting now that Addison and Prior are deeply skeptical of the attempt to get past language to something firmer, I do not mean to convert them into proto-Nietzschean or proto-Derridean rhetoricians of contradiction. From the perspective of post-structuralism both are grounded in "logocentrism." Both believe that in the beginning was the Word, the authorial will originating all subsequent meaning. Neither would know what to make of the idea that this belief should be reinscribed as "In the always-already are words." Nor would either be likely to hear more than burlesque in Beckett's version, "In the beginning was the pun."[12] But at the same time, neither Addison nor Prior seems to share Locke's nostalgia for things and ideas untouched by words or for truths too tacit to enter the shared figures and allusions of language. If these differences are significant, then it seems we would need to speak of logocentrism*s* in Augustan writing (and presumably in other literary periods) for the term to be historically useful; in the monolithic singular it is, like Locke's "wit," less descriptive of variable rhetorical practices than protective of its rhetorically constructed opposite.

---

[11] Pope's opposition of Montaigne and Locke in one of his imitations of Horace – "As drives the storm, at any door I knock, / And house with Montagne now, or now with Lock" (*Epistle I. i*, 25–26) – could have been prompted by Prior's *Dialogue*, which he read in manuscript. He mentions the work (and other prose dialogues by Prior) to Spence on Dec. 13, 1730; see Joseph Spence, *Observations, Anecdotes and Characters of Books and Men*, 2 vols., ed. James M. Osborne (Oxford: Clarendon Press, 1966), i. 92.

[12] Samuel Beckett, *Murphy* (New York: Grove Press, 1957), 65: "Not the least remarkable of Murphy's innumerable classifications of experience was that into jokes that had once been good jokes and jokes that had never been good jokes. What but an imperfect sense of humour could have made such a mess of chaos. In the beginning was the pun. And so on."

Wit versus judgment and metaphor versus metonymy

Pope's remark that the "life of a Wit is a warfare upon earth" applies as well to the word itself during his lifetime. The term ricochets from so many prefaces, poems, and pamphlets that the next step would logically seem to be backwards, to Hobbes, Davenant, Dryden, Blackmore's *Satyr against Wit*, and so on. There may be some advantage, however, in postponing that step into historical semantics if doing so keeps us from regarding ·the war of wit and judgment as a merely curious chapter in literary history, now closed by Johnson's good sense, the decline of faculty psychology, the maturation of aesthetic thought, or, mercifully, the vegetable growth of language. In this section I will try to take the Lockean opposition out of the Museum of Fixed Ideas by considering it – and its attractions – as analogous to the influential opposition of metaphor and metonymy in our era. The analogy between the dichotomies of Locke and Roman Jakobson is neither exact nor proportional; it can not be restated as Wit:Judgment::Metaphor:Metonymy. But I believe that what it lacks in exactness may be compensated for by what it suggests about the inconclusiveness of the Augustan argument and about historical continuity.

That an opposition of two figures of speech, outlined in linguistic terms and nearly buried in an essay largely about aphasia, has within a few decades entered commonroom parlance is eloquent testimony to the stature of Jakobson and to the general prestige of language theory in our century. The opposition of metaphor (including simile) and metonymy (including synecdoche) originates for Jakobson from the "twofold character" of all language, the construction of utterances by processes of *selection* and *combination*.

Speech implies a selection of certain linguistic entities and their combination into linguistic units of a higher degree of complexity. At the lexical level this is readily apparent: the speaker selects words and combines them into sentences according to the syntactic system of the language he is using; sentences in their turn are combined into utterances.[13]

We pick out words from a paradigm of words of the same function and related meanings – the noun (and potential subject) "woman," for example, rather than the kindred "person" or "lady" – and we put them together in a syntagm. Thus selection is made on the basis

---

[13] "Two Aspects of Language and Two Types of Aphasic Disturbances," in Roman Jakobson, *Selected Writings*, 8 vols. (The Hague: Mouton, 1971), ii. 239–59; the quotation is from p. 241.

of "similarity" and combination on the basis of possible "contiguity" (contiguity here meaning that linguistic units are put next to each other not randomly but as the language allows). These binary oppositions of structuralism entail others, but for the moment one more pair of terms is sufficient to trace Jakobson's path to metaphor and metonymy. There are "substitution" and "contexture," and they correspond respectively to selection and combination. Because a "selection from alternatives implies the possibility of substituting one for the other," for Jakobson selection and substitution are actually "two faces of the same operation." The same correspondence holds for combination and contexture because any "actual grouping of linguistic units binds [combines] them into a superior unit," a signifying context; and contexture is the general name for the reciprocal relations of lower- and higher-level units ("Two Aspects..." p. 243).

With these terms and assumptions in mind, we can turn to Jakobson's famous move from the twofold character of language to the "metaphoric and metonymic poles" of verbal behavior.

The development of a discourse may take place along two different semantic lines: one topic may lead to another either through their similarity or through their contiguity. The metaphoric way would be the most appropriate term for the first case and the metonymic way for the second, since they find their most condensed expression in metaphor and metonymy respectively. In aphasia one or the other of these two processes is restricted or totally blocked – an effect which makes the study of aphasia particularly illuminating for the linguist. In normal verbal behavior both processes are continually operative, but careful observation will reveal that under the influence of a cultural pattern, personality, and verbal style, preference is given to one of the two processes over the other.

("Two Aspects..." p. 254)

For literary critics this paragraph has perhaps been the most seminal passage in all of Jakobson's work, and there are immediate clues as to why this might be so. Its first sentence moves at once from the similarity and contiguity of linguistic units such as phonemes or words to the similarity and contiguity of *topics*. The rest of the paragraph quickly puts the technical account of aphasia into the suggestive context of culture, personality, and style. The dazzling progress of the next several paragraphs from children and word-association tests to oral poetry, nineteenth-century literary movements, modern painting, and film leads to the "bipolar structure" of all "semiotic systems" and finally to the inevitable conclusion that the "dichotomy discussed here appears to be of primal significance and consequence for all verbal behavior and for human behavior in general" ("Two Aspects..." p. 256).

This summary fails to do justice to either the complexity of Jakobson's argument or the fascination of his examples in this and related essays. But perhaps it is just enough to allow reflection on Jakobson's influence. Whether the magnetic attraction of his metaphoric and metonymic "poles" will continue to reach the tropics of criticism much longer is an open question, and even a guess would have to be based on conflicting signals. What is remarkable now is the extent to which Jakobson's dichotomy appears to have set a significant part of the agenda of literary theory for at least a quarter of our century. Very roughly, his influence can be seen in two phases, a first wave of studies applying the opposition of metaphor to metonymy to authorial styles (usually with minor adjustments), and, more recently, some discussions associating the adoption of Jakobson's dichotomy with an unfortunate privileging of one term over the other or with a confusion of linguistic and cognitive categories.[14] Interestingly, the paired terms remain prominent despite these reservations and despite the suspicion of binary oppositions that has characterized deconstruction. There does not seem to be a desire to discard Jakobson's opposition by, for example, relegating metonymy to its Aristotelian role as a subspecies of metaphor. That would be, according to provocative arguments by Paul de Man and Jonathan Culler, clearly the wrong move, a regression to traditional complacencies and mystifications.[15] For Culler there are already "powerful forces ...at work to make *metaphor* at once the

[14] See Willard Bohn, "Roman Jakobson's Theory of Metaphor and Metonymy: An Annotated Bibliography," *Style*, 18 (1984), 534–50, for an extensive list of studies explicitly concerned with Jakobson's position. A sampling of annual bibliographies for subsequent years suggests no decrease in the number of literary applications of Jakobson's dichotomy to subjects ranging from biblical poetry to Cuban fiction. (Interesting and recent instances in the study of eighteenth-century satire include William Bowman Piper's "Similitude as Satire in *The Beggar's Opera*," *Eighteenth-Century Studies*, 21 [1988], 334–51, and Frederick M. Keener's reading of *Candide* in *The Chain of Becoming* [New York: Columbia University Press, 1983], esp. p. 207, where metaphor is associated with teleological theorizing and metonymy with recognitions of contingency.) Jonathan Culler's argument that the dichotomy has worked to privilege metaphor is considered more fully below. Arguments that Jakobson's theory is psychologically or philosophically inconsistent are made by Hugh Bredin, "Roman Jakobson on Metaphor and Metonymy," *Philosophy and Literature*, 8 (1984), 89–103, and Leon Surette, "Metaphor and Metonymy: Jakobson Reconsidered," *University of Toronto Quarterly*, 56 (1987), 557–74. David Lodge's *The Modes of Modern Writing: Metaphor, Metonymy, and the Typology of Modern Literature* (London: Edward Arnold, 1977) is remarkable for its lucid combination of summary, application, and analysis of Jakobson's arguments; see esp. pp. 73–93.

[15] Paul de Man, "The Epistemology of Metaphor"; Jonathan Culler, "The Turns of Metaphor," in *The Pursuit of Signs* (Ithaca: Cornell University Press, 1981), 188–209. Subsequent references to Culler's essay will be made parenthetically.

opposite of tropes based on accident and the authoritative representative of figurative language in general, the figure for figurality"
(p. 199).

Culler's general argument is that regarding metaphor as "the figure
par excellence" (p. 191) supports both what I think could be called
literary institutional pieties (instanced in Proust studies and Proust
himself, recent discussions of metaphor, and traditional defenses of
poetry) and some reassuring premises "that seem basic to our culture's
way of thinking about language" (p. 207). In regard to the first, Culler
says that because it has become common to regard metaphors as the
"revelation of essences and imaginative truth," the "privileging of
metaphor over metonymy and other figures is an assertion of the
cognitive value and respectability of literary language; the accidental
play of verbal associations and contingent juxtapositions is given an
ancillary status so that it can be ignored" (p. 198). In regard to the
second point, that the elevation of metaphor reinforces conventional
notions of language, Culler concludes: "To maintain the primacy of
metaphor is to treat language as a device for the expression of thoughts,
perceptions, truth. To posit the dependence of metaphor on metonymy
is to treat what language expresses as the effect of contingent,
conventional relations and a system of mechanical processes. *Metaphor*
and *metonymy* thus become in turn not only figures for figurality but
figures for language in general" (pp. 201–02). Culler goes on to express
some interest in the possibility of putting metaphor on a level with
other tropes by regarding it as the name given to "certain interpretive
operations performed by readers when confronted by a textual
incongruity, such as the assertion of a patently false identity," rather
than as a complex structure to be described (p. 208). But like de Man
(if for different reasons) Culler feels the opposition of metaphor and
metonymy to be inescapable. Even if one moves metaphor from the
author to the reader, "there will still be the problem of distinguishing
a metaphorical move from a metonymical move, essential from
contingent relations..." (p. 209).

We might seem to have reached a point of considerable historical
irony or at least reverse symmetry. On one side of the divide called
Romanticism stand both Locke's complaints that figurative speech
masks the proper representational truth of language, and the response
of Augustan writers asserting the "cognitive value" of metaphor; on
the other are late twentieth-century objections that the ascendancy of
metaphor in modern thought obscures the truth that language is

unrepresentational. The irony is this exact, however, only if it is accurate to read Jakobson's opposition as naturally leading to a view of metaphor as the expression of "essential similarity" and metonymy as "based on a merely accidental or contingent connexion" (p. 190). I think it is not accurate and that consequently the relation of the early eighteenth-century and later discussions of figurative language is a complex mixture of partial reversals and partial repetitions.[16] I will try to justify the first assertion – namely, that Jakobson's "poles" actually favor metonymy – before considering the more general relation.

Metaphor in Jakobson's account, it will be recalled, is based on similarity; metonymy, however, is based not on "contingency" but *contiguity*. The distinction matters because the values attached can differ radically. For Culler, ascribing "contingent" relations to metonymy means seeing its relations as accidental rather than essential, superficial rather than profound, rhetorical rather than revealed, and so on – common but misguided judgments, he believes, because all figures are ultimately as contingent as metonymy. But Jakobson's "contiguity" includes things that are next to each other. While it is true that many of the "things" Jakobson describes as contiguous are adjacent within language (linguistic units occupying positions next to one another in a sequence), his readiness to speak also of contiguous topics, his appeal to perceptual experience in categorizing the often gnomic utterances of patients and his extension of those categories to the most complex arrangements of signs make clear that contiguity is an existential as well as linguistic criterion.[17] The assumption, in other words, is that we have an order of things sufficiently in mind to be certain about which ones are actually next to each other in the world and which ones are related

[16] William James occupies an interesting point between Locke and Jakobson. For James the "two fundamental laws of association" (of ideas) are the "Law of Contiguity" and the "Law of Similarity." The first governs the habitual thinking of "dry and prosaic minds"; in "witty, imaginative minds, on the other hand, the routine is broken through with ease at any moment; and one field of mental objects will suggest another with which perhaps in the whole history of human thinking it had never once before been coupled." See *Talks to Teachers on Psychology*, (first pub. 1899; Cambridge, MA: Harvard University Press, 1983), ch. 9, esp. pp. 55–56; cf. *The Principles of Psychology* (Cambridge, MA: Harvard University Press, 1981), ch. 14.

[17] This existential emphasis is even clearer in Jakobson's formulation of the opposition in "Aphasia as a Linguistic Topic," a paper first published in 1955: "The two opposite tropes, metaphor and metonymy, present the most condensed expression of two basic modes of relation: the internal relation of similarity (and contrast) underlies the metaphor; the external relation of contiguity (and remoteness) determines the metonymy." Stronger still is this formulation in "Linguistic Types of Aphasia," published in 1966: "Contrary to selection, which is based on an internal relation, combination involves the external relation of contiguity in its various forms and degrees: neighborhood, proximity, and remoteness, subordination and coordination." See *Selected Writings*, ii. 232 and 309.

merely by semantic similarity. In this respect Jakobson's opposition shares the important common feature with Locke's of providing a claim on "things as they are" that is otherwise difficult to make. The claim is especially interesting in Jakobson because it occurs at just the point where he most emphasizes the figurality of "human behavior in general." Properly speaking, however, things without language should be as difficult to reach from within linguistic structuralism as are things without ideas from within Lockean epistemology.

The point of entering as well as summarizing some of the discussion concerning metaphor and metonymy is not to suggest that our historical perspective makes Olympian adjudication possible but rather to show that we remain grounded in the history of the question. The analogy of these eighteenth- and twentieth-century battles of interpretations is imperfect but suggestive, as in the general correspondence between Locke's characterization of wit as the assertion of likenesses and Jakobson's location of poetry in the realm of equivalences.[18] There is nothing to be gained, however, by imagining that Jakobson's *metaphor* is "really" Locke's *wit*, his *metonymy* Locke's *judgment*, and so on, or in forgetting that Locke's opposition is militantly evaluative and Jakobson's insistently complementary. The oppositions that seem most instructive in juxtaposition are the basic ones, for Locke primarily operations of mind and for Jakobson primarily operations of language: Locke's *discrimination* (or "discerning") and *assemblage* ("putting together") and Jakobson's *selection* and *combination*.

In both cases, the fundamental question for the observer is whether the people he or she observes seem more inclined to select or to combine the items available to them in experience and expression. This generalization might at first seem to fit Locke better than Jakobson, since Jakobson's basic operations are cooperative as well as ethically neutral. But when we keep in mind the dominance of one operation over another not only in the extreme cases of speech disorder and in the extraordinary cases of literary modes but also in different "personalities" or "personal predilections," we see the strong desire to make characterological if not moral diagnoses. When we consider, finally, that our sense of whether another separates and combines "things" more or less as we do is likely to confirm or challenge our own claims

[18] For Jakobson's frequently quoted statement, "The poetic function projects the principle of equivalence from the axis of selection into the axis of combination," see "Linguistics and Poetics" (1960) in *Selected Writings*, iii. 27. Jakobson reformulates this point slightly differently in "Poetry of Grammar and Grammar of Poetry" (1968) by proposing that "in poetry similarity is superimposed on contiguity" (*Selected Writings*, iii. 92).

on things, it becomes easier to understand why a local debate over the status of wit would cause excitement. Whether the terms are wit and judgment (associated by Pope with "writing" and criticism, respectively), or metaphor and metonymy, or selection and combination, or others, the rival claims of assimilation and discrimination seem to mount in intensity, even, or perhaps especially, in the impatience of dismissal:

> 'Tis hard to say, if greater Want of Skill
> Appear in *Writing* or in *Judging* ill...
>
> (Essay on Criticism, 1–2)

> it's hard to say whether the distinguishers
> or the resemblancers are sillier...
>
> (A.R. Ammons, Essay on Poetics)[19]

Wit writing and wit written

·The Augustan quarrel over the province of wit is in part one transformation of the longer battle between "philosophy" and "rhetoric" alluded to earlier. Among those who have renewed the battle now – primarily by stressing the rhetorical constructs of all texts, philosophical as well as "literary" – it is common to see Socrates' attack on the Sophists as the typical territorial claim of philosophy to Truth, an illegitimate and illusory claim but one maintained successfully until very recently as the basis of "western metaphysics." This view may be the projection of a relatively modern development, the professionalization of philosophy and more particularly epistemology beginning in the seventeenth century, onto the cultural history of two and a half millennia. Its general tendency in any case is to regard Aristotelian thought, scholasticism, and Renaissance humanism as rather minor byways along the road linking Plato to Descartes. The eighteenth century of course had its own millennial simplifications, one of which was to diagnose much of what was argued (as well as built) between Cicero and the Italian Renaissance as "gothick." But when any of its inhabitants thought of a quarrel between what we would call philosophy and what it would increasingly call "poetry" they were likely to think of it as a modern rather than natural situation. For Prior, Locke has little more in common with

---

[19] A.R. Ammons, *Collected Poems, 1951–1971* (New York: W.W. Norton, 1972), 316–17.

Socrates than with Montaigne but is virtually indistinguishable from Descartes.

Prior's attack on Locke is more emblematic than typical. Many writers, including Addison and Pope, welcomed Locke on a range of topics and it quickly became common to commend his sense and moderation in contrast to Descartes's hubris and *esprit de système*. But one of the larger tendencies of the "battle" of the Ancients and Moderns was to see most of seventeenth-century philosophy as a more unified modern enterprise than the retrospective division of "Rationalism" and "Empiricism" now suggests.[20] From the Modern perspective, the enterprise was the liberation of intellect and the progress of independence; from the Ancient view it was the rejection of collective wisdom and the progress of self-absorption. At its extreme, the second perspective can become cavalier and Cavalier, which is why it has usually been regarded condescendingly as reactionary amateurism or reverentially as Taste holding out against Science. Interestingly, however, at least some current philosophers tend to share its vision of the "modern" introspective and epistemological priorities of both Rationalism and Empiricism as an arbitrary specification of certain philosophical problems. In such a view, the epistemological individualism and the abstraction of "mind" or "consciousness" that emerge in seventeenth-century philosophy are seen as historically peculiar rather than perennial concerns.[21]

The labels Ancient and Modern quickly cease to be useful in the eighteenth century and are less important in any case than the agreement that, for better or worse, modern philosophy constituted a departure from traditional authority and that its connections with the secular repository of tradition, "polite letters" or "literature," had diminished. The similar laments of the philosopher Shaftesbury and the poet Mark Akenside are illustrative; both are Modern if one is thinking of "Whiggish" libertarianism and optimism, radically so if one adds deism, while both are Ancient if the test is reverence for Greek and Roman authors. For Shaftesbury the "sprightly arts and sciences are severed from philosophy, which consequently must grow dronish, insipid, pedantic, useless, and directly opposite to the real knowledge and practice of the world and mankind." For Akenside, looking back

---

[20] Hans Aarsleff disagrees convincingly with the "pedagogically convenient and ideologically loaded separate-box distinction between rationalism and empiricism" in comparing Locke and Leibniz; see *From Locke to Saussure*, p. 9.

[21] This view of the history of philosophy is advanced in the first three chapters of Richard Rorty's *Philosophy and the Mirror of Nature* (Princeton: Princeton University Press, 1980).

from the 1740s, "Philosophy and the Fine Arts can hardly be conceived at a greater distance from each other than at the Revolution, when Locke stood at the head of one party, and Dryden at the other."[22] While their agreement is instructive, so too is the fact that they offer nearly opposite programs for the reconciliation of philosophy and poetry. The "Augustan" Shaftesbury seeks to civilize philosophy with wit, while the "pre-Romantic" Akenside seeks to philosophize poetry by separating it from wit and identifying it instead with Imagination. Since the term "imagination" appears frequently in Dryden's own criticism, often in contexts suggesting a level of wit that includes judgment, it is worth asking why he had not abandoned the troublesome word "wit" instead of repeatedly attempting to define it satisfactorily. This will entail raising the question again of why Pope follows and extends Dryden's practice not only by holding to "wit" in *An Essay on Criticism* but by calling attention to its range of meanings, even while continuing to play it off against "judgment."

Dryden's first definition of wit – in the preface to *Annus Mirabilis* (1667) – is his most striking and most complicated. It strikes, Locke might observe, because it presents a pleasing picture to the fancy. It complicates by first proposing a twofold distinction between "wit writing" and "wit written" and then merging these into a threefold description of "imagination."

> The composition of all poems is, or ought to be, of wit, and wit in the poet, or wit writing (if you will give me leave to use a school distinction) is no other than the faculty of imagination in the writer which, like a nimble spaniel, beats over and ranges through the field of memory, till it springs the quarry it hunted after; or, without metaphor, which searches over all the memory for the species or ideas of those things which it designs to represent. Wit written is that which is well defined, the happy result of thought, or product of imagination.
>
> (i. 97–98)

Wit writing is the process, "wit witting," to pursue the implied analogy of *natura naturans*, while the result might be considered as "wit witted," analogous to *natura naturata*. Coming, as we inevitably do, to

[22] Shaftesbury, *Soliloquy, or Advice to an Author*, in *Characteristics*, i. 215; Akenside, *The Pleasures of Imagination* (London: R. Dodsley, 1744), note to book II, line 30. Akenside quotes Shaftesbury, and then goes on to sketch a general improvement from the end of the seventeenth century to his own time: "But the general spirit of liberty, which has ever since been growing, naturally invited our men of wit and genius to improve that influence which the arts of persuasion gave them with the people, by applying them to subjects of importance to society."

Dryden's criticism through Romanticism, "wit in the poet" looks a good deal more interesting than wit on the page; perhaps even without the aesthetic filter the memorable spaniel would tend to cast "wit written" in shadow as a poor relation of "wit writing." "Wit written," however, will turn out to be the wit of most of Dryden's discussions, where it becomes, simply, "propriety of thoughts and words." To understand rather than regret his later shift of emphasis we need first to follow "imagination" with some care in this early analysis and find where it leads Dryden and others.

The wit appropriate to heroic or historical poetry (such as *Annus Mirabilis*) is not epigram, antithesis, or pun but the "delightful imaging of persons, actions, or things... some lively and apt description, dressed in such colours of speech that it sets before your eyes the absent object as perfectly and more delightfully than nature." Despite the active participle, "imaging," the account thus far is of wit written, that is, as experienced by a reader (the "imaging of persons..." is here the same as "persons imaged" and it is the reader's eyes from which the objects aptly described are necessarily "absent"). As the analysis unfolds formally, however, it moves toward wit writing:

So then, the first happiness of the poet's imagination is properly invention, or finding of the thought; the second is fancy, or the variation, driving, or moulding of that thought, as the judgment represents it proper to the subject; the third is elocution, or the act of clothing and adorning that thought so found and varied, in apt, significant and sounding words: the quickness of the imagination is seen in the invention, the fertility in the fancy, and the accuracy in the expression.

(i. 98)

This elaboration carries at least one significant advantage and an important disadvantage. On the one hand, it transcends the opposition of wit and judgment by simply appropriating judgment to imagination: judgment acts in such cooperation and simultaneity with "fancy" as to appear synonymous with it.[23] On the other hand, it nearly transcends language as well, separating expression in words from the intellectual discovery and construction, relegating it to last place in time and apparently in importance. The elevation of imagination comes at the expense of embracing, after all, the hostile dichotomies of modern philosophy; the implications are not essentially different from those of

---

[23] Seventeenth-century equations of wit with judgment and imagination together are surveyed briefly in D. Judson Milburn, *The Age of Wit, 1650–1750* (New York: Macmillan, 1966), 88–92.

Hobbes's opposition of judgment and fancy – "Judgment begets the strength and structure, and Fancy the ornaments of a Poem" – or from Ramus's separation of logic and rhetoric in which the latter was reduced to expression and delivery.[24]

Most of the late seventeenth- and eighteenth-century attempts to ennoble wit involve a move similar to Dryden's and lead to the same problem: judgment is appropriated to wit, which is then implicitly or explicitly redefined in broader terms as "imagination" or "genius," but which in its loftier identity finally has no visible connection with writing. The opposition that was to have been dismissed is instead displaced and intensified as a dualism of thought and language. These attempts range from Cowley's ode *Of Wit* (1668) to Johnson's Life of Cowley (1779), and include Davenant's Preface to *Gondibert*, La Rochefoucauld's dismissal of the opposition of wit and judgment as a "vulgar error," Shaftesbury's rejection of the "injudicious" use of wit and exaltation of the true poet as a "just" Prometheus, and Fielding's definition of genius in *Tom Jones* (book IX, ch. 15) as invention *and* judgment but also as a qualification for writers rather than a quality of writing.[25] The difficulties recur in slightly different forms in some twentieth-century criticism, as I think the comments of C.S. Lewis on wit reveal; but for the moment I would like to concentrate on Johnson's attempt at redefinition because it is the most rigorous and retrospective of the eighteenth-century discussions.

---

[24] Hobbes, *The Answer ...to ...Davenant's Preface*, in J.E. Spingarn, (ed.), *Critical Essays of the Seventeenth Century*, 3 vols. (Oxford: Clarendon Press, 1908–09), ii. 59.

[25] La Rochefoucauld's maxim (no. 98 in the 1706 edn. of *Moral Maxims and Reflections*) is quoted by Hooker and by Audra and Williams: "The making a Difference between *Wit* and *Judgment*, is a *Vulgar Error*. *Judgment* is nothing else but the *exceeding Brightness* of *Wit*, which, like *Light*, pierces into the very *Bottom of Things*, observes all that ought to be observed there, and discovers what seemed to be past any bodies finding out: From whence we must conclude, that the *Energy* and *Extension* of this *Light* of the *Wit*, is the very Thing that produces all those Effects, usually ascrib'd to the *Judgment*." For Shaftesbury's remark see the end of part I of *Soliloquy, or Advice to an Author*, in *Characteristics*, i. 135–36. Henry Fielding, in describing "Genius" as the power or powers of mind "capable of penetrating into all Things within our Reach and Knowledge, and of distinguishing their essential Differences," complains that "all the dull Fellows in the World" believe that invention and judgment are "seldom or never the Property of one and the same Person" (*The History of Tom Jones*, ed. Martin C. Battestin and Fredson Bowers [Middletown: Wesleyan University Press, 1975], 490–91. Interestingly, one of the most pointed objections to Locke's distinction was lodged by Sarah Fielding a few years before *Tom Jones*. In book II, ch. 6 of *The Adventures of David Simple* (1744) the intellectual Cynthia concludes: "But not withstanding all the Industry People may make use of to blind themselves, if *Wit consists*, as Mr. *Locke* says, *in the Assemblage of Ideas, and Judgment in the separating them*; I really believe the Person who can join them with the most Propriety, *will separate them with the greatest Nicety*." See *The Adventures of David Simple*, ed. Malcolm Kelsall (Oxford: Oxford University Press, 1973), 104–05.

Johnson's consideration arises from the claim that the Metaphysical writers, while not great poets, excel in wit. He then challenges even that claim in three paragraphs which are among his best known but which may bear new examination:

If wit be well described by Pope as being 'that which has been often thought, but never before so well expressed', they certainly never attained nor even sought it, for they endeavoured to be singular in their thoughts, and were careless of their diction. But Pope's account of wit is undoubtedly erroneous; he depresses it below its natural dignity and reduces it from strength of thought to happiness of language.

If by a more noble and more adequate conception that be considered as wit which is at once natural and new, that which though not obvious is, upon its first production, acknowledged to be just; if it be that which he that never found it wonders how he missed; to wit of this kind the metaphysical poets have seldom risen. Their thoughts are often new, but seldom natural; they are not obvious, but neither are they just; and the reader, far from wondering how he missed them wonders more frequently by what perverseness of industry they were ever found.

But wit, abstracted from its effects upon the hearer, may be more rigorously and philosophically considered as a kind of *discordia concors*, a combination of dissimilar images, or discovery of occult resemblances in things apparently unlike. Of wit, thus defined, they have more than enough. The most heterogeneous ideas are yoked by violence together... their learning instructs, and their subtlety surprises; but the reader commonly thinks his improvement dearly bought, and, though he sometimes admires, is seldom pleased.[26]

Most twentieth-century attention from T. S. Eliot onward has fixed on the third level of Johnson's definition, adopting the violent yoking of heterogeneous ideas as an apt description of Metaphysical poetry and sometimes, at the height of Donne's reputation, of the putatively paradoxical essence of true poetry in general. Although Johnson's quite different evaluation in the final clause of the second paragraph is usually recognized (and patronized), the definition itself has generally been welcomed, a phenomenon that I think would have surprised Dryden and Pope even more than Johnson. A definition of wit that can proceed "philosophically" only when wit has been "abstracted from its effects upon the hearer" would seem abstract beyond recognition, as puzzling as trying to define the quality of an unspoken repartee or, perhaps, to determine the wit of one of Mr. Locke's tacit propositions. Johnson might reply that he is at this point considering what Dryden

---

[26] "Life of Cowley" in *The Lives of the English Poets*, 3 vols., ed. George Birkbeck Hill (Oxford: Clarendon Press, 1905), i. 19–20.

called "wit writing," wholly apart from "wit written"; but that separation is precisely what would seem so strange.

Johnson's kinship with the Augustan discussion is clearer in the first and second paragraphs. His own preference is decidedly for the "more adequate" definition of wit as "that which is at once natural and new," and "though not obvious is...acknowledged to be just." The pertinent question is why Johnson regards this description as so much at odds with Pope's, paraphrased in the first paragraph. Johnson's explanation, that Pope "depresses" wit by isolating expression ("happiness of language") from thinking ("strength of thought") does not accord with Pope's emphasis:

> True Wit is Nature to Advantage drest,
> What oft was Thought, but ne'er so well Exprest,
> Something, whose Truth convinc'd at Sight we find,
> That gives us back the Image of our Mind...
>
> (Essay on Criticism, 297–300)

The novelty that Johnson finds lacking in Pope's account (and which Johnson in other moods would concede to be rarely compatible with general truth) resides for Pope primarily in expression because his description of wit is from the reader's point of view: the poet's "happiness of language" occasions the reader's "strength of thought." In comparison, even Johnson's first and second paragraphs have already begun to suggest that asserting the "natural dignity" of wit requires considering it "abstracted from its effects upon the hearer."

Johnson's effort to dignify wit and his abstraction of it from actual expression are not prominent again until the twentieth century, presumably because the word was already losing critical status in the later eighteenth century and disappeared almost entirely in the nineteenth century's greater abstractions of Imagination.[27] But when the term emerged again in criticism so did the tendency toward idealization. C.S. Lewis's learned but somewhat mythical history of the word's meaning may illustrate the problem and lead us back to Dryden. According to Lewis, the primary sense of wit, deriving from Anglo-Saxon wit or gewit, is mind, reason, or intelligence. This meaning is extended qualitatively during the Renaissance, partly due to the word's common use as a synonym for the Latin ingenium, to refer to a distinctive intelligence or good mind. What Lewis then calls the "ingenium

[27] Thus by the 1840s Emerson in The Poet can dismiss most of "Chalmers's collection of five centuries of English poets" as containing "wits more than poets." See Selections from Ralph Waldo Emerson, ed. Stephen E. Whicher (Boston: Houghton Mifflin, 1957), 239.

sense" or "wit-*ingenium*" is – or should be – the "foremost" meaning.
Its hereditary right is threatened, however, by the word's misleading
"dangerous sense" of jocularity and witty language, held in check
during the Renaissance but increasingly boisterous in the Restoration
and early eighteenth century. Lewis sees the attempts of Dryden,
Addison, and Pope to define "true wit" in part as efforts to exclude the
"dangerous sense" and in larger part as "tactical manœuvres to apply
a Renaissance term of approval to a very different kind of writing."[28]
Dryden's definition of wit as the "propriety of thoughts and words" is
for Lewis a particularly unfortunate narrowing of his earlier "more
Cowleyian" notion of it as an essential gift of the poet, his creativity;
and "propriety" is a "garrison word," inserted to "exclude Ovid and
Cowley and Cleveland from the highest poetical honours." Finally,
Dryden's definition defies common sense: it can be "almost safely
asserted that no human being, when using the word *wit* to talk with and
not talking about the word wit, has ever meant by it anything of the
sort" (pp. 105–06).

   This account is mythical because it casts the semantic history of a
word in the form of a contest of good and evil (roughly the native
"ingenium" of the English language itself versus "dangerous"
intrusions), posits a primitive purity of ("foremost") meaning against
which later complications are seen as heretical deviation, and simplifies
uncertainties in the interest of narrative symmetry. The general
problem begins in the beginning. What William Empson remarked of
an annotator's assertion that *pure intellect* is the "primary meaning" of
wit in the *Essay on Criticism* because it derives from "*witan*, 'to know'"
applies to Lewis's version as well: "'Primary' ... is a pun, carrying the
equation 'historically first and therefore the chief meaning in Pope's
time.' ('The first is the chief')."[29] The narrative strategy is perhaps
even more arbitrary than Empson suggests because it is not wholly
clear that the Anglo-Saxon noun or verb referred "foremost" to the
idealized "mind" of Lewis's history rather than to the senses
collectively (wits) and to sensation-knowledge. Less presumption about
the limits and purity of "primary" meaning leads to a less "abstracted"
history.

   What Lewis writes instead is an essentially spiritual history of the

---

[28] C.S. Lewis, *Studies in Words* (Cambridge: Cambridge University Press, 1960), 86–110;
additional references will be noted parenthetically.

[29] William Empson, "Wit in the *Essay on Criticism*," in *The Structure of Complex Words* (first pub.
1951i; London: Hogarth Press, 1985 [1951]), 87. Some parts of Lewis's *Studies in Words*, and
especially his remarks on wit, seem to attempt an idealist "correction" of Empson's book,
originally published in 1951.

word, in which the meanings most strongly objected to are those that put it unquestionably in the social and material world of language: jokes and "witty" remarks as well as Dryden's "propriety of thoughts and words." Lewis's own appeal to social practice in dismissing Dryden (virtually, "no human being…has ever meant by it anything of the sort") is curious and empty. If we take Dryden at his words, that wit "is a propriety of thoughts and words; or, in other terms, thoughts and words elegantly adapted to the subject" (ii. 207) – we have a definition that happily refuses to separate wit from words and conversation. And in this sense, making the barest historical allowance for the fussiness that would later attach to "propriety" and "elegantly," Dryden's wit is clearly related to the conversation of English-speaking human beings ever since.

The point of defending Dryden's practice is not to argue that redefinition of what he had called "wit written" solves all problems but that it has material advantages over the available mentalistic alternatives, Augustan or modern. Nor is it to deny, obviously, that "wit" in Dryden and Pope does sometimes mean mind, ingenuity, or imagination, but rather to challenge the idea that they (and we) would somehow be better off if it always did. The critical advantages of having a term whose "primary" referent is the poet's mind instead of the qualities of the poet's product are not self-evident. Since what the poet makes is what "makes" the poet, the move from material making to mind would seem to be of less use in the criticism of poetry *or* poets than in metaphysical assertions of the primacy of spirit over matter. Dryden's emphasis on wit as the "*product* of imagination" and as "a propriety of thoughts and *words*" is not a retreat from psychology to rhetoric but a deliberate attempt to broaden receptivity and concentrate discussion. His definition raises questions, chiefly concerning the criteria of "propriety"; but they are questions for which the matter is at hand, questions admitting of textual appeal, argument, evidence, and, as Dryden's critical practice shows, continuing conversation.

It is sometimes objected that Dryden's "propriety" broadened the definition of wit to a definition of good writing of any kind, so that it approaches the gnomic generality of Swift's later description of a good style, "proper words in proper places." Addison, in what may be a prosaic case of Bloomian misreading, quotes Dryden's definition as "a Propriety of Words and Thoughts adapted to the Subject," and remarks that according to it "*Euclid* was the greatest Wit that ever set pen to Paper" (*Spectator* 62). Addison misquotes the passage cited –

Dryden had written "*elegantly* adapted"FS25 – and he did not recall
Dryden's later elaboration: "I drew my definition of poetical wit from
my particular consideration of [Virgil]: for propriety of thoughts and
words are only to be found in him; and where they are proper they will
be delightful. Pleasure follows of necessity as the effect does the cause;
and therefore is not to be put into the definition" (Preface to *Sylvae*,
1685; ii. 22). (That misreading is likelier than ignorance is suggested by
Addison's further assertion that the definition would also prove Virgil
a much more "facetious" writer than Ovid or Martial – a quality even
further removed from any of Dryden's definitions than from Addison's.)

Dryden's influence on *An Essay on Criticism*, generally felt to be great
but difficult to locate, is perhaps most visible in Pope's consistent
adoption of the "pleasure principle" Dryden takes for granted and in
the *Essay*'s broad insistence, which also follows "of necessity," that wit
is nothing if not good *writing*. The dominance and complexity of the
word "wit" in the poem has long been observed, Empson first noting
that it occurs an average of once every sixteen lines. Less recognized is
the accompanying emphasis on "writing," which in various derivations
occurs nearly half as often (nineteen times altogether), and which
begins and ends the poem's movement from the common nuisance of
"*Writing* ... ill" (line 2) to the uncommon achievement of "*writing
well*" (line 724). If we add to these instances other references to
language – ranging from Homer's "*Text*" (line 128) to various "Parts"
of "Expression" such as "words," "music," "syllables," and so on –
the emphasis on material composition is even more conspicuous. Poetry
is always a physical labor and pleasure. The famous section on sound
and versification (lines 337–83) begins as an exposure of those who read
poetry "but to please their Ear" and then becomes a demonstration of
how to do just that – without just doing that. The reader Pope takes
into this workshop of rhymes and rhythms is one possessed of the
"*gen'rous Pleasure* to be charm'd with Wit" (line 238). The reader's
physical apprehension of the poet's physical labor is the necessary if not
sufficient condition for the charm's working. There is nothing
incongruous for Pope in moving within a paragraph from advice about
varying the vowels and excising expletives to the harmonics of
Timotheus, because small and large effects are alike "*Turns of Nature*,"
that is, discoveries and manipulations of matter.

The conjunction of human labor and human pleasure in poetry
remains conspicuous even at those moments when the subject is
inspiration. The mid-eighteenth-century poet William Collins would

ask that he might "feel" with Shakespeare. Pope's sympathy with past writers (here Homer and Virgil especially) is clearly as ardent but more intimately connected with the pleasures and production of texts:

> Oh may some Spark of *your* Coelestial Fire
> The last [i.e. latest], the meanest of your Sons inspire,
> (That on weak Wings, from far, pursues your Flights;
> *Glows* while he *reads*, but *trembles* as he *writes*) ...
>
> (195–98)

The social relation is emphatic because then "*Patriarch-Wits*" (line 479) are immediately enlisted in the project now unfolding, the *Essay* itself, whose purpose is

> To teach vain Wits a Science *little known*,
> T'*admire* Superior Sense, and *doubt* their own.
>
> (199–200)

Over the last several decades Pope's commentators have, understandably, felt it so necessary to show that *An Essay on Criticism* is a poem rather than a list of "rules" that there may be some need at this point to recall how much it is a poem about literary praxis. That is not to reduce it to technical precepts and examples. The poem can even be read (should be, I believe) as a strong narrative poem, an elaborate if subdued conjunction of cultural history and *Bildungsroman*, without losing sight of the fact that for Pope the ancient poets exist because they made poems.[30] Whatever the origin, all the "fire" in the world has meaning only as fire *in* the world, passed from one human group to another. For all his curiosity, here and notably in the Preface to the *Iliad*, about the nature of the great poet's "soul" or "genius," Pope's "Patriarch-Wits" live as "wit written." In the *Battel of the Books* Swift playfully enjoins the reader to think rather of writings – "books, in the most literal sense" – than authors: "So, when Virgil is mentioned, we are not to understand the person of a famous poet called by that name, but only certain sheets of paper, bound up in leather, containing the words of the said poet; and so of the rest." The remark must be transposed to another key to accord fully with the suggested narrative of *An Essay on Criticism*, but Pope's story of wit is closer even in its more exalted moods to Swift's context of writings than to the figures of ghostly influence in Collins, Gray, Blake, or Wordsworth.

---

[30] I have discussed the narrative element of Pope's *Essay* in "Theory and Story in *An Essay in Criticism*," in Christopher Fox (ed.), *Teaching Eighteenth-Century Poetry* (New York: AMS, 1990), pp. 237–48.

It is not accidental that for these later writers the word "wit" could hardly be a synonym for poetry. Pope's own usage remains elusive but is somewhat clearer when seen in terms of primary emphasis, as a stubbornly social term for poetry on the page rather than poetry *in potentia*. Wit written, as Dryden had insisted, does not mean simply the sting of epigram. And yet it does not *not* mean epigram. One might think of it as a manner or fabric which makes epigram possible, which epigram helps complete. It is tempting in this respect to begin to speak of the "spirit" of wit, but we may be closer to home with Dryden's "propriety." The most powerful moments in Augustan writing are not triumphs over matter but triumphs of matter, in which the labor of getting the best words in the best places gives proprietary pleasure. Unless such proprietary claims are seen at once as provisional as well as "final," unless, in other words, brevity is their soul, the claim of collaborative clarity dissolves into dull control, "ease" into strained facility. When the claim succeeds, however, it is a moment of quickness in which matter does not disappear but rather bears visible traces of human labor and purposiveness. The "materialism" of Augustan wit operates in several ways, some of which I will try to analyze in practice in the following chapter. Here a general point about *An Essay on Criticism* and the theoretical use of "wit" it suggests should be clarified. Empson's assertion that "there is not a single use of the word in the whole poem in which the idea of a joke is quite out of sight" is overstated, but it is more promising than interpretations of wit as "really" meaning something unrealized, a quality of the poet's mind. If we conclude that for Pope "wit" nearly always has in sight the idea of forceful writing that gives pleasure, we will be consistently close to his meaning in *An Essay on Criticism*. We may also move a step closer to understanding the social commitments of his contemporaries who found the troublesome word so useful.

3

On the matter of wit

I can very well suppose men may be frightened out of their wits, but I
have no apprehension they should be laughed out of them.
Shaftesbury, *Sensus Communis; An Essay on the Freedom of Wit and
Humour*

It may be noted by the way that there is no better start for thinking than
laughter. And, in particular, convulsion of the diaphragm usually
provides better opportunities for thought than that of the soul. Epic
theater is lavish only in occasion for laughter.
Walter Benjamin, "The Author as Producer"

Laughter is a vital factor in laying down that prerequisite for fearlessness
without which it would be impossible to approach the world realistically.
As it draws an object to itself and makes it familiar, laughter delivers the
object into the fearless hands of investigative experiment – both scientific
and artistic – and into the hands of free experimental fantasy.
Mikhail Bakhtin, "Epic and Novel"[1]

Because they criticize the emergent political economy of capitalism
and sometimes parody the experimental and descriptive procedures of
natural science, the "Tory satirists" of the early eighteenth century are
often considered as anti-materialist writers. If materialism means greed
or denial of immortality, they are. If materialism means a belief that
the questions most often worth writing about are, to use an important

---

[1] Shaftesbury, *An Essay on the Freedom of Wit and Humour*, in *Characteristics*, i. 65; Benjamin,
Reflections: Essays, Aphorisms, Autobiographical Writings, ed. Peter Demetz (New York: Harcourt
Brace Jovanovich, 1978), 236. Bakhtin, *The Dialogic Imagination: Four Essays*, trans. Caryl
Emerson and Michael Holquist (Austin: University of Texas Press, 1981), 23.

Swiftian word, "fundamental" problems of the relations of bodily
beings to their environment, products, and each other, then they
clearly are not anti-materialists. At this date it should not still have to
be recalled that the point of Swift's "Celia, Celia, Celia shits" is not
that Celia does but that Cassinus thought she didn't. Similarly, the
point about the "enthusiast" is not that he has a body but that he
pretends it is only his "outward Man." Ignorance of the body and of
bodies is the origin of abstraction, the real target, one version of which
is activity that looks foolish not because it is materialist but because it
is mentally mechanistic. Like the problematic labels themselves,
characterizations of the supposed "gloom" of the "Tory satirists" as a
rearguard "humanism" on the part of authors "bitterly opposed to the
scientific trends of their day" (Bredvold, Fussell, Davie) are beginning
to appear to have more to do with modern literary-critical nostalgias
than with Augustan literature.[2]

Laughter rather than gloom is the response the satirists tend to
regard as normative. There are disagreements in the period about the
occasion for laughter, but writers as different as Rochester and Addison
or Shaftesbury and Swift could agree on its importance. All but the
grave tend to see it as the necessary counterforce to "gravity," a word
to which we will return. I have juxtaposed Shaftesbury and Benjamin
above not to confuse their politics but to suggest the materialist
implications of laughter in even so "Platonized" an Augustan as
Shaftesbury. The assumption in both views is that laughter is
intellectually liberating, makes critical thought possible, because it
grounds us in our senses ("wits"). For Benjamin laughter is the
potential "alienating" of the public "through thinking, from the
conditions in which it lives." For Shaftesbury it leads to "humanity
and common sense" by countering the "different systems and schemes
imposed by authority," under which citizens might "wholly lose all
notion or comprehension of truth." By the time of Fielding's Preface to
Joseph Andrews, laughter is beginning to look more sentimental than
subversive – it is "wholsome physic" that purges away "spleen,
melancholy, and ill affections" – but even so the path from the body

<hr/>

[2] I refer in this paragraph to the influential essay by Louis I. Bredvold, "The Gloom of the Tory
Satirists," in James L. Clifford (ed.), *Eighteenth-Century English Literature: Modern Essays in
Criticism* (New York: Oxford University Press, 1959), 3–20, to Paul Fussell's elegiac emphasis
in *The Rhetorical World of Augustan Humanism: Ethics and Imagery from Swift to Burke* (Oxford:
Clarendon Press, 1965), and to the claim by Donald Davie that "a great deal of the finest
writing of the period, in verse and prose alike … is produced by men like Swift and Pope, who
were bitterly opposed to the trend of scientific development in their day" (*The Language of
Science and the Language of Literature, 1700–1740* [London: Sheed and Ward, 1963], 23).

politic is clear: "I will appeal to common observation, whether the same companies are not found more full of good humour and benevolence, after they have been sweeten'd for two or three hours with entertainments of this kind [i.e. burlesques], than when soured by a tragedy or a grave lecture."[3] (Fielding may be deliberately down-playing the political element in his own stage burlesques, written up to the Licensing Act of 1737, and to which Benjamin's ideas concerning Brechtian "epic theater" might be applied.)

Not all wit, of course, aims at laughter. According to Dryden, Virgil's poetry has more wit than Ovid's, and Pope could regard the *Iliad* as a "Work of Wit" as well as *Mac Flecknoe*. I begin with laughter, first, because so many Augustan works arouse it and, secondly, because much of the point of the argument over "wit" seems to have been to hold on to a word for good writing of various kinds which does not (like "art," for example) almost automatically *exclude* the likelihood of laughter. Similarly, the body is not the only material norm invoked by Augustan writing, but it is the best place to start.

Wit's body and bodies

The presence of the body in Augustan writing is so widely recognized that it may seem superfluous to insist on it once again. One thinks readily of Rochester's sprawling fornicators in St. James's Park, Dryden's sewage-laden Thames, Pope's dunces plunging into Fleet Ditch, the Yahoos, and in the next moment of the long history of testimony, usually disapproving, to these images – from Johnson's judgment that "Pope and Swift had an unnatural delight in ideas physically impure, such as every other tongue utters with unwill-ingness," to less censorious but perhaps more condescending verdicts in this century about the "schoolboyish" humor of the age.[4] Increasingly close attention has been given to the function of scatology in satire generally and in Swift's work particularly, with the result that the

---

[3] *Joseph Andrews*, ed. Martin C. Battestin (Boston: Houghton Mifflin, 1961), 9. Fielding makes a point here of taking a more tolerant position than Shaftesbury toward burlesque, "not because I have had some little success on the stage this way, but rather as it contributes more to exquisite mirth and laughter than any other."

[4] Johnson, "Life of Pope," in *The Lives of the English Poets*, 3 vols., ed. George Birkbeck Hill (Oxford: Clarendon Press, 1905), iii. 242. William Empson refers to the early eighteenth century as "that rather schoolboyish period" in his otherwise sympathetic "Wit in the *Essay on Criticism*;" see *The Structure of Complex Words* (first pub. 1951; London: Hogarth Press, 1985), 85.

subject now is less ethically and emotionally charged within critical
discussion. That is progress, although whether wholly without loss is
debatable, for one might suspect that "scatology" itself is a somewhat
self-protective term as well as technically useful. In either case
(prosecution or defense), the emphasis has tended to fall on the grosser
bodily images used as a means of satiric denigration. What need further
consideration are the perhaps less striking but significant uses of the
body as a positive norm.

As suggested above in speaking of Swift, the body figures often as a
measure of various kinds of abstraction. Since one of the more obvious
kinds of abstraction exists in philosophical writing, it is not surprising
that we can find a ready example in the remaining few pages of Prior's
burlesque of Locke. The concluding section of "Lock and Montaigne"
sinks – or rises – to a hypothetical "Farce" sketched out by Montaigne.
The scene resists paraphrase.

> Suppose, Mr: Lock, you returned to your own Chamber from the Business, the
> Visits, and pleasures of the Day. Your Night gown on, Your Books before You.
> John, say you to Your Man, You may go down and Sup, Shut the Door. John,
> who ...has been dabbling in your Book, and consequently Admired the
> Wisdom of it, reasons thus upon the matter. The Senses first let in particular
> Ideas into the Sensorium, the Brain, or as my Master admirably expresses it
> to the Drawing Room, which are from thence conveyed to the... Cabinet of
> the Mind, right! The vibration of the Air and its' Undulation Strike the
> Tympanium of my Ear, and these Modifications being thus Conveyed to my
> Sensorium, certain words in the English Language ...produce a determined
> Conception. John You may go down and Sup; shut the door. Now *John* has
> been a common Appellative to Millions of Men thro many Ages, from
> Apostles, Emperors, Doctors and Philosophers, down to Butlers and Valets de
> Chambre and Persons of my Quality ...Now to none of these could my Master
> Speak, for they are either Dead or Absent; it must therefore be to me; doubtful
> again: for my Masters own Name is John, and being a Whimsical Person, he
> may probably talk to himself. No that cant be neither....
>
> (Prior, i. 635–36)

From one point of view this farce is of course unfair to Locke, who
had after all acknowledged that ratiocination is inappropriate to much
of common life. The text works by insisting on another point of view,
one dominated by details excluded from introspective analysis: the
author in his nightgown, the routine of the day, an untheoretical room
with a substantial door, two bodily beings unabstracted from social
relationship (master and servant), who have yet to eat supper. The

physical and social details – the body among bodies – accumulate as
the scene progresses.

Let us now imagine the Door shut, and John safely arrived in the Kitching,
Margaret the Cook Maid sets the cold Beef before Him, Robin the Butler gives
Him a Bottle of Strong Beer, and they proceed Amicably to the News of the
Day, If the Regent is at Madrid, or the King of Spain upon the Coast of
Scotland. If Digwell the Gardiner Stole two of Sir Thomas's Spoones, or the
Match holds between my Lord Truemadam's Coachman and Prue the Dairy
Maid.

   This conversation goes on cheerfully until John, stroking the
greyhound by his chair, asks Margaret whether she thinks a dog can
form complex ideas. "Truly," she says, "I neither know nor care."

John proceeds, and Margaret tho you have Stewed many a Barrel or quart of
Oysters, You never examined if an Oyster was capable of thinking, and tho
you have seen many a hundred Old Men, You never found out that an Old
Man who has lost his Senses is exceedingly like an Oyster, As like as he is to
a rotten Apple, says the Butler. John pittying the Butlers Ignorance continues
his Discourse to the Maid, Do you believe Margaret that there are any
Original Characters impressed upon a Child in the Womb? Prethey John,
replyes She, let us talk of our own Concerns, what have You or I to do with
Children in the Womb? Stil John goes on; I would fain make you perceive
Margaret, that my Body is a Solid Substance endued with an Extension of
parts, and that You have in your Body a Power of communicating Motion by
impulse, that motion will produce an intense heat, and then again that heat
– Look You John, says Margaret, I have often told you of this: When ever you
get half Drunk you run on in this filthy baudy manner.

   The opposition of colloquial talk to "discourse" is clear enough.
Under or in it is the suggestion as well that John has taken precisely the
wrong way to assert the solidity of his body. His "extension" and
Margaret's "warmth" are, for Prior, perfectly healthy until abstracted.
As the butler enters the fray, the overextended John asks him in "what
Predicament" he considers the "human Species."

Sirrah, Robin Answers in great Anger I scorn your words; I am neither
Predicament nor Species any more than your Self; But I wont Stand by and
see my fellow Servant affronted. Here, Mr: Locke, you find Bella plus quam
Civilia. John and Margaret form their different Alliances, the whole Family
is set into a flame by three leaves of Your own Book, and you may knock Your
heart out for Your Boyled Chicken, and Your Roasted Apples.

                                                    (Prior, i. 636–38)

   Prior in fact seems to have thought Locke's method more perverse than inflammatory. His strategy in these later exchanges is a more graphic form of the strategy of the work as a whole, which is to "refute" the conclusions of monologue with kinetic dialogue. The force of the method is to assert that the important truths are all relational, that a psychology of introspection begins to go wrong as soon as it leaves the social context and the negotiation of human needs – epitomized here in kitchen conversation. This norm implies skepticism not of personal individuality but of individualism without persons. Robin and Margaret do not understand Locke but know where they are and thus emerge in the dialogue as more solid and substantial bodies than John. Robin's comic protest against being turned into a complex idea ("I am neither Predicament nor Species") and his affirmation of communal connection ("I wont ...see my fellow Servant affronted") seem to speak for Prior's sense of human identity as fundamentally physical and interpersonal.

This is not to suggest that the body is never suspect. Humans are of course fallen, and there is no thoroughgoing naturalism or primitivism in the period which ignores the likelihood that raw self-assertion will be raw. Perhaps the clearest example in ironic writing is Swift's claim, in *An Argument against Abolishing Christianity*, that most doctrinal disputes are really attempts to evade necessary "Restraints on human Nature," a point illustrated by anecdote: "This was happily expressed by him, who had heard of a Text brought for Proof of the Trinity, which in an antient Manuscript was differently read; he thereupon immediately took the Hint, and by a sudden Deduction of a long *Sorites*, most logically concluded; Why, if it be as you say, I may safely whore and drink on, and defy the Parson."[5] The position is not confined to explicitly Christian arguments. Something like an aesthetic version of the fall is expressed by Pope in *Peri Bathos, or the Art of Sinking in Poetry* – "The Taste of the *Bathos* is implanted by Nature itself in the Soul of Man" – and in the *Dunciad* whenever the dunces are seen as escaping the "restraints" of civilization and resorting to what comes naturally.

But the stronger current runs in the other direction, toward the trust of the body's "honest instinct" that flows from Rochester's *Satyr against Reason and Mankind* to *An Essay on Man*. Humans may have innate tendencies toward dullness but true bathos is an "Art"; the "Genius of no Mortal whatever, following the meer Ideas of Nature, and unassisted with an habitual, nay laborious Peculiarity of thinking,

[5] Antepenultimate paragraph of *An Argument against Abolishing Christianity*, *PW* II. 38.

could arrive at Images so wonderfully low and unaccountable."
Rochester's Artemisia uses nature and art in much the same antithesis:

> Nature's as lame in making a true fop
> As a philosopher; the very top
> And dignity of folly we attain
> By studious search, and labor of the brain,
> By observation, counsel, and deep thought:
> God never made a coxcomb with a groat.
> We owe that name to industry and arts...
>
> (*Artemisia to Chloe*, 154–60)

Rochester is often considered the extreme case, but the general tone
of his "libertine" praise of bestiality is, as the ending of *Tunbridge Wells*
reminds readers, close to Swift's:

> Ourselves with noise of reason do we please
> In vain: humanity's our worst disease.
> Thrice happy beasts are, who because they be
> Of reason void, are so of foppery.
> Faith, I was so ashamed that with remorse
> I used the insolence to mount my horse;
> For he, doing only things fit for his nature,
> Did seem to me by much the wiser creature.

Arguments in which the body is normative – either through the
analogy of animals, who perceive but are unaffected with reason, or of
uneducated humans, who have knowledge but not "art" – generally
risk anti-intellectualism which, taken to its logical conclusion, would
lead the reader to stop reading. One does not stop, however, because
the works in which such appeals are strong are typically strong as well
in argumentative ingenuity.

The paradoxical process of asserting a bodily norm by conspicuously
intellectual or "artful" means is part of the game of parody and
burlesque, which work only if an author manages to display mastery of
the modes "contained" by the representation. The question of the full
meaning and effect still remains, and might be put in terms of whether
the bodily norm is finally cancelled out by the example of verbal
dexterity. Is a rational argument against rationality, for instance,
simply an argument for better rationality? Rochester suggests as much
by restricting "right" reason to sensation:

> That reason which distinguishes by sense
> And gives us rules of good and ill from thence,

That bounds desires with a reforming will
To keep 'em more in vigor, not to kill.

(*Satyr against Reason and Mankind*, 100–03)

The question abides because the poem continues, like most other powerful arguments, to employ reason in ways that could not be redefined as essentially sensory prudence, just as the poem's eventual range of ethical concerns belies the speaker's posture of immediate self-interest.

But to conclude that the norm of the body yields to the norm of intellectual example seems to involve deciding that at some point in the texts body becomes "apparent" and intellect "real," which draws the line in the wrong place. Some of the most interesting Augustan works question one's ability to divide experience into ready categories of body and mind or matter and spirit. Swift's works do so more systematically than most, but two brief examples from Pope may show how dichotomies of physical and spiritual, earthly and heavenly, are persistently equivocated. The first is from the *Epistle to Bathurst* and involves the eschatological question Pope raises and to which the tale of Balaam is in some ambiguous sense a reply. The question is whether for prodigals and misers there "are other worlds prepar'd? / Or are they both, in this their own reward?" (lines 335–36). One plausible reading would regard the question as in fact a statement, roughly to the effect that the vicious are miserable here as well as hereafter. An equally plausible interpretation takes the question as real, admitting the possible answer that even divine justice would require no more than leaving such thwarted people to their worldly ends. The second example concerns the status of the sylphs in *The Rape of the Lock*. When the speaker in Belinda's dream asks "What guards the Purity of melting Maids, / In Courtly Balls, and Midnight masquerades ... ?" and then answers, "'Tis but their Sylph, the wise Celestials know, / Tho' *Honour* is the Word with Men below" (lines 71–78), Pope suggests more ontological alternatives than any analytic translation is likely to capture. One of these, however, is an assertion that *Honour* is no less mysterious and no more material than the sylphs, which in turn does not necessarily mean that it is immaterial. The sylphs present this sort of problem continually: one cannot read the poem for long without taking the sylphs seriously and one cannot take them seriously for long without beginning to sound like Bottom explicating his "dream." I will return to them, no less flat-footedly, later in this chapter.

Mechanical operations

The legend of Swift barely passing logic at Trinity College has an appeal like that of Einstein nearly failing arithmetic. Swift's parodic mastery of argumentative techniques has become a critical subject (in the phrase of one of his voices) of "uncontrollable demonstration." In the following paragraphs I will concentrate on *The Mechanical Operation of the Spirit* because its argument bears directly on the oppositions of matter and spirit. It has not often been followed as closely as the arguments of *A Tale of a Tub, An Argument against Abolishing Christianity*, and, of course, *A Modest Proposal*. The work receives less attention for understandable reasons; it is overshadowed by *A Tale of a Tub*, which it and *The Battel of the Books* accompanied, and it is advertised on the title page as "A Fragment." Despite that description and its close relation to *A Tale of a Tub* (especially the section on the "Aeolists"), I think the argument of *The Mechanical Operation of the Spirit* is as autonomous and complete as any in Swift. It is in any case brief enough to let us attempt to see its structure in some detail.

The essay progresses by establishing oppositions and then complicating them to the point of collapse or redefinition. (There is some advantage in speaking of what the essay does rather than of its impersonated author, a complacently modern virtuoso, since this debatable "persona" nearly disappears after the epistolary preface, as "he" acknowledges by the fifth paragraph.) The instability of dichotomies is suggested at large by the division of the work into two roughly equal sections, the first ostensibly about recent "fanatic" assemblies, the second about their teachers; in fact, much of the latter is a "brief Survey of some Principle Sects among the *Fanatics* in all ages" (II, paras. 11–15). This instability begins with the writer's first major distinction, between literal and allegorical meanings, closely followed by another, between "particular" and "universal" subjects. Everything after the story of Mahomet and his ass will be told "by way of Allegory" (to avoid "Offence to any Party whatever"), but with the usual opposition so turned that the "real" subject of the work is to be Mohammedanism, while the discussion of the Dissenters will supposedly be merely an allegorical veil (I, para. 3). The next paragraph opposes writings suited for "particular Occasions and Circumstances of Time, or Place, or of Person" to this text's allegedly higher concern with "universal Nature, and Mankind in general." But two paragraphs later the subject will become the mechanical operation of the spirit "as it is at present performed by our *British Workmen*," the only surprise being how neatly the phrase drops the particulars of time, place, and persons into order.

Oppositions remain unstable but operate more rigorously in the other parts of the work. Having defined Enthusiasm as *"A Lifting up of the Soul or its Faculties above Matter,"* the author applies this definition to religion, "wherein there are three general Ways of ejaculating the Soul": "The first, is the immediate Act of God, and is called, *Prophecy* or *Inspiration*. The second, is the immediate Act of the Devil, and is termed *Possession*. The third, is the Product of natural Causes, the effect of strong Imagination, Spleen, violent Anger, Fear, Grief, Pain, and the like." The effect of this remarkable list is to offer and withdraw distinctions simultaneously. Nothing could be further apart than God and the devil, yet the acts of both are supernatural and therefore conflated. Nothing could be more clearly opposed than supernatural and natural causes (the first and second vs. the third), yet all three are alike (*a*) in being so well understood (!) as to require only perfunctory acknowledgment and (*b*) in standing together as what is *not* the subject of this discourse.

The declared subject, then, the "fourth Method of *Religious Enthusiasm* ... as it is purely an Effect of Artifice and *Mechanic Operation* (I, para. 5), is opposed to all three of the others simply by being worth discussing; but it is also explicitly defined against the third method only, which is "purely an Effect of Nature," while the mechanical operation is "wholly an Effect of Art" (I, para. 7). The distinction between nature and art controls the rest of the work, alternately subsuming and subverting the accompanying opposition of matter and spirit. One's impression of the essay's riskiness comes, I think, from the growing sense that the controlling opposition is itself nearly "uncontrollable."

Before attempting to follow Swift further, however, a reader might note that even if the work were indeed a fragment and ended right here, a kind of indeterminacy principle would already be apparent. Underneath all of the argumentative dichotomies lies the arresting suggestion that any of the four ways of "transporting" the soul "beyond the Sphere of Matter" might be as material, or immaterial, as any other on the same list – which includes, of course, the "immediate Act of God ... called ... Inspiration." At this level, there seem to be only two logical possibilities: either mechanical operation is as "spiritual" as inspiration, or divine inspiration is an affair of matter. The first is obviously unacceptable, the second equally so, unless what is under attack includes assent to conventional definitions as well as the behavior of unconventional Dissenters. Given Swift's commitments, the second path is as perilous as the first, but the rest of the work seems to show why it is preferable.

Like body and spirit, "nature" and "art" are put under strain as soon as they appear. The "Longheads" (whose practice of binding infants' heads eventually resulted in a race of "macrocephali") are obviously a ludicrous club raised against the "Roundheads"; but they also introduce the idea that "Custom, from being a second Nature," may "proceed to be a first," since what "in its Original, was purely an Artifice ... Through a long Succession of Ages, hath grown to be natural" (I, para. 7). The next brief paragraph uses this idea more seriously than we may be expecting, and its complexity is easily missed. In it the "curious Reader" is asked to attend to two dichotomies: "First, between an Effect grown from *Art* into *Nature*, and one that is natural from its Beginning; secondly, between an Effect wholly natural, and one which has only a natural Foundation, but where the Superstructure is entirely Artificial" (I, para. 8). Since the treatise claims the first and last of these as its proper subject, it is worth trying to sort out the three "Effects" in relation to their supposed causes:

(1) artificial cause ⟶ natural effect
(2) natural cause ⟶ natural effect
(3) natural cause ⟶ artificial effect.

But the curious reader will notice that Swift does not use the word "cause" in the first two cases, simply implying it by "effect" and the preceding "Longhead" paragraph, and that he does not use "effect" in the third case, where the terms are rather "foundation" and "superstructure." If we try applying this latter pair of terms to the other instances we end up with perhaps a plausible reformulation in the case of number two (natural foundation for a natural superstructure) but a very difficult revision of number one (artificial foundation for a natural superstructure). All that seems to be clear is that the middle set (the "wholly natural") is normative for the moment, while the other two that concern the essay are artificial in either origin or effect. They are, so to speak, half artificial. They are also, to pursue the same logic, half natural. What is striking here is not that Swift sees so much artifice but so much nature. It would seem easier to have arranged things to include a fourth category, the "wholly artificial" (artificial effects of

artificial causes), if the aim were purely to make the Dissenters appear
as unlike the rest of humanity as possible. By not taking this easy step
Swift instead makes the distinction between "them" and "us" more
tenuous. The result of the mock precision that distinguishes "natural"
from "artificial" effects is to put the distinction in question. One is
forced to take refuge in the simple but paradoxical recognition that
artifice is natural.

By now even the very curious reader may have begun to feel that the
present discussion is taking the long way around to the recognition that
Swift has an unsettling ability to implicate his audience in his attacks,
as collaborators one moment, as part of the target the next. The object
here is not to emphasize Swift's peculiar power, however, but to
identify a general tendency of his work in exploring more explicitly and
intricately the tensions empowering many Augustan works. Swift's
remarks on the Longheads, for example, raise questions that flutter
more coyly around Belinda's curls. As we wade through the problematic
"clarifications" that follow it, the Longheads' collective artifice begins
to appear extreme only because it is so visible (producing children's
heads "in the Form of a Sugar-Loaf"), not because it begins at birth.
The distinction between nature and artifice – or, in current formula,
nature and nurture – is invoked and put to ethical use, but its pursuit
is also recognized as something likely to lead back to a legendary
"original," borrowed from a traveller's tale or an eccentric doctrine.
Both works, in other words, emphasize the artificiality of the
"superstructure" of modern life – the "artificial Extasies" of low
culture and high – without taking seriously a historical state of nature
as its alternative.

But if the road back to an origin is blocked and mocked, the road
down remains open, and leads to a "foundation" in the human body.
In *The Rape of the Lock* the bodily basis is present all along as
metaphorical sexuality – explicated by Belinda's "Hairs less in sight"
(III. 176) – but its moral, in Pope's phrase, is finally opened "more
clearly" with Clarissa's speech on mortality (v. 9–34), where "Curl'd
or uncurl'd" – and in or out of sight – "Locks will turn to grey." *The
Mechanical Operation of the Spirit* assumes both death and sexuality as its
starting point (Mahomet riding his italicized *ass*) and then sets off in a
chase of wit after the true "Business of Flesh and Blood" (II, para. 15).
Swift's search for the "real foundation" or "fundamental point" of
enthusiasm in the closing paragraphs (where the terms are repeated six
times) proceeds so insistently toward sexuality as nearly to obscure the

more "basic" position it illustrates: "Too intense a Contemplation is not the Business of Flesh and Blood; it must by the necessary Course of Things, in a little Time, let go its Hold, and fall into *Matter*" (II, para. 15). The Dissenters clearly are the object of attack, but the attack is coherent (and not simply vehement) because it works them into the consistent principle that those who "abstract themselves from Matter" (I, para. 13) "bind up" the wits of whatever inspiration God has granted modern humans, "all their sense." It is not accidental that the maxim of art that Swift uses in his memorable deflation of spiritual pride – "in *Life* as in *Tragedy*" it is a "great Defect ... to interpose the Assistance of preternatural power without an absolute and last Necessity" (II, para. 1) – is also roughly the law of parsimony in the material sciences. The search for "one material and fundamental point" (II, para. 11) in human action is a tautological quest, since the fundamental is the material.

The "material point" of Augustan wit requires more exact definition if it is to be distinguished from other views, which may also be regarded as versions of materialism, that Swift, Pope, and other writers either do not share or actively oppose. Before trying to discriminate materialisms theoretically, however, I would like to explore further some ways in which several works of the period take as the matter closest at hand the human body.

Big bodies and little bodies (Swift, Gay, Pope)

Johnson's remark that "once you have thought of big men and little men, it is very easy to do all the rest" has at least the virtue of locating the imaginative origin of *Gulliver's Travels* in the play of physical proportion. From this visual premise, much of the rest does seem easy, although in Pope's sense rather than Johnson's, that is, so apparently artless as to appear inevitable. Swift plays the game of sizes so largely that Gulliver's epiphany in Brobdingnag – "Undoubtedly the Philosophers are in the Right when they tell us, that nothing is great or little otherwise than by Comparison" – begins to seem little in comparison. Swift did not play the game alone, however. There is more than a pleasant symmetry in the fact that one of the greatest poems of the period works in its own way by juxtaposing big and little bodies; the introduction of the sylphs into *The Rape of the Lock* seems so far from being an afterthought because they are an imaginatively logical extension of the original juxtaposition of big poetry and "Little Men"

(I. 11). Whether Swift learned from Pope is debatable, but Pope's appreciation more than a decade later of Swift's ironic ability to "magnify Mankind" is eagerly sympathetic, as both the dedication of the *Dunciad* and his poems on *Gulliver's Travels* make clear. Gay's mock-heroic *The Fan*, a slighter work than Pope's or Swift's, uses miniature actors to magnify "trivial Things" and appeared between the sylphless and sylphic versions of *The Rape of the Lock*. The vision is most compatible with satiric fictions; but more directly didactic works, such as *An Essay on Man* and Mandeville's *Fable of the Bees*, insist that we alternately see human society large and small – now a bubble, now a world, London as Everywhere, London as beehive – to get the perspective right. Getting it right, as the *Epistle to Burlington* suggests, is the work of both visual and ethical sense; otherwise the human actor is dwarfed by his Brobdingnagian "things." In its bodily humor as well as its Palladianism, the period is an Age of Proportion.

If we think of the visual fields they create, magnification and miniaturization are techniques of optical manipulation, as closely related as two ends of a telescope, or the telescope and microscope. And, as with any abrupt shift of perspective, the first effect noticed will be visual defamiliarization, common things made uncommonly vivid. In this regard, the Lilliputians' inventory of Gulliver's pockets establishes Swift as the dean of defamiliarization, although this title, unlike the alternative praises Pope offers in the opening lines of the *Dunciad*, would probably not soothe Swift's ear. As the example suggests, the more memorable instances of things are likelier to involve magnification, for the good reason that miniaturization may startle – the world shrinks to a bubble, for example – but allows less room for detail the more it does so. Defamiliarization itself is selective but not necessarily evaluative.

But because big and little are also terms of value, defamiliarization by scale is of course frequently judgmental as well as descriptive. Big-heartedness and small-mindedness are obvious examples. But we do not need to reflect long, even at the same level of everyday speech, to recognize that big and little as terms of value do not automatically or necessarily correspond to praise and blame respectively. The fact that diminutives can commonly express condescension *or* endearment gives pause. At the other end, the magnification of a person clearly signifies his or her importance, but even the magnifier may not know whether what is clear is good or evil. In other words, while for the purpose of analysis we may concentrate on the images projected by techniques of enlarging or diminishing, a reader is always likely to sense that the relation of big and little is reciprocal, that changing the size of the object in some sense changes the size of the viewer. The terms of size have meaning, as Gulliver announces on the shore of Brobdingnag, only by "Comparison"; but the reader already knows that the first term of the comparison is oneself.

It is plain, then, that such bodily comparisons may readily arouse powerful and conflicting feelings – as the history of responses to *Gulliver's Travels* suggests. The feelings often conflict not only because readers vary from each other but because, in Pope's phrase, we vary from ourselves. Being "enlarged" at one moment may mean glory or conspicuous humiliation. The feelings are powerful because, in any case, responses to the body are likelier to be ambivalent than neutral, especially when the body in question is one's own. At this point, the issue of proportion leads from the language of optics to the language of dreams.

Although it is fitting that Gulliver falls asleep into Lilliput and awakens out of Brobdingnag, the dreamlike quality of *Gulliver's Travels* depends less on such structural devices or on a consistent atmosphere (which is often pure daylight and Defoe) than on arresting moments of surreal isolation. Such moments can occur anywhere in the work and sometimes within a single sentence, as in this detail among many concerning Lagado: "The People in the Streets walked fast, looked wild, their Eyes fixed, and were generally in Rags." Most of the fuller scenes one might associate with dreams, however, take place in the first two books, and the larger share of those in Brobdingnag. That is where Gulliver is most vulnerable and where, as John Traugott has recently observed, the "stuff of nightmare" is always near.[6] The following list of brief episodes from book II is mine, and partial, but most of the incidents seem to be remembered as well by students who have just read the work for the first time: Gulliver mistaken for a weasel or other "small dangerous Animal" and put back down on all fours by the farmer who discovers him; the attack by two rats, each the "Size of a large mastiff"; the descriptions of the boxes built to house Gulliver (there are three, one of them padded on all sides); Gulliver dropped into a bowl of cream and swimming for his life until rescued by Glumdalclitch; a pet monkey carrying Gulliver up the sides of the

---

[6] John Traugott, "The Yahoo in the Doll's House: *Gulliver's Travels* the Children's Classic," in Claude Rawson (ed.), *English Satire and the Satiric Tradition* (Oxford: Basil Blackwell, 1984), 127–50; the phrase is on p. 133.

palace to the rooftop, 500 yards high; the king's speech describing
Gulliver's kind as the "most pernicious Race of little odious vermin
... upon the Surface of the Earth"; Gulliver and traveling box dropped
into the ocean, where he fears drowning or starvation, until he is pulled
out four hours later.

Freud repeatedly insisted that there is no "key" to the interpretation
of dream symbols since a useful interpretation must be undertaken in
the context of the analysand's associations and with his or her
collaboration. But Freud also concluded that a few images do recur
with less variability than others and comprise a fairly small, fixed
vocabulary of symbols:

The range of things which are given symbolic representations in dreams is not
wide: the human body as a whole, parents, children, brothers and sisters,
birth, death, nakedness – and something else besides. The one typical – that is
regular – representation of the human figure as a whole is a *house*, as was
recognized by Scherner, who even wanted to give this symbol a transcendent
importance which it does not possess. It may happen in a dream that one finds
oneself climbing down the façade of a house, enjoying it at one moment,
frightened at another. The houses with smooth walls are men, the ones with
projections and balconies that one can hold on to are women. One's parents
appear in dreams as the *Emperor* and *Empress*, the *King* and *Queen* or other
honoured personages; so here dreams are displaying much filial piety. They
treat children and brothers and sisters less tenderly: these are symbolized as
small animals or *vermin*. Birth is almost invariably represented by something
which has a connection with *water*: one either falls into the water or climbs out
of it, one rescues someone from the water or is rescued by someone – that is to
say, the relation is one of mother to child. Dying is replaced in dreams by
departure, by a *train journey*, being dead by various obscure and, as it were, timid
hints, nakedness by *clothes* and *uniforms*. You see how indistinct the boundaries
are here between symbolic and allusive representation.[7]

Only the train is missing from *Gulliver's Travels*.

Enough misapplied psychoanalysis has been visited upon Swift to
require a careful distinction between the psychic power of the text and
the psychic life of the author. Seeking the "real" Swift with Freud's
summary in hand would lead to a number of unreal questions. Does
Gulliver fear drowning in his box because Swift's memories of birth
were unusually clear? or because his nurse carried him soon after across

[7] *Introductory Lectures on Psycho-Analysis*, Lecture 10 ("Symbolism in Dreams"), in *The Standard
Edition of the Complete Psychological Works of Sigmund Freud*, 24 vols., ed. and trans. James Strachey
(London: Hogarth Press, 1966–74), xv. 153.

the Irish Sea? The commonality Freud attributes to these images should remind us that any clues they may offer here point to the work's well-known appeal to children rather than to the childhood of the artist. Concerning Swift, they allow us to conclude little more than that he had a childhood and, like many great writers, seems to have gotten a lot out of it. In psychoanalytic terms, he appears to have been able to "regress" more productively than most people.

Concerning the text and audience, the clues are more helpful. They point to a middle ground between reductive biographical speculations (Swift's voyage through the birth canal, etc.) and equally reductive appeals to narrative realism (for example, Gulliver fears he will drown because sailors do). This middle ground comprises a large landscape, only a small part of which pertains directly to the play of proportion. The extraordinary concentration of elementary dream images in book II of *Gulliver's Travels* suggests that defamiliarization by scale begins very much at home, with the most familiar of prospects. The fiction's play is a game of calculation, but what it is first calculated to is the body. The most vivid instances of defamiliarization seem to be moments of refamiliarization.

While miniaturization of the perceiving subject tends to magnify individual bodies and things, miniaturization of what is perceived tends to emphasize corporate bodies and physical relationships. This again is simple enough as an optical shift, analogous to the difference between cinematic close-ups and long shots. Gulliver says of the Lilliputians that "They see with great Exactness, but at no great Distance," and of course the reverse is true of him in their world, while in Brobdingnag Gulliver will see "exactly" but rarely very far. This fact contributes as much to Gulliver's anxieties in Brobdingnag as does the likelihood of being stepped on; in Lilliput, on the contrary, he is delighted by the "entertaining Prospect" as soon as he can stand up: "The County round appeared like a continued Garden; and the inclosed Fields ...resembled so many Beds of Flowers ... I viewed the Town on my left Hand, which looked like the painted Scene of a City in a Theatre." Even when the focus is in both cases on large groups the emphasis is predictably different. Viewing, as best he can, the Brobdingnagian cavalry with swords aloft, Gulliver has the overwhelming impression of "ten thousand Flashes of Lightning ...darting at the same time from every Quarter of the Sky." What he sees in Lilliput, however, is the "best military Discipline I ever beheld."

As the examples may suggest, change of perspective is simpler in principle than in effect. It is not a question of whether something will be seen large or small but of which things will be seen as real. There is, in other words, a politics as well as an optics of looking up or looking down. The former will emphasize "parts," the latter the "whole." The words require quotation marks because parts and wholes are not simply discovered but constituted by perspective (something recognized when we speak of perspectives as taken rather than given). That there are political as well as visual definitions might best be illustrated for the moment by considering two contrasting perspectives in a work far removed from satire, *The Prelude*, where the opposing impressions of city and country often reflect differences of altitude as well as attitude. Seen from the street level, London is a "second-sight procession" of isolated faces passing in "blank confusion." From a sufficient height, the discrete bodies no longer have but are parts, members of a visible body politic. From the mountains that, like the poet, "now from high / Look down upon them," the villagers at Grasmere Fair become a "little family of men."[8]

Such melodies are rarely sought or found in Augustan literature, but the perspectives of Lilliput, *The Rape of the Lock*, and Gay's *The Fan* all include "entertaining Prospects" of material harmony. I use this awkward phrase to suggest that the shift of emphasis from the individual to collective body is indeed playful but in a way that makes play normative. All three are, in this loose sense, pastoral visions, and in each of them political mutations tend to occur. The first is the conversion of work itself into something so apparently voluntary, ordered and absorbing as to become more like play than labor. Closely related to this transformation is a tendency to see the body's products as artifacts rather than excretions. The third transformation concerns the status of these "things"; now magnified, they are seen less as objects of personal property than as communal achievements. But from this rather solemn summary it may be appropriate to turn now to the diminutive proportions of mock-heroic.

The "hero" of *The Fan* is the "new Machine" invented by Venus as a lover's gift and fashioned by her cupids. Like other poems and various periodical essays, including Pope's contribution to *Spectator* 527 ("On a Fan"), it ironically and affectionately surveys the artifacts associated with modern ritual romance. And like *The Rape of the Lock*, its epic parallels play the arms of love against the arms of war. In Gay's poem

---

[8] *The Prelude: A Parallel Text*, ed. J. C. Maxwell (New York: Penguin, 1971); in the 1805 text the lines are VII. 602, 695, and VIII. 7, 57–58.

the closest parallels emerge as diminutive reflections of Vulcan's armory in book VIII of the *Aeneid*. But unlike *The Rape of the Lock* of 1712, the epic background of *The Fan* extends rather than creates the effects of miniaturization, which depend primarily on Gay's own visual scale. By painterly convention, the "busie Cupids" are already small, and Gay immediately pictures them in "Lilliputian" relation to tools of presumably human proportion. To sharpen their darts, "Some with joint Force whirl round the stony Wheel," while several laborers are required to "work the File" or "the Graver guide" (I. 107, 132). Their size is appropriate to a world of delicate objects:

> A diff'rent Toil another Forge employs;
> Here the loud Hammer fashions Female Toys,
> Hence is the Fair with Ornament supply'd,
> Hence sprung the glitt'ring Implements of Pride;
> Each trinket that adorns the modern Dame,
> First to these little Artists ow'd its Frame.
>
> (I. 111–16)

The catalogue grows to include toys of males as well:

> Here the yet rude unjointed *Snuff-box* lyes,
> Which serves the railly'd Fop for smart Replies;
> There Piles of *Paper* rose in gilded Reams,
> The future Records of the Lover's Flames;
> Here clouded *Canes* 'midst heaps of Toys are Found,
> And inlaid Tweezer-Cases strow the Ground.
> There stands the *Toilette*, Nursery of Charms,
> Compleatly furnish'd with bright Beauty's Arms;
> The Patch, the Powder-Box, Pulville, Perfumes,
> Pines, Paint, a flatt'ring Glass, and Black-lead Combs.
>
> (I. 119–30)

The relation of *The Fan* to *The Rape of the Lock* is complicated but apparently reciprocal. Most of the artifacts Gay presents are already present in the first version of Pope's poem, often more pointedly used. (Even with his snuff box and clouded cane, for example, Sir Plume falls short of smart replies.) What *The Rape of the Lock* lacks until 1714, however, is a visual scale that would allow fully the oscillation between satire and celebration that Pope achieves when, to take one example, a lapful of sylphs spread their wings, "Trembling and conscious of the rich Brocade." Gay's cupids are less evocative figures than the sylphs, but the "joint Force" of these "little Artists" suggests the concerted efforts of Pope's light militia and the engaging military discipline Gulliver finds in Lilliput. As Venus places her order for a contrivance fitted to the human hand but unfolding to show a "Miniature Creation," discipline becomes spontaneous and pacific. Nearly invisible swords are beaten into nearly invisible ploughshares.

> Th' expecting *Loves* with Joy the Model view,
> And the joint Labour eagerly pursue.
> Some slit their Arrows with the nicest Art.
> And into Sticks convert the shiver'd Dart;
> The breathing Bellows wake the sleeping Fire,
> Blow off the Cinders, and the Sparks aspire;
> Their Arrow's Point they soften in the Flame,
> And sounding Hammers break its barbed Frame:
> Of This, the little Pin they neatly mold,
> From whence their Arms the spreading Sticks unfold...
>
> (i. 177–86)

The art of miniaturization is both analytic and synthetic. It divides conventional wholes into parts by making a big thing into many little things; thus the image of Gulliver's body in Lilliput almost immediately "becomes" a multitude of little bodies, his pain becomes visible as hundreds of tiny arrows, or in *The Rape of the Lock*, the normally monolithic Honour is "really" hosts of sylphs. It also makes many little things into a big thing, allowing a play of synthesis rarely available in more sober contexts. One of Gulliver's pleasantest prospects, for example, is his first view of the Lilliputian nobility: "The Ladies and Courtiers were all most magnificently clad, so that the Spot they stood upon seemed to resemble a Petticoat spread on the Ground, embroidered with Figures of Gold and Silver." The description momentarily replaces the image of many forms with the image of one, much as Gulliver's earlier impression of the landscape combined countless farms and forests into a single garden. Both ideas seem apt, just pretty enough, and Gulliver on imaginative terra firma. Closer to London, however, both comparisons are precisely the sort Pope and Swift would ridicule. "When a true Genius looks upon the *Sky*," Pope writes, "he immediately catches the Idea of a Piece of *Blue Lutestring*, or a *Child's Mantle*," and then quotes Blackmore. The narrator of *A Tale of a Tub* asks rhetorically, "What is that which some call *Land*, but a fine Coat faced with Green? or the Sea, but a Wastcoat of Water-Tabby?" These are instances of what Scriblerus would call the "*Diminishing* Figures." But in a miniature world, such impositions of

the human form or artifacts on what is normally vast or varied may
pass for accuracy rather than bathos.

That miniaturization affords the author a holiday from decorum is
less significant (since various mock-genres do so by definition) than the
peculiar contract it extends to the reader. As the images discussed
suggest, one is required to adopt anthropomorphic and animistic
"views," usually ascribed to primitive peoples and children. Gulliver's
"entertaining Prospects" must be *entertained* if one is to make sense of
his narrative. This demand is fairly clear in the case of *Gulliver's Travels*,
where we have the experience of children's responses to books I and II
as a rough illustration. But the complexity of the contract presents itself
clearly, too, in the form of a familiar classroom dilemma. What does
one say, exactly, to the student who declares, for example, that "this
book is not at all what I thought it was"? The area between gullibility
and skepticism is of course what we tend to mean by critical
intelligence, but one that both *Gulliver's Travels* and *The Rape of the Lock*
define as a peculiar composition of visual innocence and rhetorical
sophistication. Since the latter is usually the path of least resistance in
critical analysis, perhaps especially so in the discussion of Augustan
works, the appeal to innocence seems worth more emphasis. Ernst Kris
suggested that art in general works as "regression in the service of the
ego." The literary contract of works of visual scale might be thought of
as an especially explicit pact of mutual regression.[9]

Like much else in *The Rape of the Lock*, including its sexual humor, its
appeal to an innocent reading is at once equivocal and explicit. The
work does not interest actual children, of course, at least none of less
than Popean precocity. As suggested earlier, however, to find it
intelligible requires that we entertain the prospects of its miniature
world. As with *Gulliver's Travels*, this receptivity involves contradictions
more extreme than the acceptance of fiction normally designated by
the "willing suspension of disbelief," a notion which, from Aristotle to
Coleridge, rests heavily on the assumption that probabilities may be
substituted for actualities. Accepting the immediate visual incongruity
presented in the Lilliputians or sylphs is more like granting the premise
of a joke than believing that a man on a stage is Oedipus. But it is
complicated further by the requirement to "believe" as well as

---

[9] For Kris's comparison and differentiation of states in which the "ego abandons its supremacy
and the primary process obtains control" (such as dreaming or psychosis) and artistic
inspiration as "regression in the service of the ego" see his *Psychoanalytic Explorations in Art* (New
York: Schocken Books, 1964), esp. pp. 59–63, 177, 220–22, 253–54, 263, 311–12.

"grant." If one forgets the sylphs are a joke, one joins the Rosicrucians instead of the laughter. If one decides they are only a joke (not being true), one joins the hopeless company of dogmatic readers like the bishop who said of *Gulliver's Travels* that "for his part, he hardly believed a word of it."[10] And if one follows the likelier course of trying to have it both ways at once, then the last four of these lines from Ariel's speech to the sleeping Belinda are as challenging as any in the poem:

> If e'er one Vision touch'd thy infant Thought,
> Of all the Nurse and all the Priest have taught,
> Of airy Elves by Moonlight Shadows seen,
> The silver Token, and the circled Green,
> Of Virgins visited by Angel-Pow'rs,
> With Golden Crowns and Wreaths of heavn'ly Flow'rs,
> Hear and believe! thy own Importance know,
> Nor bound thy narrow Views to Things below.
> Some secret Truths from Learned Pride conceal'd,
> To Maids alone and Children are reveal'd:
> What tho' no Credit doubting Wits may give?
> The Fair and Innocent shall still believe.
>
> (I. 29–40)

The "joke" of the final lines is plain and has become more conspicuous in recent years as the sort of urbanity that might be called coffeehouse condescension; enough of it flows through the "cosmopolitanism" and "humanism" of the *Spectator* and countless other works to remind one that "polis" and "human" are often merely the historian's synonyms for men and man. The joke's assumptions are clearly masculine: everyone knows that the "learned" group is overwhelmingly male (proud or not), that young women may be as credulous as children, that doubting wits are right not to believe in elves, and so on. But if the sarcasm is plain, the irony is not.[11] The most immediate complication is the emphasis of the passage itself on female education rather than temperament. This miseducation (criticized by writers ranging from Addison to Mary Astell) is evoked by Pope as one in which males and females conspire, and his image of their collaboration

---

[10] Swift to Pope, Nov. 27, 1727, in *The Correspondence of Jonathan Swift*, ed. Harold Williams (Oxford: Clarendon Press, 1963–65), iii. 189.

[11] Of this passage Valerie Rumbold remarks, "We are free to infer that women never grow up, but at the same time Pope takes the opportunity to tease the judicious reader with such eminently respectable precedents as Jesus's 'of such is the kingdom of God,' and the conventional disdain of the gentleman for the pedant"; see *Women's Place in Pope's World* (Cambridge: Cambridge University Press, 1989), 76.

– "all the Nurse and all the Priest have taught" – begins to specify the subject further as the miseducation of Roman Catholic girlhood. It also broadens it to the relation of "Vision" and belief. Who is responsible for the equation of elves and fairies with saints and angels? There are a number of candidates: Belinda's old teachers, her new teacher (it is Ariel who will later equate staining honor and brocade), Belinda herself (mixing her lessons like Bibles and billets-doux), or Pope (the liberal Catholic poet in an "advanced" mood). The likeliest suspects seem, however, to be the group put in the climactic place, men whose learning is pride and whose wit is doubt. That "doubting Wits" may be a loaded phrase in Augustan writing – suggesting pseudo-skeptics, complacent or undiscriminating doubters – can be gathered from the anticlerical Shaftesbury as well as from Swift.[12] Within *The Rape of the Lock*, the complex term "wits" itself is used to undercut modern male prowess. In the lunar sphere, "Heroes' Wits are kept in pondrous Vases, / And Beaus' in Snuff-boxes and Tweezer-Cases" (v. 115–16), and all such masculine powers are, in the Olympian balance, found wanting:

> Now *Jove* suspends his golden Scales in Air,
> Weighs the Men's Wits against the Lady's Hair;
> The doubtful Beam long nods from side to side;
> At length the Wits mount up, the Hairs subside.
>
> (v. 71–74)

Canto v may seem a long way to go to resolve a joke from canto I, but the irony of gender appears to run the length of the poem, at least as long as Pope chooses to "keep the Machinery in view." Ariel's first speech is, like Prospero's in *The Tempest*, more to the audience than to the immediate auditor. It is a necessary piece of exposition, but in this case the history to be retraced – if the story is to follow and be followed – involves intellectual as well as narrative regression. Ariel's speech establishes conditions of belief for the poem's readers, who, if they are to see any further into the poem, must implicitly contract to "credit"

---

[12] Shaftesbury speaks at several points in his *Miscellaneous Reflections* of the "forward wits" of the present age who find "justness and accuracy of thought too constraining." His own "jocular method" of "lay-wit" attempts (as does Swift in *A Tale of a Tub*) to "find means to laugh gentlemen into their religion who have unfortunately been laughed out of it," reclaiming those members of the "polite world, who have been so long seduced by the way of raillery and wit." See esp. Miscellany v, ch. 2, in *Characteristics*, ii. 326–38. Shaftesbury and Swift are compared more fully in ch. 4.

what they have forgotten in their urbanity. As befits his stature, Pope's Ariel flatters rather than commands mortal ears, but he flatters, and thus implicates, the coffeehouse wits as well as Belinda. In order to proceed, readers will have to agree to become like "Maids" or "Children" again: the male wits can take their pick.[13]

Before considering just what properties the sylphs offer readers who agree to look, I would like to examine Pope's interest in bodily scale in a simpler but instructive context, the group of poems written in delighted recognition of *Gulliver's Travels*. Of these five poems (all but one published in a 1727 edition of Swift's work), four play on the relation of big and little; the most ambitious, *Mary Gulliver to Captain Lemuel Gulliver*, is of special interest here because its survey of visual episodes from Lilliput and Brobdingnag suggests the imaginative kinship of *Gulliver's Travels* and *The Rape of the Lock*. For Pope, Swift's miniaturization and magnification of bodies immediately open an area of sexual comedy, in which the familiar and instinctual body is normative. In terms of twentieth-century interpretations of *Gulliver's Travels*, Pope is the first member of the "soft" school (I will return to the troublesome dichotomy of "hard" and "soft" readings of satire in chapter 5); that is, he assumes that Gulliver's rejection of his kind is an absurd triumph of Enthusiasm over Sense. Against a background of simple religion and appropriate passion – "'Tis said, that thou shouldst cleave unto thy Wife; / Once *thou* didst cleave, and *I* could cleave for Life" (lines 9–10) – Gulliver's rejection of the eligible body naturally becomes perverse rather than "tragic":

> Not touch me! never Neighbor call'd me Slut!
> Was *Flimnap*'s Dame more sweet in *Lilliput*?
> I've no red Hair to breathe an odious Fume;
> At least thy Consort's cleaner than thy Groom.
> What mean those Visits to the *Sorrel Mare*?
> Say, by what Witchcraft, or what Daemon led,
> Preferr'st thou *Litter* to the Marriage Bed?   (25–32)

Mary's amorousness has its own humor (the poem is a mock-Ovidian

---

[13] In "Sense and Sensibility: The Child and the Man in *The Rape of the Lock*," *Modern Language Review*, 78.2 (Apr. 1983), 273–84, Charles Martindale makes an interesting argument for the coexistence of the "adult world of sense" and the "child's magic vision" in the poem. I disagree with Martindale's contention that these two readings "cannot really be combined to provide a satisfying wholeness of vision, because they tend in opposite directions" and with his notion that Pope's problem was "how to write imaginatively-alive poetry in an Age of Reason"; but his emphasis on mock-heroic as a mode in which childlike naiveté and adult sophistication can be proposed simultaneously is helpful and apt (pp. 282–84).

"expostulating, soothing, and tenderly-complaining Epistle"), but her bodily good sense is clearly what prompts her empathetic "Remembrance" of Gulliver's physical predicaments:

> How did I tremble, when by thousands bound,
> I saw thee stretch'd on Lilliputian Ground;
> When scaling Armies climb'd up ev'ry Part,
> Each step they trod, I felt upon my Heart.
> But when thy Torrent quench'd the dreadful Blaze,
> King, Queen and Nation, staring with Amaze,
> Full in my View how all my Husband came,
> And what extinguish'd theirs, encreas'd my Flame.
>
>   .   .   .
>
> When in the *Marrow-Bone* I see thee ramm'd;
> Or on the House-top by the *Monkey* cramm'd;
> The Piteous Images renew my Pain,
> And all the Dangers I weep o'er again!
> But on the *Maiden's Nipple* when you rid,
> Pray Heav'n, 'twas all a wanton maiden did!
>
>   (67–74, 83–88)

That the "frolicksome" Brobdingnagian maid did "many other Tricks" ("wherein the Reader will excuse me for not being over particular") reminds one that Pope had only to follow Swift to find sexual humor in Gulliver's lack of proportion.[14]

Pope's memory of Gulliver caught in a marrow-bone, on the other hand, might have as much to do with his own work as with Swift's scene. Gulliver tells of being "wedged" there by the queen's thirty-foot dwarf immediately after relating how on another occasion the same "malicious little Cubb" had dropped him into a bowl of cream. In *The Rape of the Lock* Ariel had warned that careless sylphs might be "plung'd in Lakes of bitter *Washes*... Or wedg'd whole Ages in a *Bodkin's* Eye,"

---

[14] *Gulliver's Travels*, part II, ch. 5, in *PW* xi. 119. Pope follows Swift in emphasizing the humor of Gulliver's sexual vulnerability and pride, which Swift suggests quite early in Lilliput (part I, ch. 3) when Gulliver stands as a colossus for the emperor's troops to march under: "His Majesty gave Orders, upon Pain of Death, that every Soldier in his March should observe the strictest Decency, with regard to my Person; which, however, could not prevent some of the younger Officers from turning up their Eyes as they passed under me. And, to confess the Truth, my Breeches were at that Time in so ill a Condition, that they afforded some Opportunities for Laughter and Admiration."

or hang in suspense above a "Sea" of hot chocolate (III. 127–28, 135–6). This is one of the several points of contact either between *The Rape of the Lock* and *Gulliver's Travels* or between *The Rape of the Lock* and the group of Gulliver poems. All are small (appropriately), but they help bring to the surface some common "views" underlying the larger interest in perspective that Pope and Swift share. The comic emphasis given to minute gradations, for example, finds similar expression in the description of Ariel as "Superior by the Head" to lesser sylphs and in Gulliver's observation that the emperor of Lilliput is "taller by almost the Breadth of my Nail, than any of his Court; which alone is enough to strike Awe into the Beholders." The crowd of nobles in Lilliput spread out against the ground like a petticoat may call to mind both the merging of the sylphs with Belinda's rich brocade and the "Fifty chosen *Sylphs*, of special Note" assigned the "important Charge, the *Petticoat*" (II. 118). Gulliver's peculiar reverence for the chairs he caned with the "Combings of her [Brobdingnagian] Majesty's Hair" parallels the obsessive concern of the sylphs (and mortals) for Belinda's lock.

From Pope's perspective, even Gulliver as a "diminutive Insect" in the king of Brobdingnag's hand evokes something of the sylphs, who "to the Sun their Insect-Wings unfold" (II. 59); in the dramatic monologue he made of this episode, Pope's king sees Gulliver as proof "in Miniature" of "*Nature's* Power," which "wings the Sun-born Insects of the Air." A final response from another of the poems on *Gulliver's Travels* suggests a more general connection between physical magnification and the big language of mock-heroic. The couplet "Yet lovely in her Sorrow still appears: / Her Locks dishevell'd, and her Flood of Tears…" might almost describe Belinda, but comes instead from *The Lamentation of Glumdalclitch*, where the "flood" is then promptly compared to an English rain. In *The Rape of the Lock* Belinda's eyes are not only like the sun but like suns ("When those fair Suns shall sett, as sett they must…"). The distance is not great, as Pope recognized, between such exaltation and Brobdingnagian heights: pining for her Grildrig, Glumdalclitch "sobb'd a Storm, and wip'd her flowing Eyes, / Which seem'd like two broad Suns in misty Skies."

The sylphs as the image of wit

There is more to *The Rape of the Lock* than the sylphs and more to them than their size. They and it require further thought here, however, for three basic reasons. First, *The Rape of the Lock* has, from

Pope's day on, commonly been felt to epitomize Augustan wit, even by
readers, such as the Wartons, who have wanted to distinguish wit from
"pure poetry."[15] Second, it is difficult to imagine the poem fully or
adequately representing Augustan wit without the sylphs. Third, it is
impossible to imagine the sylphs as other than small. Without
attempting to reduce the poem to its smallest denominators, then, we
can try to see more clearly how the nearly bodiless sylphs appear to
embody wit. That way of putting the question perhaps presupposes one
answer: that the "lightness" or "quickness" so frequently attributed to
wit (and on this much Locke and Dryden would agree) is readily
figured as "nimble" or "airy" bodily movement, the body grown
nearly weightless, as in the dancer's "easiest" motion in *An Essay on
Criticism*. Dryden's ranging spaniel, the dancer, and the sylphs all
suggest freedom of the body, and not freedom from but in or through
it. The simultaneous recognition and refinement of physicality is
balanced nicely in the sylphs' "Airy Substance" (III. 152). It may be
useful to concentrate on their substantial littleness before attempting
the fields of air.

The tendency of miniaturization to turn things into representations
or models of "themselves" (as toys or artifacts) is shown in Gulliver's
feeling that the Lilliputian capital is "like the painted Scene of a City
in a Theatre," an impression he never has in Brobdingnag or anywhere
else. The sylphs are associated with artifice and representation in
several ways, ranging from their identity as small male characters now
standing for absent women to their connection with the cosmetic
adornment of living women and the "moving Toyshop of their Heart."
The sylphs are not witty in themselves; Ariel is as unconscious of his
zeugmas as his fellow sylph is of his cartoon heroism in the scissors'
mouth, where "Airy Substance soon unites again." But they are the
cause of wit in others. As Ariel says of the heart's Toyshop, "This erring
Mortals Levity may call, / Oh blind to Truth! the Sylphs contrive it
all" (I. 103–04). These lines, too, turn on both sarcasm and irony,
neither intended by Ariel. The sarcasm means roughly that the
fickleness of coquettes is indeed their fickleness ("Levity") and not the
contrivance of Providence. The irony suggests two propositions. The

---

[15] In the prefatory epistle to *An Essay on the Genius and Writings of Pope* (1756, 1782) Joseph Warton
expresses assurance that his addressee, Edward Young, would not have expected to be
"denominated a poet" had he written only the satires that mark him as "a man of wit and
a man of sense" rather than proceeding on to "the sublime and the pathetic," those "two chief
nerves of genuine poesy." Joseph Warton's text is most easily consulted in Scott Elledge (ed.),
Eighteenth-Century Critical Essays (Ithaca: Cornell University Press, 1961), ii. 718–19.

first is that, whether providential or not, the appetite for variety probably does more than is commonly recognized to "save" the young from other appetites. The second (and more self-conscious or metapoetic) proposition is that earnest theology about such toys as wigs and sword-knots is exactly the kind of vision that contrives the pleasure of novelty which readers and writers call sometimes levity and sometimes wit.

Keeping in mind the sylphs' size and that their earnestness in the presence of "Brobdingnagian" artifacts is therefore "natural," we might infer that the wit they help define is a verbally established viewpoint which gives pleasure by simultaneously impressing the audience as natural and artificial. That this may sound close to a description of poetry or literary art in general would not, as we have seen, disturb Dryden or Pope; but we can specify it somewhat further by putting more emphasis on artificial than natural. The compositions one is likeliest to point to as works of Augustan wit call attention to the artifice of their representations. Such works may do so thematically by describing actors in whom "form" appears to have triumphed over "content," such as Swift's "most devoted Servant of all Modern Forms," Locke's servant in Prior, Pope's Cloe "in Decencies for ever." But more important, they advertise artificiality by displaying their own impositions of form. The imposition is most clearly "foregrounded" through deliberate disproportions of manner and subject, as in burlesque, parody, and mock-heroic writing, but any conspicuous show of structure and symmetry may have similar effects. This is why we regard the couplet, once its balances have been adjusted, as a more appropriate idiom than blank verse (unless used parodically), and it is also why the larger artificialities of structural arrangement – "books," prefaces, chapters, and so on – are as much in place in Swift or Fielding as they would be out of place in the illusionistic narratives of Defoe or Richardson.

This emphasis on deliberate artificiality may seem in direct conflict with Dryden's insistence that the general "propriety" of words and thoughts (and not merely epigrammatic sharpness, for example) should define wit or with the Horatian dictum, so often repeated in the period, that art should conceal art. But one meaning of that paradoxical dictum is that art will always be conspicuous to a discerning reader, the more so the more it "hides" itself, just as propriety becomes visible (and a subject for discussion) when one is most aware of potential "improprieties" being avoided. The issue is one of emphasis. The more likely we are to be comfortable in calling a composition a work of wit the more likely it is to remind us continually of its composition and humanly arbitrary ordering. This is of course a necessary rather than sufficient condition; but the mutual recognition of the material's "reduction" – reduced in both the particularly Augustan sense of clarification and in the more general sense of diminution or distancing – seems to be essential alike to the success of both the epigram and the "comic epic in prose." When the reader does not feel that the writer recognizes the partiality of the reduction, or does not accept provisional reduction as appropriate to the context or subject, wit will appear as superficial or as failed philosophy. Thus the problems of tone posed by *An Essay on Man*, and thus, to take a simpler case, Johnson's dismissal of Gay's epitaph. It seems not to have occurred to Gay that the "last words" he composed for his final mock-genre might be read as an attempt at finality concerning last things.

We come back to sylphs then, because they seem to do for wit written what Pope said of writing in general: they "materialize our Ideas" by "making the Voice become visible."[16] Visualized, if just barely, as frankly equivocal and "originally" derivative compositions, they play rather literally at doing what we seem to expect other works of wit to manage in various linguistic ways, to "keep the machinery in view." That the machinery is both new and inherited dramatizes the historical contingency of wit, the recognition Prior grants Montaigne but not Locke, that writers compose rather than create. Mock-epic in general is an advertisement not only of the triumph of literary form over small content but also of the desirability of historical experience over innocence. If oral epics are "primary" epics and their literary counterparts "secondary," mock-epics in poetry and comic epics in prose are tertiary works, no longer bound to mask their social modernity and human making. Theoretically, a late twentieth-century reader might be prepared to see the littleness of Pope's sylphs as an emblem of lamented "lateness"; but the poem offers nothing to support such a reading, for the sylphs are figures of free and available energy. If Pope ever asked himself the question sung by Frost's ovenbird – "What to make of a diminished thing?" – *The Rape of the Lock* suggests that the answer was to make a miniature world and to make it new. A few last attempts to define the sylphs' charm may help

---

[16] Pope's *Guardian* essay (no. 172) on "the origin of letters" is reprinted in *The Prose Works of Alexander Pope*, i, ed. Norman Ault (first pub., 1936; repr. New York: Barnes & Noble, 1968), 141–44. The quoted phrases are on p. 142.

clarify the relationship between artificial miniaturization and "natural" energy.

It may be that the word "charming" comes up so often in discussions of *The Rape of the Lock* because the poem is about charm; that is, it not only presents beautiful objects but analyzes the processes and pleasures of perception. Raising this peculiarly modern subject – a compound of recent epistemological, optical, and aesthetic concerns – to the level of explicitness is achieved by means of those "vehicles of Air" Pope revised into his poem in 1714. The addition of the sylphs allowed Pope more room for philosophical as well as narrative play, or, as he might rather have seen it, room for a more deeply playful imitation of Homer. Like many readers of Homer from antiquity to the nineteenth century, Pope praised Homeric poems as repositories of all the learning of the poet's time. For Pope, "those innumerable Knowledges, those Secrets of Nature and Physical Philosophy" in the supposed allegory of the *Iliad* are further proofs of Homer's unrivaled invention. That the intellectual *Iliad* of Pope's day can be reduced to an apparent nutshell is part of the comedy of diminution (modern wits in tweezer-cases). But miniaturization also lets Pope allegorize, as seriously as the poem will bear, at least three of the large scientific and philosophical issues of the period. Of these, perception seems to me the most thematically pertinent to the poem as a whole, but the two others are closely connected with it. They are the principle of causation and the question of "action at a distance," both of which attained new complexity in the debates prompted by Newtonian science, and particularly by the accounts of gravity.

The first of these, the principle of causation, is introduced into the poem with Ariel's first speech on the origin, elemental identity, and function of the sylphs, a discourse whose airy learning relates interestingly to Pope's remarks on Homer's intellectual allegory in the Preface to the *Iliad*. There Pope would praise the "fertile ... Imagination ... able to cloath all the Properties of the Elements, the Qualifications of the Mind, the Virtues and Vices, in Forms and Persons; and to introduce them into Actions agreeable to the nature of the Things they shadow'd." In Ariel's account, the sylphs are the transformed souls of coquettes, inhabitants of air, and guardians of mortal maidens. As the poem progresses, it becomes clear of course that their guardianship is purely "allegorical," impotent as soon as required. One way of putting this is that they are emblems of the poetry which, in Auden's sense, "makes nothing happen," at the same time that what they cause is much of the poem's best poetry. Within the context of either Pope's human narrative or the learning of his day, Ariel's revelation of the "Properties of Elements" and of the sylph's contrivance of events is obviously pseudoscience; but it is pseudoscience that points to a serious problem of scientific narrative.

The issue of causation is associated most closely in the modern history of philosophy with Hume, whose argument in the *Treatise on Human Nature* (1739–40) would question the idea of "necessary connexion" and demote claims of causality from deductive to inductive status. (The point, roughly, is that what we call "necessary" relations between events are actually habitually observed relations; causes and effects are related only in our contingent experience rather than logically.) But the issue, raised in less exacting terms by Cartesian dualism generally, was a basic part of Berkeley's so-called "immaterialism" (to which I will return in the following chapter) and his critique of mechanistic explanation. Since "solidity, bulk, figure, motion, and the like" are ideas rather than agents, they "have no *activity* or *efficacy* in them so as to be capable of producing any one effect in nature," Berkeley argued in 1710. In the language of experience, the connection of ideas "does not imply the relation of *cause* and *effect*, but only of a mark or *sign* with the thing *signified*"; thus fire, for example, is not the cause of the pain I suffer upon my approaching it, but the mark that forewarns me of it.[17] In relation to the bodies they purportedly "guide" (II. 88) the sylphs cause nothing but signify a great deal. I do not mean by this observation to suggest that Berkeley "caused" the sylphs but that Pope's machinery plays with a central problem of mechanistic science, physical causation, as well as with "am'rous Causes."

The question of "action at a distance" is in a sense the problem of causation seen in physical, spatial terms. The question it raises is how one body can affect another without touching it, either directly or through an intervening medium. Descartes had solved the problem by positing space as a *plenum* of matter rather than a void, but the Newtonian rejection of Cartesian mechanics quickly raised the question again. Newton himself was led to theorize a subtler ether than Descartes's, through which force might be communicated. In some contexts he refers to this rarified matter as "spirit," in others as an "etherial substance," apparently on the analogy of gases, which he

[17] *A Treatise concerning the Principles of Human Knowledge*, ed. Colin M. Turbayne (Indianapolis and New York: Bobbs-Merrill, 1957), 52–54 (paras. 61, 65).

calls "aerial substances."[18] The "Aerial Kind" of *The Rape of the Lock*
range from the "Fields of purest Æther" to the "grosser Air below" (II.
75–90). They are often regarded, impressionistically, as bringing
"atmosphere" to the poem. They do so, scientifically, by constituting
a subtle medium through which impressions may be communicated
from one body to another. Failing to insulate their "Charge" from
other mortals, they succeed instead in extending the contact of her
attractive force through the poem.

Pope's analysis of perception seems to me to have been lying in wait
of development in the original version of the poem, but it is best seen
in the atmospheric descriptions which the sylphs allow. Of these the
most sustained is the description of Belinda and her party travelling by
barge to Hampton Court.

> But now secure the painted Vessel glides,
> The Sun-beams trembling on the floating Tydes,
> While melting Musick steals upon the Sky,
> And soften'd Sounds along the Water die.
> Smooth flow the Waves, the Zephyrs gently play,
> *Belinda* smil'd, and all the World was gay.
> All but the *Sylph* – With careful Thoughts opprest,
> Th' impending Woe sate heavy on his Breast.
> He summons strait his Denizens of Air;
> The lucid Squadrons round the Sails repair;
> Soft o'er the Shrouds Aerial Whispers breathe,
> That seem'd but *Zephyrs* to the Train beneath.
>
> (II. 47–58)

The last couplet picks up the thread of mock-explanation running
through the first canto (what seems like "Honour" or "Levity" from
below is really the sylphs from above, I. 67–104) and weaves it into a
more sensuous fabric of appearances. The transformation of pleasant
but lifeless zephyrs into an animated society of speech ("Aerial
Whispers") is one way of analyzing a synthesis that has already
occurred, as the combined phenomena of sunlight, music, and the
motion of air and water flow toward and then from Belinda's smile.
The moment studied, in other words, is one of aesthetic apprehension,
an energy of fusion, such as Pope associates in *An Essay on Criticism* with

---

[18] These phrases are from a letter to Robert Boyle, in *Newton's Philosophy of Nature*, ed. H.S.
Thayer (New York: Hafner Press, 1953), 112–15. A very helpful note on Newton's place in the
controversy between "void" and *plenum* theorists is provided by H. Bunker Wright and
Monroe K. Spears in connection with Prior's *Alma*, III. 53ff; see Prior, ii. 970–71.

"Rapture" and the "gen'rous Pleasure to be charm'd with Wit" (lines 235–38). There, too, the elusive but unmistakable unity coalesces in the human face:

> In Wit, as Nature, what affects our Hearts
> Is not th' Exactness of peculiar Parts;
> 'Tis not a *Lip*, or *Eye*, we Beauty call,
> But the joint Force and full *Result* of all.
>
> (243–46)

The descriptive mingling of sylphs and sunlight is often regarded as one of the most painterly passages in Pope; but it is at least as much a "science" of the subject of painting – forms in light – as a demonstration of technique. It offers a playful miniaturization of Newton's "New Theory about Light and Colours":[19]

> Some to the Sun their Insect-Wings unfold,
> Waft on the Breeze, or sink in Clouds of Gold.
> Transparent Forms, too fine for mortal Sight,
> Their fluid Bodies half dissolv'd in Light.
> Loose to the Wind their airy Garments flew,
> Thin glitt'ring Textures of the filmy Dew;
> Dipt in the richest Tincture of the Skies,
> Where Light disports in ever-mingling Dies,
> While ev'ry Beam new transient Colour flings,
> Colours that change whene'er they wave their Wings.
>
> (II. 59–68)

The equivocation in the last line as to whether the sylphs reflect or cause color builds on the ambiguity in the rest of the passage (especially lines 61–62) as to whether they are for the moment seen or not, even by the poet, and whether they are bodies in the light, the medium of light, or bodies of light. Newton avoided categorical distinctions where possible, advancing the supposition that "light is neither ether nor its vibrating motion, but something of a different kind propagated from lucid bodies," while allowing as reasonable that "others may suppose it multitudes of unimaginable small and swift corpuscles of various sizes springing from shining bodies ... and continually urged forward by a principle of motion" (p. 91). Nothing in or out of Pope's passage

---

[19] Newton's early paper on this subject, first published in the *Philosophical Transactions of the Royal Society* in 1672, is available in *Newton's Philosophy of Nature*, pp. 68–81. His *Opticks* was first published in 1704. For a very different association of *The Rape of the Lock* (and other poems) with Newton's discussion of color see Ruth Salvaggio's chapter "Pope, Newton, and the Problem of Color," in her *Enlightened Absence: Neoclassical Configurations of the Feminine* (Urbana and Chicago: University of Illinois Press, 1988).

suggests that he had any interest in whether the "corpuscular" theory might hold; what he is strongly interested in embodying is the modern discovery that the apparent unity of pure light is a compound of many colors. Pope's own experiment in refracting light through "lucid Squadrons" into its parts and then refocussing it back into its "joint Force" moves from a playful physics of phenomena to a phenomenology of attractive unity.

What I mean to suggest by that phrase is that while Pope's various analyses of moments of rich perceptual unity tend to show unity to be a composition of parts, they do so to attend to its effects rather than its causes. Thus the cosmetic "causes" of Belinda's fragile construction of herself are all laid out on the dressing table to be seen but vanish suddenly in the face of unity. This is not to ignore the exposure of the sacred rites of pride but to acknowledge the revelation of rising "charms" which for the moment brings Belinda's beauty into an atmosphere of attraction like that surrounding Minta Doyle in *To the Lighthouse*:

And so tonight, directly he laughed at her, she was not frightened. Besides, she knew, directly she came into the room that the miracle had happened; she wore her golden haze. Sometimes she had it; sometimes not. She never knew why it came or why it went, or if she had it until she came into the room and then she knew instantly by the way some man looked at her. Yes, tonight she had it, tremendously...[20]

The passage in the first version of the poem which seems to me to point most distinctly to both the miniaturization and aesthetic focus Pope would develop was a piece of pretty sententiousness serving as the transition from Belinda's curls to the Baron's desire. In the revised poem it still plays that role but also helps set the tone for the sylphs-and-sunlight passage that soon follows. From the close-up of "shining Ringlets" and "smooth Iv'ry Neck" the narrator moves to this reflection:

> Love in these Labyrinths his slaves detains,
> And mighty Hearts are held in slender Chains.
> With hairy Sprindges we the Birds betray,
> Slight Lines of Hair surprize the Finny Prey,
> Fair Tresses Man's Imperial Race insnare,
> And Beauty draws us with a single Hair.

(II. 23–28)

[20] Virginia Woolf, *To the Lighthouse* (New York and London: Harcourt Brace Jovanovich, 1927), 148.

The progress from lovers' compulsions to the attraction of beauty is in keeping with the revised emphasis of the poem and particularly of this canto, which the sylphs soon take over. In the lines themselves the crucial movement is from hairs to hair, that is from individual hairs used to catch birds or fish to the "single Hair" and thus to the attractive unity humans call simply "hair." Whether attraction is produced by unity or produces it is a nice question in much of Pope's poetry. The lines in *An Essay on Criticism* on beauty as the "joint Force and full *Result*" suggests the first alternative. The sylphs in *The Rape of the Lock* often suggest the second, since their "Care" of Belinda is not protection but attention. In either case, the ability to discover or create wholeness depends on sensuous predisposition (owning to "*gen'rous Pleasure* to be charm'd with Wit," for example) and cultural sense. Pursuing an isolated curl and swearing by *Atalantis*, the Baron is a "man of parts" – only parts.

Pope's "allegory" of perception is unusual in its subtlety, but it has much in common with the concerns of other eighteenth-century works. We have seen similar problems raised in *Gulliver's Travels* especially, and in the next chapter I will turn to other works to study norms of perception as those are used to question "abstraction," a fondness for which the voices of wit tend to associate with "gravity." Before we move to those topics, a final illustration of the interplay of proportions, perceptions, and realities may help define the epistemological range of Augustan writing. The illustration consists of a pair of incidents, one from the second and one from the fourth book of *Gulliver's Travels*. As Gulliver longs to leave Blefuscu he sees in the water "somewhat that looked like a Boat"; wading to it, he is overjoyed to find it to be a "real Boat" – that is, a boat his size. (A few chapters later, of course, Gulliver's rowboat will be a Brobdingnagian toy.) About to leave Houyhnhnmland, Gulliver looks out to sea toward what he thinks may be an island and, with the aid of his pocket-perspective, decides that it is one. His friend the sorrel nag sees only a blue cloud, however, "For, as he had no Conception of any County beside his own, so he could not be expert in distinguishing remote Objects at Sea, as we who so much converse in that Element" (ch. 10). The explanation is partly in the interests of narrative plausibility, but it analyzes as well as accounts for the Houyhnhnms' blissful insularity. Swift's phrasing constructs an interesting thematic connection between received ideas and "ideas." Unless the images are vividly insistent, it is likely that conception will determine perception.

By examining and bringing together texts by Prior, Rochester, Swift, Gay, and Pope, I have tried thus far to literalize the idea that Augustan wit *embodies* concerns that comprise a materialist understanding of experience. Through argument and imagery this writing brings forward questions pertaining to physical proportion, causation, agency, and perception, stressing in its treatment of all of these what in our day might be called the *givenness* of the body. Augustan wit calls attention in many ways to the bodies of people and things to insist that the truly human environment be recognized. It tends to portray the desire to transcend or penetrate the surfaces of bodies available to humans as in fact the most hazardous superficiality.

This theme will become clearer in the consideration of "abstraction" in the next chapter, but I hope it is now clear that there is no compelling reason to regard these works as nostalgic or reactionary. If they appear "antiscientific" it may be because the emerging scientific orthodoxy was already beginning to look like the latest form of spiritual pride. It could reasonably appear so not because it was presumptuous but because, as the founder of modern "ecological" psychology, James J. Gibson, has argued, the Newtonian view that space and time are independent of perceiving agents is a "convenient myth" about the world. The myth obviously works well for science, but it is arbitrary in regarding pure space and time as primary reality, an order Gibson seeks to invert: "Time and space are not empty receptacles to be filled; instead, they are simply the ghosts of events and surfaces." The Newtonian world and the ecological world afforded us should not be confused with each other. "The environment is not the same as the physical world, if one means by that the world described by physics." Because of that important difference the "science of the environment has its own facts."[21] The works surveyed here and those to be considered in the next chapter depend on a distinction between material life and physics. In Augustan writing an alternative human science insinuates its own facts, unsystematically but collectively, as an ecology of wit.

---

[21] In order, these quotations are from *The Ecological Approach to Visual Perception* (first pub. 1979; Hillsdale, NJ: Lawrence Erlbaum Associates, 1986), 100–01, 15, 18.

4

Gravity, abstraction, and crackpot materialism

The task consists in forcing the *thinglike* environment, which mechanically influences the personality, to begin to speak, that is to reveal in it the potential word and tone, to transform it into a semantic context for the thinking, speaking and acting (as well as creating) personality...A thing, as long as it remains a thing, can affect only other things; in order to affect a personality it must reveal its *semantic potential*, become a word...

Bakhtin, "Toward a Methodology for the Human Sciences"[1]

Gravity and the fall into abstraction

The pun on gravity lurking in Augustan writing is not an expression of deathbed wit, as in Mercutio's "Ask for me tomorrow, and you shall find me a grave man," but a way of naming the dull weight opposed to wit, as in Pope's account of small spite – "The graver Prude sinks downward to a *Gnome*" – or large mindlessness: "None need a guide, by sure attraction led, / And strong impulsive gravity of Head" (*The Rape of the Lock*, I. 63; *Dunciad*, IV. 75–76). Pope is unique in working out the pun so fully (much of the "plot" of the final *Dunciad* is gravitational), but the general idea of the dull man as one who has no counterforce to his own weight is farcically visible in Shadwell's "large bulk" and Flecknoe's "sinking" (*Mac Flecknoe*, lines 195–96, 214) and grimly so in the fall "headlong down" of Rochester's reasoning engine. "Pride drew him in," Rochester says, as it of course draws in most of the objects of ethical attack, authored by grave and witty writers alike. But in the metaphorical world of Augustan wit, it is gravity that goes before a fall.

Gravity is also what wit must overcome, not by ignoring but by

---

[1] M.M. Bakhtin, *Speech Genres and Other Late Essays*, trans. Vern W. McGee (Austin: University of Texas Press, 1986), 164.

continually recognizing its force. Since wit is so frequently defined against gravity, we may leave the scientific metaphor for the time being and try to catch the values implied in the antithesis. These range from rather simple remnants of seventeenth-century contrasts of wits and "Cits" to more complex evaluations of individual and cultural temper. Shaftesbury, who wrote more theoretically than anyone about the opposition of "wit and humor" to "gravity and seriousness," suggests much of the range within his own essays (*Characteristics*, i. 232). Wit is clearly preferable to gravity; in fact it is a kind of moral as well as literary virtue, since "*gravity* is of the very essence of imposture" (i. 10). But it is not always clear whether an excess of gravity is due to "breeding," constitutional moroseness (wit versus the "melancholy way of treating religion," for example, i. 24), interested calculation, or cultural attributes. Shaftesbury at one point anticipates Arnold's Hellenism and Hebraism by contrasting the "witty Athenians" with the Jews, "naturally a very cloudy people" who could "endure little raillery in anything" (i. 22–23). More often, he stresses the voluntary nature of either wit or gravity, maintaining that true religion has nothing to fear from the former and that the latter tends, unless tested by ridicule, to the "imposture of formality" – in other words, self-delusion and dogmatism.

This last emphasis, reminiscent of Rochester's disdain for the "formal" clergyman and "formal lies" of authoritarian moralists (*Satyr against Reason and Mankind*, lines 46, 177), may have been what Swift regarded as the "free Whiggish thinking" of *A Letter concerning Enthusiasm*; but Swift also found it "very well writ" and seems not to have been offended that several readers believed it had been written by the author of another anonymous work, *A Tale of a Tub*.[2] Swift's aggressive Apology for "sallies" in *A Tale of a Tub* that "might not suit with maturer years, or graver Characters" concedes more to gravity than usual. As "not the gravest of divines," Swift tends to find gravity in "dull divines" who resent genius "And deal in vices of the graver sort, / Tobacco, censure, coffee, pride, and port."[3] Within *A Tale* it is a Bedlamite who is seen "gravely taking the Dimensions of his Kennel" and who "intreats your Penny with due Gravity" (p. 177). Elsewhere in the same Digression the "pretended Philosophy which enters into the Depth of Things …comes gravely back with Informations and Discoveries, that in the inside they are good for nothing" (p. 173). This

---

[2] See *Tale*, p. 6, where Swift's letter to Ambrose Philips (Sept. 14, 1708) discussing Shaftesbury's anonymously published work is quoted.

[3] "Stella's Birthday (1727)," line 14; "The Author upon Himself," ll. 21–22.

difficult passage will be discussed more fully below, but we might note here that even Martin appears capable of "Gravity" enough to contribute to the "reader's *Repose, both of Body and Mind*" (pp. 139–40).

Gravity` may stand primarily for pompous emptiness, as in Rochester's "Nothing! who dwellst with fools in grave disguise" or Sterne's "Gravity is a mysterious carriage of the body intended to conceal the defects of the mind"; but it typically occurs in contexts suggesting hypocrisy and pseudomorality. Pope's "grave Sir Gilbert," for example, "holds it for a rule, / That 'every man in want is knave or fool'" and thus leaves the poor to Providence (*Epistle to Bathurst*, lines 103–04). Catius, "ever moral, ever grave," refuses to associate with real knaves, except "just at dinner." The "talkative and grave" interpreters of conduct may not be hypocrites but are too slow and self-sure to be ethically perceptive (*Epistle to Cobham*, lines 5, 51, 136). By this time, "grave Epistles" are for Pope comfortable things, "Such as a King might read, a Bishop write" (*Imitations of Horace, Satire II. i*, lines 151–52). In Fielding's *Jonathan Wild*, Shaftesbury's "essence of imposture" is entirely deliberate; one of Wild's maxims is "To maintain a constant gravity in his countenance and behaviour, and to affect wisdom on all occasions."[4] Through the late seventeenth and early eighteenth century "grave" becomes so loaded that it is likely to be used either in direct attack or in self-deprecation. Instances of the latter include Rochester's Artemisia "gravely" advising herself not to write poetry and several of Swift's verse portraits of the artist (e.g. "I gravely sat me down to think: / I bit my nails, and scratched my head, / But found my wit and fancy fled"). The word tends to become a sign that wit is at work, as in *A Modest Proposal*'s footnote identifying "a grave author" as Rabelais.[5]

The fate of Shadwell in *Mac Flecknoe* is re-enacted again and again in Augustan writing: a person of gravity rises above "sense" and falls into a waiting trap. The landing place may be a stale ditch or a fresh grave (Swift's Marlborough "Turn'd to that Dirt from whence he sprung"), but the *ways* up and down are the same. Typically a character tries to transcend matter and sinks abruptly into it. The career of Rochester's philosopher who ends "huddled in dirt" is a complex elaboration of the idea; its simplest emblem is Gulliver attempting to jump over Brobdingnagian cow dung and falling short ("just in the Middle up to my Knees"). Even where the commentary

---

[4] Henry Fielding, *Jonathan Wild*, ed. David Nokes (London: Penguin Books, 1982), 216 (book IV, ch. 15).

[5] "Stella's Birthday (1723)," lines 4–6; *A Modest Proposal*, para. 13.

or picture is not so clear about the recognition of physical bodies, attention is drawn to the character's lack of bodily wits as well as wit. Shadwell's claim to "Nonsense," for example, may be primarily stylistic, but the atmosphere of "potent ale," "fogs," and "poppies" keep him in sensory as well as literary "oblivion" and "tautology," functioning much like the smoke Swift's visionaries inhale "to abstract themselves from matter."

The criticism of abstraction as a deviation from "sense" is neither Augustan nostalgia nor anti-intellectualism but a consciously modern attempt to define an intelligent materialism. Before considering its implications (primarily in Rochester, Swift, Berkeley, Prior, and Pope) we should look at another of Gulliver's falls, for it points to the relation of mental and physical gravity and suggests the metaphorical differences between gravity and wit. The fall in question closes a paragraph of minor misfortunes, each of them interesting for Gulliver's reaction or explanation: "I likewise broke my right shin against the Shell of a Snail, which I happened to stumble over, as I was walking alone, and thinking on poor *England*" (II. v). The graver fall is the one in the final phrase, into the bathos of abstract and implausible patriotism.

The alternative to stumbling gravity is not flight but, as Pope's figure for the "ease" of good writing suggests, the recognition and use of bodily weight epitomized in dance. This metaphor takes an interesting turn in *Alma: or, the Progress of the Mind* (1718), as Prior praises his great predecessor in poetic burlesque, Samuel Butler:

> His noble Negligences teach,
> What Others Toils despair to reach.
> He, perfect Dancer, Climbs the Rope,
> And balances your Fear and Hope:
> If after some distinguish'd Leap,
> He drops his Pole, and seems to slip;
> Straight gath'ring all his action Strength,
> He rises higher half his Length.
> With Wonder You approve his Slight;
> And owe your Pleasure to your Fright.

(II. 7–16)

As a description of style the lines apply more directly to burlesque than to mock-heroic, but they suggest a more general pleasure of wit in the observation of seeming falls and continual recoveries. If the reader's "fear" for the burlesque writer is that his pseudo-doggerel will fall into real doggerel, the corresponding "hope" in reading mock-heroic or mock-georgic verse is that the high style will *almost* be overbalanced by low subjects. The pleasures of flirting with gravity were elaborated further in 1734 in an anonymous poem "On a Female Rope-Dancer" (recently rescued from oblivion by Roger Lonsdale) reminiscent of Prior and suggestive of Yeats:

> Whilst in her prime and bloom of years
>   Fair Celia trips the rope,
> Alternately she moves our fears,
>   Alternately our hope.
>
> But when she sinks, or rises higher,
>   Or graceful does advance,
> We know not which we most admire,
>   The dancer, or the dance.[6]

The difference between this image and the body swayed to music in Yeats's *Among School Children* is as marked as that between the "moving Toyshop of their Heart" in *The Rape of the Lock* and the heart's "foul rag and bone shop" of *The Circus Animals' Desertion*. That is, the Augustan emphasis is on the immediate recognition of motion and artifice rather than on their possible transcendence.

Prior's lines on Butler may, of course, recall a considerably less positive image of acrobatic mastery:

When a great Office is vacant, either by Death or Disgrace, (which often happens) five or six of those Candidates petition the Emperor to entertain his Majesty and the Court with a Dance on the Rope; and whoever jumps the highest without falling, succeeds in the Office. Very often the chief Ministers themselves are commanded to shew their Skill, and to convince the Emperor that they have not lost their Faculty.

                                              (*Gulliver's Travels*, part i, ch. 3)

What separates praise from blame in these two dances is the line between recognized and unrecognized metaphor. A reader of course recognizes Swift's metaphor – or rather completes it – by transferring the description to Europe, but Gulliver and the Lilliputians see it only as reasonable fact. Were one to pause and try to account for the political practice instead of drawing the parallel, one might imagine that at some point a Lilliputian emperor decided that since ministering

---

[6] This anonymous poem is reprinted from *The Honey-Suckle*, no. 3 (1734) in Lonsdale's *The New Oxford Book of Eighteenth-Century Verse* (Oxford: Oxford University Press, 1984), 282.

requires "balance" the candidates should balance. This is the kind of
projective reasoning that Colin Turbayne in another context calls
being used by metaphor rather than using it, and that Swift tends to
call projecting. I have pointed in the first chapter to Gulliver's own
difficulty with metaphor and will turn later to book III where, as the
Tale's speaker says of "zeal," abstractions tend to ripen from a word to
a notion to a tangible substance. More generally, writers of the period
tend to assume that the ability to recognize and use metaphor reflects
a proper recognition and use of the body; correspondingly, they tend
to portray those who disregard or disdain metaphor as those most likely
to build on it the structures hailed as "systems," and "schemes" or
simply "reason."

The opposition is put in these terms directly and, I believe, by
allusion in Rochester's *A Satyr against Reason and Mankind*. There the
"Reason" of philosophy is a self-imposed barrier between proud
humans and the "light of nature, sense." It is thus "an *ignis fatuus* in
the mind" (line 12). This metaphor for reason seems to challenge
Hobbes's metaphor for metaphor: "Metaphors ... are like *ignes fatui*"
(*Leviathan*, I. v. 116). It is generally agreed that Rochester adopts much
of Hobbes in this poem, but he seems to differ decisively on the issue of
reason. While the celebration of reason assigned to the poet's
philosophical interlocutor (lines 48–71) is more idealistic than any
statement in *Leviathan*, Hobbes's account is antithetical to Rochester's
norm. For Hobbes, reason (I. v. 110–11) is essentially arithmetical
"reckoning" (which is why metaphor is a deviation from it); for
Rochester, right reason "distinguishes by sense" (line 100) rather than
by number:

> My reason is my friend, yours is a cheat;
> Hunger calls out, my reason bids me eat;
> Perversely, yours your appetite does mock:
> This asks for food, that answers "What's o'clock?"

> (106–09)

The lines turn back on the interlocutor his celebration of "Reason, by
whose aspiring influence / We take a flight beyond material sense"
(lines 66–67). For Rochester, anything beyond material sense is
nonsense; and the man most eager to get there will be the champion of
"reason" and enemy of "wit" (line 54).

Rochester's attack, it is sometimes noted, extends in other poems to
mindless fornication (thus often to himself) as well as to bodiless
"nonsense" (*Satyr*, line 89). The critique of sexual pursuit complements

Rochester's intellectual satire by showing that what poses as materialism (supposedly uninhibited pursuit) is in fact not materialist enough, because it abstracts desire into "formal" distortions. "Thoughts" are for "action's government," and "our sphere of action is life's happiness" (*Satyr*, lines 94, 96); but for the second claim to be meaningful, "action" must include emotion as well as motion. Of modern lovers, the slightly sentimental but decidedly witty Artemisia says,

> To an exact perfection they have wrought
> The action, love; the passion is forgot.
>
> (*Artemisia to Chloe*, ll. 62–63)

It was with *Artemisia to Chloe* in view that Pope would come to speak of Rochester and Swift in the same Horatian breath:

> If, after all, we must with Wilmot own,
> The cordial Drop of Life is Love alone,
> And Swift cry wisely, 'Vive la Bagatelle!'
> The Man that loves and laughs, must sure do well.
>
> (*Epistle I. vi.* ll. 126–29)

Delusions of a partial skepticism: Shaftesbury and *A Tale of a Tub*

Pope's arresting association of writers in many ways so different as Rochester and Swift seems plausible for him, I think, because both writers express a restless skepticism that is anti-idealist rather than anti-idealistic. Rochester faults the man who "falls" to philosophic disillusionment in the *Satyr* for "aiming to know that world he should enjoy" (line 34), but the norm of unquestioned pleasure is obviously in tension with the assault on complacency in most of the poem. A similar tension runs through much of Swift's work, sometimes tightened to the breaking point, as in the *Tale*'s "Digression concerning ... Madness," where the climactic celebration of "Credulity" is clearly ironic but notoriously unclear in its application. For all the work's individuality, *A Tale of a Tub* is inescapably central to a more general skepticism in Augustan writing; but its relations to the climate of wit are perhaps as elusive as some of its own rhetorical turns. In the Apology Swift added in 1710 he accounted for any excesses in the *Tale* on the grounds that the author "was then [i.e. in 1696] a young Gentleman much in the World, and wrote to the Taste of those who were like himself; therefore in order to allure them, he gave a Liberty to his Pen..." (p. 4). Given Swift's eagerness to vindicate himself from charges of impiety, it is natural that this remark is usually read as hindsight more than history;

but it is worth taking seriously the claim that the work was intended to speak first to a rising generation of young gentlemen "much in the World," with a "tast" for "Productions of Wit" (p. 18). From this perspective, "the Wits of the present Age" (invoked in the opening phrase of the Preface) include not only foolish writers to be parodied but a more extended group of readers the work undertakes to "allure" to something truer. The views of Shaftesbury, another young gentleman much in the world at the turn of the century, are helpful here. His assessment of the prevailing taste in wit at this time and the project he envisioned for true wit help one gauge the currents in which Swift chose to swim.

Shaftesbury's discussion of wit runs through not only *Sensus Communis: An Essay on the Freedom of Wit and Humour* (1709) but also *A Letter concerning Enthusiasm* (1708) and *Soliloquy, or Advice to an Author* (1710), all three of which were collected in *Characteristics* (1711). In general Shaftesbury finds much to praise in modern wit and more that is promising. The punning "false sort of wit, which so much delighted our ancestors," has nearly vanished, and the remaining dross will "refine itself" if left unconstrained: "For wit is its own remedy ... The only danger is, the laying an embargo" (*Characteristics*, i. 45–46). "In these latter days of wit," the enthusiasms of gallantry and knight-errantry have been corrected by ridicule; if "saint-errantry" is still strong, that is because religious enthusiasms has been treated less freely (i. 16).

But censorship is not the only obstacle to free intellectual trade for Shaftesbury, because the advances in ridicule have been one-sided. While it may be true that there was never "in our nation a time when folly and extravagance of every kind were more sharply inspected, or more wittily ridiculed," Shaftesbury registers an important reservation: "If the knowing well how to expose any infirmity or vice were a sufficient security for the virtue which is contrary, how excellent an age might we be presumed to live in!" (i. 9). If, we might add, wit were really on a self-correcting course, it would need only legal protection and not philosophic guidance. Instead, Shaftesbury sees modern wit as restricted by its own complacency:

The fault is we carry the laugh but half-way. The false earnest is ridiculed, but the false jest passes secure, and becomes an errant deceit as the other. Our diversions, our plays, our amusements become solemn. We dream of happiness and possession, and enjoyments in which we have no understanding, no certainty; and yet we pursue these as the best known and most certain things in the world. There is nothing so foolish and deluding as a partial scepticism.

(i. 56)

Shaftesbury's own skeptical observation that "the most ingenious way of becoming foolish is by a system" (i. 189) has passed into the popular domain; but the remark seems intended less in the spirit of Emerson's "a foolish consistency is the hobgoblin of little minds" than as a further exposure of "partial scepticism." In the argument where the reflection on "system" occurs Shaftesbury attacks both Descartes and Locke as representatives of a "super-speculative philosophy" (i. 190–96), by which he means one that does not take purposive action as its subject. His criticism of Descartes is especially interesting because Shaftesbury does not emphasize the "geometrical" spirit of the *Meditations* or *Discourse on Method* but what we might call the behaviorism of the *Treatise of the Passions*. Just as an observer who notes everything about a watch except its "real use" will never understand its "real nature," a philosopher who examines only the effects of the passions on the body "might possibly qualify himself to give advice to an anatomist or limner, but not to mankind or to himself; since ... he considered not the real operation or energy of his subject, nor contemplated the man, as real man, and as a human agent, but as a watch or common machine" (i. 190–91). Shaftesbury's position toward Descartes is similar to Rochester's toward Hobbes (and, I believe, to Swift's toward both): the "speculative" philosophy is wrong not because it is materialist but because it is mechanistic. Were the speculative philosophy fully rather than partially skeptical it would see the abstraction of its underlying metaphor of the machine, and were it fully rather than selectively materialist it would not seek precision by regarding agency as immaterial. These are not, of course, Shaftesbury's terms; but the seriousness of his position is clearer when its emphasis on social and material practice is recalled. The "super-speculative" philosophy is inferior to the "more practical sort" because it ignores the question of "real use," not because it fails to fit elegantly into a humanist's handbook.

Many of Shaftesbury's views are close to *A Tale of a Tub* and *The Mechanical Operation of the Spirit*, from the description of modern prophesying as a "puppet-show" of "motion of wires and inspiration of pipes" (i. 21) to the recurring association of solemnity and self-delusion. The topics are common enough in anti-Puritan satire to render the question of influence irrelevant. Intentionally or incidentally, Shaftesbury describes much of the "real operation or energy" of Swift's *Tale*: its carrying the laugh much more than half way, ridiculing the "false jest" of solemn amusements as well as the "false earnest," probing the delusions of "partial scepticism" as well as of whole dogmatism, and referring, finally, its radical probing to the question of what is of "real use" to the "real man ... as human agent."

The concentrated analysis of happiness in "A Digression on Madness" starts in the middle of the ninth paragraph with the sentence, "Those Entertainments and Pleasures we most value in Life, are such as *Dupe* and play the wag with the Senses," and runs for a little over 800 words to the end of the tenth paragraph (pp. 171–74). It is typical of *A Tale of a Tub* that the passage often regarded as the heart of the mystery should be a digression within a digression, begun shortly after a flurry of asterisks and closed by a transition at once emphatic and dubious: "But to return to madness." Much of the uncertainty about the interruption (it does not, properly speaking, advance the account of "the Original, the Use and Improvement of Madness in a Commonwealth") comes down to whether to read it as a lucid interval in its entirety or in small part. There is no doubt that at least some of the narrator's zany unreliability remains and no doubt that he also speaks at least some of the time for Swift. That is true, of course, of any section of *A Tale of a Tub*, but here the stakes seem higher and the proportions more critical. Most readers are likely to consider the opening definition of happiness as "*a perpetual Possession of being well Deceived*" as carrying Swift's weight but to wonder whether Swift or his creature is responsible for the concluding endorsement: "This is the sublime and refined Point of Felicity, called, *The Possession of being well deceived*; the Serene Peaceful State of being a Fool among Knaves." The line between these two points in the text is short but evidently not straight. In the progress from psychology to ethics how far has the laugh been carried and at whose expense?

The question is all the more difficult because Swift produces not only bad logic (which we can, if not always easily, straighten out) but also apparently bad logic that turns out to be straighter than it looked. The latter is the intellectual equivalent to the pseudo-doggerel of his poems, and it is a more elusive affair than false syllogisms. The first instance of "pseudo-error" is the narrator's jump from sensation (entertainments "dupe" sight or hearing as "tickling" dupes touch) to the "Understanding" and his reduction of the latter to memory and imagination, the realms of "Things past" and "Things conceived." This looks like a double error – introducing sensation only then to ignore the "excluded middle" of its objects, things present – but in fact the rest of the paragraph quickly corrects the momentary omission by turning the full force on sensation:

Again, if we take this Definition of Happiness, and examine it with Reference to the senses, it will be acknowledged wonderfully adapt. How fade and insipid do all objects accost us that are not convey'd in the Vehicle of *Delusion*? How shrunk is every Thing, as it appears in the Glass of Nature? So that if it were not for the Assistance of Artificial *Mediums*, false Lights, refracted Angles, Varnish, and Tinsel; there would be a mighty Level in the Felicity and Enjoyments of Mortal Men. If this were seriously considered by the World, as I have a certain Reason to suspect it hardly will; Men would no longer reckon among their high ·points of Wisdom, the Art of exposing weak Sides, and publishing Infirmities; an Employment in my Opinion, neither better nor worse than that of Unmasking, which I think, has never been allowed fair Usage, either in *The World* or the Play-House.

The final clauses are easily bad logic – this is not the way to use the analogy of world and stage – but they do not seem to undercut anything else. They may even function like the line "She spoke, and no applause ensued" following Clarissa's speech in *The Rape of the Lock* (although the case is admittedly simpler there), to preserve the opening of the "moral" from gravity. The passage begins with a note of potential self-importance (the definition will be "acknowledged wonderfully adapt"), and the use of two rhetorical questions immediately following suggests for a moment that it will develop into a familiar chord. But that is not the music one hears, partly because the questions quickly drive the old theme of happiness as delusion (commentators have suggested echoes of Horace and Bacon as well as Prior) into the newer science of optics and Newtonian physics, where the distinction between primary and secondary qualities of "Objects" had been revived persuasively enough, as we have seen, to play a crucial role in Lockean epistemology. The brief answer to the question moves from semiscientific phrases to the homely and homiletic "Varnish" and "Tinsel" to the climactic "Felicity and Enjoyments of Mortal Men." Since the narrator is not thoughtful of mortality, the last phrase sounds like recollection rather than tautology. It has occurred once before in the "Digression on Madness," in another burst of sobriety: "Let us next examine the great Introducers of new Schemes in Philosophy, and search until we can find, from what Faculty of the Soul the Disposition arises in mortal Man, of taking it into his Head, to advance new Systems with such an eager Zeal, in things agreed on all hands impossible to be known" (para. 5; p. 166). Mortality is normative in both cases, but more complexly in the discussion of felicity; it is clear that for Swift mortal man and metaphysical certainty are mutually exclusive ideas, unclear that mortal "Wisdom" should *not* depend on "exposing weak Sides, and publishing Infirmities" – activities that play no small part in *A Tale of a Tub*.

The fact that these activities are challenged by the same man who objects to "unmasking" as impolite in any theater leads one to want to dismiss his argument entirely. The narrator states the point twice more in the next paragraph, however, each time more forcefully. I have quoted part of the first of these formulations earlier in the discussion of gravity; the complete sentence (which immediately follows the remark on unmasking) is this: "In the Proportion that Credulity is a more peaceful Possession of the Mind, than Curiosity, so far preferable is that Wisdom, which converses about the Surface, to that pretended Philosophy which enters into the Depth of Things, and then comes gravely back Informations and Discoveries, that in the inside they are good for nothing" (p. 173). The second is the conclusion reached by the narrator as a result of his observation of a "Woman *flay'd*" and the "Carcass of a *Beau* ... stript": "That whatever Philosopher or Projector can find out an Art to sodder and patch up the Imperfections of Nature, will deserve much better of Mankind, and teach us a more useful Science, than that so much in present Esteem, of widening and exposing them (like him who held *Anatomy* to be the ultimate End of *Physick*)" (p. 174).

I single out these two statements because they seem more difficult, finally, than the more celebrated "entrapment" of the final sentences of the section, where the narrator recommends Epicurean contentment with "*Superficies* of Things" and then defines the "refined Point of Felicity" as "the Serene Peaceful State of being a Fool among Knaves." For there Swift offers two ways out. One is to reject the equation of felicity and serenity, as, for example, Hobbes had done: "Felicity is a continuall progress of the desire, from one object to another."[7] The other way out is to reject the assumption that felicity is necessarily the highest attainment of mortal agents. Young gentlemen much in the world may be likelier to choose the first alternative, but that is at least a more promising starting place for moral reflection (as in the poem "Desire and Possession" or the sermon "On the Poor Man's Contentment") than the version of Epicurean detachment offered at the close. In short, rejecting the conclusion that felicity is

---

[7] *Leviathan*, ed. C.B. Macpherson (London: Penguin, 1968), 160 [part I, ch. 11]. Cf. pp. 129–30 [part I, ch. 6]: "For there is no such thing as perpetuall Tranquillity of mind, while we live here; because Life it selfe is but Motion, and can never be without Desire, nor without Feare, no more than without Sense."

serenity and serenity all does not require concluding that the narrator must have gone so far wrong earlier that his contrast of "that pretended Philosophy" and "a more useful Science" is really backwards.

The second statement is explicit about the criterion of use, but it is crucial in the first as well. The philosophy which "enters into the Depth of Things" and "gravely" concludes that "in the inside they are good for nothing" ignores the question of real use (good for what?) while pretending to answer it categorically (good for nothing). The remark on the usefulness of soldering and patching rather than widening and exposing anticipates Shaftesbury's specific reservation that current wit knows better "how to expose any infirmity or vice" than how to provide "sufficient security for the virtue which is contrary" as well as his general concern about partial skepticism. It also anticipates, in phrasing and sentiment, the Brobdingnagian king's conviction "that whoever could make two Ears of Corn, or two Blades of Grass to grow where only one grew before; would deserve better of Mankind, and do more essential Service to his Country, than the whole Race of Politicians put together" (II. vii, para. 5).

These parallels can not assure that the line of wit in the *Tale* describes a similar curve, but they are consistent with the proposition that "*Anatomy*" should be subservient to "*Physick.*" In the interval between his two pronouncements the narrator explains why he is about to describe his experiments in dissection; the results are offered "to save the Charges of all such expensive Anatomy for the Time to come." Swift has few illusions about "all" of anything being eradicated for "Time to come," and one imagines him thinking of "charges" differently than his teller might think of them. But the haunting phrase remaining in the middle suggests what the *Tale* works to divert for Swift, as well as what it would become in his life: such expensive anatomy.

Both "Depth" philosophy and the philosophy of "Superficies" are inadequately materialist. Proponents of the first "abstract themselves from matter" by expecting it to be of the "same consistence quite thro'" and misconstruing the question of use. Devotees of "*Films* and *Images*," on the other hand do not ignore the question but misplace it, locating it in the individual abstracted from society. Swift's many references to Epicurus and his disciple Lucretius tend to be either neutral or critical of them as visionaries rather than materialists, and he seems more concerned with the implications of social than scientific atomism. The man who could "content his Ideas" with the sort of

"sublime and refined ...Felicity" the *Tale*'s narrator finally recommends would have to imagine himself not an Epicurean materialist but
an Epicurean deity, detached from matter, mortality, and social
morality. It is in this spirit of sublime refinement that Pope's "high
Priori" philosophers are willing to

> Let others creep by timid steps, and slow,
> On plain Experience lay foundations low,
> By common sense to common knowledge bred,

that they argue for a "Mechanic Cause," profess to "See all in *Self*
and but for self be born," and ask Dulness to

> hide the God still more! and make us see
> Such as Lucretius drew, a God like Thee:
> Wrapt up in Self, a God without a Thought...
>
> (*Dunciad*, IV. 464–66, 483–85)

Abstraction from the body in Pope and Prior

In a deeply thoughtful discussion of *The Rape of the Lock* David Morris
calls attention to the "abstracted sexuality" of its actors, essentially a
sexuality "refined" into narcissism, displaced into fetish, ritualized into
mechanistic predictability.[8] This insight can be modified and extended
to much of Pope's later poetry, where the subject is frequently
abstracted materialism, that is, a mixture of conduct and doctrine
professing material ends but exposed as pursuing them without
reference to the healthy individual body or the body politic. Thus the
dunces, for example, espouse the simplest materialism, favoring "solid
pudding" over "empty praise" (I. 54) but are apparently determined
to starve in order to devote themselves to their "grave" and abstract
mother, who in her turn inspires a poetry that goes (in Rochester's
phrase) "beyond material sense" to unwrite and eventually uncreate
the natural environment. Similarly, the corrupted "Millions" of the
Epilogue to the Satires are on one level anarchists of self-interest ("'Tis
Av'rice all, Ambition is no more!") but are ultimately "Slaves" of the
abstraction, Vice Triumphant, whom they have constructed by means
of "reverential Awe" (*Dialogue I*, lines 145–170).

Abstract Vice or Dulness are in part satiric conveniences, ways of

---

[8] David B. Morris, *Alexander Pope: The Genius of Sense* (Cambridge, MA: Harvard University
Press, 1984), 91–95.

giving fictional unity to disparate targets. But they are also extensions of motifs running through many of Pope's poems of the 1730s, such as the fallen displacement of natural and social reverence, in *An Essay on Man*, onto the superstitious tyranny of "Pow'r unseen" (III. 245–52) or the devotion of selfish but self-denying misers to "Some Revelation hid from you and me" (*Epistle to Bathurst*, line 116). Enough commentary has called attention to Pope's treatment of wealth to allow us merely to observe here that he finds the miser not only useless (so is the spendthrift Buckingham, "this lord of useless thousands") but also the willing victim of an abstraction: a man for whom the variety of available enjoyments has frozen into the singularly inaccessible "Gain."[9] Pope tends to associate with possessiveness what Blake would associate with piety, the "Human Abstract." For Pope the liberation from abstraction lies in *use*, the explicit subject of the third and fourth *Epistles to Several Persons* (both subtitled "Of the Use of Riches") and the implicit subject of the first and second, concerned with the use of "character" both in action and interpretation.

Anyone who chooses to write on ethical subjects will, of course, have to consider the use of things, but Pope's insistence that use be referred to material practice is strong even when he is writing at the greatest level of generality. Thus the discussion of man "with respect to *Society*" (Epistle III of *An Essay on Man*) begins from a celebration of "plastic Nature" where "atoms each to other tend," all life flows from and to the "sea of matter," and "nothing is foreign." This passage (lines 7–26) is often regarded as another version of The Great Chain of Being; if it is (Pope speaks here of the "chain of Love"), it is hardly a static image of hierarchy. Its implications instead are egalitarian ("one centre still, the gen'ral Good"), dynamic ("See life dissolving vegetate again"), and ecological ("nothing stands alone"). This perspective and the praise of "instinct" (lines 79ff) lead to Pope's account of the state of nature as one in which humans and animals together "hymn'd their equal God" (line 156). In the union of matter rather than somewhere above it, humans come as close as they may to the "equal eye" of God's sense of the whole or to the "equal sky" of the Indian's hope, "whose untutor'd mind ... proud Science never taught to stray"

[9] See esp. Earl R. Wasserman, *Pope's 'Epistle to Bathurst': A Critical Reading with an Edition of the Manuscripts* (Baltimore: Johns Hopkins Press, 1960); Peter Dixon, *The World of Pope's Satires* (London: Methuen, 1968), 122–52; Howard Erskine-Hill, "Pope and the Financial Revolution," in Peter Dixon (ed.), *Writers and Their Background: Alexander Pope* (Athens: Ohio University Press, 1972), 200–29; Morris, *Alexander Pope: The Genius of Sense*, pp. 179–213.

(Epistle i, 87, 99–101). It is in the historical fall from equality that the political task of poetry becomes that of exploding "Th' enormous faith of many made for one" and teaching "Pow'r's due use to People and to Kings" (Epistle iii, 242, 289).

Pope's view of human history as a fall from instinctual action and sensuous apprehension is similar in an important respect to Prior's account of the "Progress of the Mind." In most respects, *Alma* and *An Essay on Man* are poems of entirely different orders. Prior's Hudibrastic amble burlesques philosophical argument from Aristotle's *De Anima* to Locke's *Essay* and ends with a call for wine, more in the spirit of Housman's "Malt does more than Milton can / To justify God's ways to man" than of attempted theodicy. Yet for all its parody of "system," the poem is remarkably learned and, in its fashion, ambitious. Prior's own rope dancing is easier to applaud than describe, but the general impression is that the major philosophical problem of mind and body has been *entertained*, not dismissed. Prior sets the problem as the question of the soul's location – in the head or heart? or "All in All"? – and he "solves" it for all time to come with the theory that the soul is in no one place permanently but rises in "ascending Stages" through the phases of life. It enters at the feet (thus the kicking and running of infants and children), reaches loinward by young adulthood (thus the special vigor of youth), finds the heart in middle age, and the head at "Sixty" or so, until eventually

> Stun'd and worn out with endless Chat,
> Of WILL did this, and NAN said that,
> She finds, poor Thing, some little Crack,
> Which Nature, forc'd by Time, must make....
>
> (iii. 524–27)

The relation of this "Progress of the Motion" (i. 269) to Pope's progress of man in society must obviously be drawn lightly, but it lies in the association of reason with detachment from the body and of reason's ascendancy with the latter-day human role as "foe to Nature" (*Essay on Man*, iii, 163). The "motions" of earlier life are comic but robust in Prior's view; it is not until the soul reaches the head that he speaks of frauds, crimes, malice, and "Thy Pride of being great and wise" (iii. 473–78). It is in this advanced stage that the "Farce of Life" properly begins, in which "We err by Use, grow wrong by Rules; / In gesture grave, in Action Fools" (iii. 498–99). "Use" in the first line of the couplet seems to mean habit or convention rather than making use, because it is only in Prior's late age of reason that desire becomes separated from the use of things which might gratify it:

> L'AVARE not using Half his Store
> Still grumbles, that He has no more...
> And eats To-day with inward Sorrow,
> And Dread of fancy'd Want To-morrow.
>
> (III. 424–25, 428–29)

Collecting is a less miserable absorption but equally compulsive and functionless, including the speaker's own: "And Trifles I alike pursue; / Because They're Old; because They're New" (III. 462–63). As the aging man comes to live by "borrow'd Sense," the projects of the head become further removed from utility, history, and probability:

> With endless Pain This man pursues
> What, if he gain'd, He could not use:
> And T'other fondly Hopes to see
> What never was, nor e'er shall be.
>
> (III, 509, 494–97)

But to return to gravity.

Prior refers twice to Newtonian gravity in *Alma*, both times in contexts that imply skepticism about its finality in any exhaustive explanation of motion. The first occurs as "Mat" waxes systematic (II. 222ff) in defense of "Impulsive Force" as what controls men and things alike. In the following lines, the word for gravity is "attraction" (more common at the time in scientific and philosophic writing, although Newton himself used the words interchangeably), and "Dick" is Richard Shelton, the interlocutor whose objections throughout the whole poem are often normative:

> Thus to save further Contradiction,
> Against what You may think but Fiction;
> I for Attraction, DICK, declare:
> Deny it those bold Men that dare.
> As well your Motion, as your Thought
> Is all by hidden Impulse wrought:
> Ev'n saying, that you Think or Walk,
> How like a Country 'Squire you talk?
>
> (II. 243–50)

The argument of this section is against zealous Newtonianism rather than Newton, an eager transfer of mechanism from planets to persons, which Prior depicts as a flight beyond the material sense of common language. But the suggestion that the scientific basis of the misguided metaphor may itself be "but Fiction" lingers into the next canto, where Newton appears in the company of system makers whose explanations rest on a single, and apparently arbitrary, principle:

> From great LUCRETIUS take His void;
> And all the World is quite destroy'd
> Deny DES-CART His subtil Matter;
> You leave Him neither Fire, nor Water.
> How oddly would Sir ISAAC look,
> If you, in Answer to his Book,
> Say in the Front of your Discourse
> That things have no *Elastic* Force?
> How could our *Chymic* Friends go on,
> To find the Philosophic Stone;
> If You more pow'rful Reasons bring,
> To prove, that there is no such thing?

$$\text{(III. 53–64)}$$

Prior's final comparison of Newtonian and "chymic" explanations may look less extreme in light of recent attention to Newton's vast manuscript writings on alchemy.[10] Similarly, Swift's treatment of the theory of gravitation in *Gulliver's Travels* should have begun to look less like scientific philistinism three decades after Thomas Kuhn's *Theory of Scientific Revolutions*. The ghost of Aristotle, having noted that the physical systems of Descartes and Gassendi are now "exploded" (like his own), "predicted the same Fate to *Attraction*, whereof the present Learned are such zealous Asserters. He said, that new systems of Nature were but new Fashions, which would vary in every Age; and even those who pretend to demonstrate them from Mathematical Principles, would flourish but a Short Period of Time, and be out of vogue when that was determined" (III, ch. 8, para. 2). "Fashion" is a more evaluative term perhaps than "paradigm," and there is often some suspicion, I think, that Swift has turned out to be "right" (at least in our Short Period of Time) by accident. But both his and Prior's views are close to those of an earlier philosopher of science whose critique of Newtonian physics lacks neither systematic rigor nor sophistication: George Berkeley.

---

[10] See Betty Jo Teeter Dobbs, *The Foundations of Newton's Alchemy* (Cambridge: Cambridge University Press, 1974).

The "doctrine of abstraction": Berkeley and book III of *Gulliver's Travels*

Berkeley's fullest discussion of gravity is in *De Motu*, 1721, but his reservations are clear in his first and most enduring philosophical work, *A Treatise concerning the Principles of Human Knowledge*, published in 1710:

> The great mechanical principle now in vogue is *attraction*. That a stone falls to the earth, or the sea swells toward the moon, may to some appear sufficiently explained thereby. But how are we enlightened by being told this is done by attraction? Is it that that word signifies the manner of the tendency, and that it is by the mutual drawing of bodies, instead of their being impelled or protruded toward each other? But nothing is determined of the manner of action, and it may as truly (for aught we know) be termed *impulse* or *protrusion* as *attraction*.[11]

Berkeley's criticism of mechanistic explanation is part of a larger argument against what he calls the "doctrine of *abstraction*" (para. 100), an argument it is now time to consider in relation to another work which has abstraction as its primary subject, book III of *Gulliver's Travels*.

Berkeley called his position immaterialism. Since in what follows I will regard him as committed in fact to the materialist assumption of much Augustan writing, it is necessary to begin by recalling what meaning these terms have for Berkeley. The materialism he attacks is roughly what I have referred to as abstract materialism. According to Berkeley, the "patrons of matter" err fundamentally by positing the existence of a "corporeal substance" somehow under or independent of those "accidents" of things (such as extension, figure, solidity, and motion) always present in perception (paras. 18, 67). The supposition of a "substance without accidents" for Berkeley is "no less absurd" than "accidents without a substance" (para. 67), and matter independent of perception is "an incomprehensible somewhat," defined by its patrons much as we would define a "*nonentity*" – which in fact it is (paras. 47, 68; cf. 75, 80).

Berkeley repeatedly attributes this erroneous materialism to the "doctrine of abstract ideas." "For can there be a nicer strain of abstraction than to distinguish the existence of sensible objects from

---

[11] *A Treatise concerning the Principles of Human Knowledge*, para. 103, quoted from *The Works of George Berkeley*, ed. A.A. Luce and T.E. Jessop (London: Thomas Nelson and Sons, 1949), ii. 86. Since paragraph numbers are used in various editions, subsequent parenthetical references will refer to paragraph rather than page for convenience.

their being perceived, so as to conceive them existing unperceived"
(para. 5). The doctrine of abstraction is the belief that we form general
ideas by "abstracting entirely from [a particular idea] and cutting off
all those circumstances and differences which might determine it to any
particular existence" (Introduction, para. 9). This belief is "remote
from common sense," for Berkeley, because the mind does not work in
such a way. We do not frame a general idea of a triangle, for example,
in the manner Locke describes – by imagining a triangle "neither
oblique nor rectangle, neither equilateral, equicurral, nor scalenon, but
all and none of these at once" (Introduction, para. 13, quoting *Essay*, IV.
vii. 9) – but rather by conceiving a particular triangle and letting it
"stand for" others (para. 15). Similarly, we may have a general but
not abstract idea of man, because the "idea of man that I frame to
myself must be either of a white, or a black, or a tawny, a straight, or
a crooked, a tall, or a low, or a middle-sized man" (Introduction, para.
10). Locke believed that abstractions were possible, and peculiarly
human, due to language; Berkeley, however, replies that "a word
becomes general by being made the sign, not of an abstract general
idea, but of several particular ideas, any one of which it indifferently
suggests to the mind" (Introduction, para. 11).

As even this partial account will suggest, Berkeley's attack on the
"doctrine of abstraction" implies a theory of imagination, symbolism,
and language that deserves more careful consideration than it usually
receives in histories of critical thought. For the purposes of the present
argument the following points concerning abstraction are most
pertinent: (1) abstraction rests on mistaken notions of language and
mind; (2) it in turn supports a materialism "abstracted ...from
perceiving and being perceived" (para. 81); (3) materialism thus
abstracted is the "very root of scepticism" (para. 86; cf. para. 92)
because it teaches that things are never as they appear (para. 35–40);
(4) *general* ideas are possible and necessary; general *abstract* ideas are
neither; (5) ethical abstraction, in which words such as "happiness" or
"justice" are taken to "stand for general notions, abstracted from all
particular persons and actions," makes "morality difficult, and the
study thereof of less use to mankind" (para. 100); (6) natural
philosophies should consider not only effects but "final causes" or the
"various ends to which natural things are adapted" since they may
direct us to the "proper uses and applications of things" (para. 107);
(7) philosophers enamored of abstraction have overvalued mathematics, but we should regard "all inquiries about numbers only as so

many *difficiles nugae*, so far as they are not subservient to practice and promote the benefit of life" (para. 119). The last three points, which refer explicitly to ethical *use*, are the most clearly related to Swift (and Prior and Pope), but all of these strands of Berkeley's argument may help us see the coherence of Swift's treatment of abstraction in book III and, in turn, redefine its relation to the whole of *Gulliver's Travels*.

Like book II, book III sprouts from a seed planted a few pages before it begins. In the first case the man who "would gladly have taken a Dozen of the Natives" of Blefuscu back to England (I, ch. 8) soon finds himself in the role that would have awaited each of them, a curiosity among giants. By a similar comic logic, then, the Gulliver who complained of the Brobdingnagians that "as to Ideas, Entities, Abstractions and Transcendentals, I could never drive the least Conception into their Heads" is soon after "drawn up" into the company of men whose heads contain little else. Abstraction is so strong in the atmosphere of the floating island that only a Laputan gentleman would need a critical Flapper to put him in mind of it (the Laputan women, with their "Abundance of Vivacity," and the unlearned males remain uninfected, as in Prior's "Lock and Montaigne"). Gulliver himself seems inspired by its philosophic air even before his ascent; temporarily abandoning homely comparisons, he tells of having "perceived a vast Opake Body," which "appeared to be a firm Substance," capable of "progressive Motion" – although he was not "at the time, in a Disposition to philosophise upon this Phaenomenon" (ch. 1, paras. 10–11). Gulliver's diction will in fact fluctuate, sometimes from one sentence to the next, between the familiar and the learned, just as his perspective will alternate between sensible and projective observation. The bladders carried by Flappers, for example are "fastned like a Flail to the End of a short Stick" and contain "dried Pease, or little Pebbles," but their function is to apply "some external Taction upon the Organs of Speech and Hearing" (ch. 2, para. 1). The atmosphere is clearly contagious; the more difficult problem is to find its consistency.

The fact that book III lacks "unity of place" seems often to lead readers to ignore an obvious structural question about it: why does Laputa come first? The question has perhaps been obscured too by the assumption that book III, completed last, contains many loosely connected satiric leftovers. But on the safe assumption that Swift was concerned with getting proper scenes as well as proper words into proper places, we may begin by looking at what precedes the Laputan sojourn and consider the question of whether what follows it follows from it.

The normative role of the king of Brobdingnag is generally recognized; our understanding of the reversal of values in Laputa may be clearer if we recognize it particularly as well. I have mentioned the Brobdingnagians' imperviousness to "abstractions," but it is important to recall that their ideal king is hardly anti-intellectual. Not only is he interested in law and polity, but learned in "Philosophy and particularly Mathematicks" and even fond of that Laputan art, music (ch. 3, paras. 5–7; ch. 6, para. 3). He does not, of course, fiddle to the music of the spheres, and, like his subjects (and Berkeley or Arbuthnot) he believes mathematics should be useful; but Swift goes out of his way to make the king an intellectual as well as a patron of learning. It has been said, in discussions of book III that Swift is opposed to theoretical science and to attempts to "manipulate" nature; but the king's views suggest that Swift's targets are more specifically defined. The king wants two blades of grass where one grew before, and he emerges as a philosopher-king (rather than, say, an agricultural engineer) because of his interest in intellectual generality. He believes no more than Berkeley in abstract ideas but takes *general* ideas to be vital.

The difference between the two kinds of ideas seems to depend on whether an idea derives from or escapes from particular perceptions, whether it seeks to include or transcend physical experiences. Turning away from experience is no more satisfactory than its mere accumulation. Curious about the education of lawyers, the Brobdingnagian king asks Gulliver "whether those pleading Orators were Persons educated in the general Knowledge of Equity; or only in provincial, national, and other local Customs" (ch. 6, para. 13). This remark is less quoted than Swift's comments on the corruption and sophistry of lawyers, here and in book IV, but it is the more difficult challenge intellectually. The "general Knowledge of Equity" is theoretical in so far as it is based on principles rather than precedents; the latter will be defined in book IV as "all the Decisions formerly made against common Justice and the general Reason of Mankind" (ch. 5, para. 14). General knowledge or reason, then, would seem to be common sense uncommonly broadened by philosophical and historical insight, a kind of philosophical anthropology. It is neither abstract in Berkeley's sense – that is, the illusory "cutting off of all those circumstances and differences which might determine [an idea] to any particular existence" (Introduction, para. 9) – nor a collection of unevaluated facts. In casual speech we often use "abstract" and "general" roughly synonymously and oppose both terms to "specific." Swift tends to distinguish generalizations from abstraction and, in the Academy of Lagado especially, to portray abstraction and the quest for "specifics" as two sides of the same counterfeit coin.

The view that general ideas occupy a reasonable middle ground between disembodied abstractions and particular perceptions is suggested by much of the satire on speculation and antiquarianism in *The Memoirs of Martinus Scriblerus*. But the subject is treated most directly in the account of Martin's education in "Rhetoric, Logic, Metaphysics" in chapter 7:

Martin suppos'd an *Universal Man* to be like a Knight of a Shire or a Burgess of a Corporation, that represented a great many Individuals. His Father ask'd him, if he could not frame the Idea of an Universal Lord Mayor? Martin told him, that never having seen but one Lord Mayor, the Idea of that Lord Mayor always return'd to his mind; that he had great difficulty to abstract a Lord Mayor from his Fur, Gown, and Gold Chain; nay, that the horse he saw the Lord Mayor ride upon not a little disturb'd his imagination. On the other hand Crambe, to shew himself a more penetrating genius, swore that he could frame a conception of a Lord Mayor not only without his Horse, Gown, and Gold Chain, but even without Stature, Feature, Colour, Hands, Head, Feet, or any Body; which he suppos'd was the abstract of a Lord Mayor. Cornelius told him he was a lying Rascal...[12]

Charles Kerby-Miller, the modern editor of the Scriblerus *Memoirs*, argues (against Warburton and others) that this section satirizes scholasticism rather than Locke (pp. 253–54); but it is in fact close to Berkeley's criticism of Locke and to Prior's dialogue between Locke and Montaigne.

Putting Laputa first, then, achieves two purposes in Swift's intellectual and political satire. By juxtaposing the king of Brobdingnag and the Laputan court intelligentsia, it allows a finer contrast of philosophical orientations than might emerge, say, if the narrative went directly from Brobdingnagian sobriety to experiments with excrement. The contrast between general and abstract thinking in turn establishes an intellectual set of principles against which many of the academicians' errors can emerge as Error: not simply wrong but *consistently* wrong. It may be argued that neither Swift nor the reader

[12] See *The Memoirs of Martinus Scriblerus*, ed. Charles Kerby-Miller (New Haven: Yale University Press, 1950; repr. Oxford: Oxford University Press, 1988), 120.

needs to establish such principles because everybody knows the experiments are "impractical." This argument leads, however, to the view that Swift saw much bad science around him, made no serious effort to distinguish good from bad, and therefore (simple man or brave humanist, according to the reader's biases) opposed "modern science." While I do not propose that Swift was a systematic philosopher of science, I believe he provides an episodic argument to the following effect: that the Laputans are wrong not because they are theoreticians but because they are bad theoreticians, that the difference between good and bad theory is roughly the difference between generalization and abstraction, and that the bad science of Lagado is a series of attempts at applied abstraction.

Berkeley's assault on the doctrine of abstraction begins, it will be recalled, with an appeal to imagination. We cannot really imagine an "abstract" triangle or an "abstract" man, Berkeley argues, because we cannot form ideas contrary to all sense experience. We may combine and separate ideas, by imagining a green man, or a body without a head, but cannot imagine a man with no body. We can of course "imagine" we imagine such abstractions, as Locke and others have done, but we have stopped attending to our experience when we do so. Although freer than narration, true imagination always derives from the human senses, the "inlets of perception" (para. 81), in whose reliability Berkeley has full belief: "That what I see, hear, and feel doth exist, that is to say, is perceived by me, I no more doubt than I do of my own being ... We are not for having any man turn *sceptic*, and disbelieve his senses; on the contrary, we give them all the stress and assurance imaginable..." (para. 40). The dependence of imagination on the human body is as complete for Swift as for Berkeley. It is not accidental that the Laputans are both out of their wits and without wit. Closing their inlets of perception (until "flapped") and abstracting their minds from their bodies, they have no "Imagination, Fancy, and Invention." Not surprisingly, they are "very bad Reasoners" (ch. 2, para. 11).

Illustrated in the figure of the Laputans, the view that reason and imagination are properly corroborative rather than competitive and that both should be continually grounded in perception is established as a normative principle before we are allowed off the island. This view is quite compatible with Berkeley's analysis of abstraction and philosophically incompatible with Locke's distrust of wit, and it is the general principle worked out in book III. Swift's bad reasoners on and below Laputa tend to make four interconnected mistakes. They abstract by ignoring or schematizing the body, by overlooking questions of usefulness or ends, by becoming fixated on the future, and by misunderstanding language and metaphor.

The last point emerges fully in the language projects, but we may see the connection of all four mistakes in political and scientific experiments as well. The man proposing to cure colic with a bellows, for example, is unconcerned with a living body before him and with whether the cure works ("the Dog died on the Spot"), is convinced that the experiment somehow will succeed with enough repetition ("we left the Doctor endeavouring to recover him by the same Operation"), and is the victim of a metaphor gone literal (colic is "wind," thus, in homeopathic theory, the cure must be wind). Similarly, the political projector of "Remedies for all Diseases and Corruptions" of nations offers this rationale: "Whereas all Writers and Reasoners have argued, that there is a strict universal Resemblance between the natural and the political Body; can there be anything more evident, than that the Health of both must be preserved and the diseases cured by the same Prescriptions?" (ch. 6, para. 2). No rationale is given for "extracting Sun-Beams out of Cucumbers" (ch. 5, para. 2), but we might imagine it to be that what is *in* something can be taken out of it. The error is not only a misjudgment of practicality or use (the usual human way of getting solar energy "out" of a cucumber being to eat it) but of language; like the next projector, who is trying to extract the "original Food" from excrement, he apparently assumes that *in* has an invariable meaning: sunlight must be in the cucumber as a fish, rather than water, is in a pond. In this way, Swift's extractors are Berkeley's abstractors. They try to "abstract one from another, or conceive separately, those qualities which it is impossible should exist so separated" (Introduction, para. 10), and they proceed accordingly to the Berkeleian absurdity of supposing "a substance without accidents" (para. 67).

As we have seen, Berkeley finds the source of the belief in abstract ideas in misunderstandings of language. We may consider his argument in more detail in connection with the two projects that comprise Swift's "School of Languages" (ch. 5, paras. 19–23). The first is given in a sentence and is in effect a premise to the second; it is "to shorten Discourse by cutting Polysyllables into one, and leaving out Verbs and Participles; because in Reality all things imaginable are but Nouns." The second is to abolish "all Words whatsoever." Since Words are only Names for *Things*, it would be more convenient for all Men to carry about them, such *Things* as were necessary to express the particular Business they are to discourse on." The rationale is often taken as a parody of the Royal Society's ideal, according to Thomas Sprat's *History*, of a style in which the number of words would approach the number of "things" conveyed. Berkeley's argument concerning language and abstraction suggests that Swift's subject includes more contemporary and philosophically controversial issues than those presented by a manifesto published nearly sixty years before *Gulliver's Travels* was composed.

Berkeley argues that two received opinions concerning language are the "source" of the error of abstraction (Introduction, paras. 18–20). The first is that every "name" has or should have "one only precise and settled signification" and that every general name therefore signifies a fixed abstract idea. But the fact is that no general name has a definite signification; instead it signifies "indifferently" many particular ideas. In his comments on Locke, Berkeley implies that he differs at bottom from Locke in regarding a general term as a linguistic convenience rather than as the mirror of something in the mind (cf. Introduction, paras. 9–13, which quote or refer to Locke's *Essay*, ii. xi. 10, iii. iii. 6, and iv. vii. 9). We use a general name meaningfully, in any case, by keeping it within a consistent definition, not by making "it stand everywhere for the same idea": a fixed correspondence of word and idea would be "useless and impracticable."

The second error for Berkeley is the assumption that the sole end of language is "communicating ideas." Armed with this assumption (and presumably with the fact that we do generally make sense to each other), philosophers intensify their conviction that "every significant name stands for an idea" or image in the mind. Neither of these mutually reinforcing beliefs is correct. What we might now call the mimetic or representational function of language ("the communicating of ideas by words") is not its "chief and only" use. "There are other ends, as the raising of some passion, the exciting to or deterring from an action, the putting in mind in some particular disposition – to which the former is in many cases barely subservient, and sometimes entirely omitted, when these can be obtained without it…" Even in less emotive contexts, names often "stand for" rather than "excite" ideas; that is, they refer to them but need not "occasion" a mental "view" of what they mark. For "in reading and discoursing, names [are] for the most part used as letters are in algebra, in which, though a particular quantity be marked by each letter, yet to proceed right it is not requisite that in every step each letter suggest to your thoughts the particular quantity it was appointed to stand for."

In making this last point Berkeley does not refer to Locke; in fact, his analogy suggests what may be their deepest difference. As argued earlier, Locke's distrust of wit is part of a more general uneasiness about the imprecision of language, a limitation which he hopes philosophy will overcome by finding its "algebra." Prior seems to be responding to this desire for extralinguistic purity when he has "Montaigne" tell "Lock" that simile is the algebra of discourse. Berkeley goes even further: in its common as well as uncommon uses, language is everywhere and already algebraic. That does not mean that it cannot mislead; it will, indeed, gravely mislead those who, having chastened their style, imagine that where there are words there must be ideas. Berkeley means instead that there is no reason to discard our subtle instrument of generality by dreaming of something finer.

Swift's projectors embrace the errors Berkeley describes by assuming fixed correspondences between words and ideas ("useless and impracticable" for Berkeley) and by regarding the communication of ideas ("things" in the mind for Berkeley, things in the pack for Swift) as the sole purpose of language. The "other ends" of language are insisted upon again in book IV when Gulliver immediately notices that the Houyhnhnm language "expressed the Passions very well" (ch. 1, para. 8). Here those ends are asserted through the absurdity of humans thinking they will have done the "Business they are to discourse on" once they have shown their "Things." This illusion is based on the theory of "one only precise and settled signification" ("since Words are only Names for Things...") as well as on a reductive theory of communication. The language professors figuratively carry on their backs the received opinions Berkeley analyzes. To see whether the errors lead for Swift, as for Berkeley, to abstraction, we may pause to consider what they are literally carrying.

To complete the fantasy Swift sketches, one would need to grant for the moment his professors' reasoning, which supposes that: (1) "in Reality all things imaginable are but Nouns," (2) nouns are "Names for Things," and (3) that imagining things primarily means seeing them. (While some of the contents of one's thing-hoard might be heard or, depending on the degree of intimacy, touched, smelling and tasting seem unlikely.) How do they look? They have to be small enough to be carried and big enough to be visible – Lilliputian perhaps. Do they have color? Or, if one wants to communicate the idea of a brown horse does one show a colorless horse and then a patch of brown? And to show the idea of an unusually large brown horse? Even resolutely limiting the inventory to simple visual ideas, we quickly find that the *things* "requisite to furnish Matter for this ... artificial Discourse" must approach either infinity or the abstractedness Berkeley attributes to modern "matter" – that is, they would not be things at all but "substance without accidents."[13] We plainly do not need Berkeley's theory or a brown horse in order to realize that the language project is a bad idea; but Berkeley helps show how attempts to transcend the use, or rather uses, of language begin and end with a bag full of abstract ideas.

The importance of distinguishing between generalization and abstraction can be seen in much of the intellectual satire of book III; it begins to acquire unmistakable ethical force in Gulliver's fantasy of abstracting himself from his body (had he but luck enough to be a Struldbrugg) and then from the general body of society in Houyhnhnm-land. Since we will need to return to this issue as a central problem posed by Augustan satire (including several episodes in book III and most of book IV), it may be useful to observe here the similar responses of Berkeley and Swift to that stubborn abstraction, "man." Here is Berkeley's account of how philosophers have wrongly persuaded themselves that such an abstraction is a real idea: "the mind, having observed that Peter, James, and John resemble each other in certain common agreements of shape and other qualities, leaves out of the complex or compounded idea it had of Peter, James, and any other particular man that which is peculiar to each, retaining only what is common to all, and so makes an abstract idea wherein all the particulars equally partake – abstracting entirely from and cutting off all those circumstances and differences which might determine it to any particular existence" (Introduction, para. 9). But this is all non-sense, inconceivable and misleading. Belief in the existence of such abstractions, Berkeley later argues, has "rendered morality difficult" (para. 100). Swift's argument is simpler but compatible. Abstraction makes morality difficult because "all my love is towards individualls." There is an acute epistemology as well as sensibility behind Swift's familiar pronouncement: "principally I hate and detest that animal called

---

[13] Bertrand Russell argues that "no sentence can be made up without at least one word which denotes a universal" and that the history of philosophy has been skewed by the tendency to recognize only those universals named by nouns and adjectives, not those named by verbs and prepositions. These express "relations"; of their omission Russell remarks, "it is hardly too much to say that most metaphysics, since Spinoza, has been largely determined by it." See *The Problems of Philosophy* (first pub. 1912; Oxford: Oxford University Press, 1967), 53–54.

man, although I hartily love John, Peter, Thomas and so forth. This is
the system upon which I have governed my self many years (but do not
tell)…" (September 20, 1725).

Crackpot materialism

The notion of "crackpot materialism" I invoke is adapted from C.
Wright Mills, who, in praising Thorstein Veblen's social analysis,
points to Veblen's insight into "what one might call 'crackpot
realism.'" According to Mills, Veblen "believed that the very Men of
Affairs whom everyone supposed to embody sober, hard-headed
practicality were in fact utopian capitalists and monomaniacs; that the
Men of Decision who led soldiers in war and who organized civilians'
daily livelihoods in peace were in fact crackpots of the highest
pecuniary order. They had 'sold' a believing world on themselves; and
they had – hence the irony – to play the chief fanatics in their delusional
world." As the "only comic writer among modern social scientists,"
Veblen "teaches us to be aware of the crackpot basis of the realism of
those practical Men of Affairs who would lead us to honorific
destruction."[14]

It seems helpful to consider much of Augustan writing as directed
against abstract or "crackpot" materialism because the tendencies
these texts criticize are mechanistic and idealist rather than sensibly
materialist. From the perspective of "material sense," Augustan wit
regularly defines its values against the graver conduct of characters
who regard the body as irrelevant or as something to be transcended,
and it regularly insists that the question of "use" be kept central. Its
targets typically include "men of decision" who, like the Laputan king
and unlike his Brobdingnagian predecessor, have no curiosity about
social practice or the conditions of material life. Receptivity to social
experience is its aesthetic as well as political norm, as we see in Pope's
ironic advice to the "profound" poet to write about either the "Sun,
Moon, Stars, &c." or the "Treasures of the Deep," since "all that lies
between these, as Corn, Flowers, Fruits, Animals, and Things for the
meer Use of Man, are of mean price, and so common as not to be
greatly esteem'd by the curious: It being certain that any thing of
which we know the true Use, cannot be Invaluable."[15]

---

[14] C. Wright Mills, Introduction to Thorstein Veblen, *Theory of the Leisure Class* (New York: New
American Library, 1953), pp. vii–viii, xix.

[15] *Peri Bathos: or … The Art of Sinking in Poetry*, ch. 4, para. 3, in *The Prose Works of Alexander Pope*,
ii, ed. Rosemary Cowler (Oxford: Basil Blackwell, 1986), 191.

We hear much about the common sense of Augustan writing, of course, but perhaps not enough about the intellectual demands of the Augustan's conception of that uncommon virtue. In stressing their philosophical as well as rhetorical intelligence, I do not mean to claim prescience for the Augustan wits. The "fanatics" they depict are not the same ones Mills has in mind, nor is the specter of "honorific destruction" that has brooded over this century's vast abyss the same abstraction who triumphs at the close of the *Dunciad*. The differences are important, and the historical specificity of Augustan satire will be the principal concern of the next chapter. On the other hand, Mills's formulation may remind us that opposition to a prevailing modern "practicality" need not be a nostalgic spiritualism. To minimize the material sense of Augustan wit is to prefer nostalgias of our own to historical engagement.

5

That satire is art, only more so

Critical evasions

Although the question "Is Satire Art?" may be considered officially dead, its assumptions have transmigrated to modern versions of the desire to protect literature from politics and rhetoric.[1] It is probably more accurate to speak of a protective desire rather than a position, because actual arguments for a clear distinction between "literary" and "non-literary" writing have become increasingly rare. In relation to this question as to many others, ours is the Age of Quotation Marks. At the same time, we continue to feel the attractions of such an opposition, which can be traced back through at least one strain of Modernism to at least one strain of Romanticism and to the fitful invocations of "pure poetry" clustering in the 1740s.[2] We might consider, for example, the lingering appeal of Yeats's claim that "We make out of the quarrel with others, rhetoric, but of the quarrel with ourselves, poetry." Or the allure of the distinction drawn by Stephen Dedalus between the "static" emotion of proper art and the "kinetic" modes of didacticism or pornography, on the grounds that the latter make us want to *do* something. Or the elegiac economy of Frost's remark that politics is about "grievances," poetry about "griefs." Or Northrop Frye's characterization of a literary work as an "autonomous verbal structure" and non-literary writing as "words used instru-

---

[1] "Demonstrations of the satirist's skillful handling of language and management of single effects have made suspect the once popular examination question, 'Is Satire Art?' but we are still left with a satirist who is only an artist *manqué*, a contriver of farragoes rather than articulated wholes"; see Alvin Kernan, *The Cankered Muse* (New Haven: Yale University Press, 1959), 5.

[2] "Pure poetry" is the phrase used by Joseph Warton in 1756 to advocate more emphasis on "fancy" and less on "wit" and to try to separate poetry from politics; I discuss this lyric ideal in *Literary Loneliness in Mid-Eighteenth-Century England* (Ithaca: Cornell University Press, 1982), esp. pp. 81–96, 128–46.

mentally."[3] Underlying each of these declarations are Romantic projections of the autonomy of the imaginative "self" and of the autonomy of "imaginative" literature.

Such claims are not last glimmers of Modernism but operate, if more subtly, in Postmodernist discussions as well. For the difference between emphasizing the self-expressive function of literature and seeing literature as primarily a discourse of self-referentiality is often not very great. Geoffrey Hartman asks whether "literary language" is not "the name we give to a diction whose frame of reference is such that the words stand out as words (even as sounds) rather than being, at once, assimilable meanings?"[4] The question is rhetorical but skirts questions of rhetoric. The proposition it advances depends on the Romantic proposition that the literary essence is lyric poetry.

This is not to suggest that all of Romanticism leads to the idea that literature is most literary as it aspires to the condition of music. When Marilyn Butler writes that "The problem is that all modern professional persons of letters are Romantics, one way or another, and the premises on which most of our procedures rest are biased in favour of aestheticism," she is in fact arguing against a selective legacy, "English Romantic writing as we habitually represent it: without its critical element, its corrections, critiques, parodies, satires… "[5] The partial inheritance remains deeply influential in twentieth-century criticism, and I will return to some of the theoretical problems it entails. At the moment, we do not need to scrutinize a theory of literature which has the effect of making satire marginal to see that the assumptions sketched here would present immediate problems for practical criticism of Augustan satires. We clearly cannot get very far by approaching *A Modest Proposal*, for example, as a work that is powerful because it arises from Swift's quarrel with himself rather than

---

[3] Yeats's remark is in the "Anima Hominis" chapter of *Per Amica Silentia Lunae* (1917); see *Mythologies* (New York: Collier Books, 1969), 331. For Stephen Dedalus's dichotomy see *A Portrait of the Artist as a Young Man*, ed. Chester G. Anderson (New York: Penguin, 1977), 205. Frost's contrast is drawn in "On Extravagance," a talk given at Dartmouth in 1962 and reprinted in his *Poetry and Prose*, ed. Edward Connery Lathem and Lawrance Thompson (New York: Holt, Rinehart and Winston, 1972), 447–59: "I've been thinking lately that politics is an extravagance, again, an extravagance about *grievances*. And poetry is an extravagance about *grief*. And grievances are something that can be remedied, and griefs are irremediable" (p. 449). For Frye's opposition of "autonomous" and "instrumental" writing see *Anatomy of Criticism* (Princeton: Princeton University Press, 1957), 74.

[4] *Saving the Text: Literature/Derrida/Philosophy* (Baltimore: Johns Hopkins University Press, 1981), xii.

[5] "Satire and Images of Self in the Romantic Period: The Long Tradition of Hazlitt's *Liber Amoris*," in Claude Rawson (ed.), *English Satire and the Satiric Tradition* (Oxford and New York: Basil Blackwell, 1984), 209–25. The quotation may be found on p. 224.

others, or because it brings us to emotional stasis and does not make us want to do anything, or because it concerns griefs rather than grievances, or because it offers words which stand out at once as words rather than as readily assimilable meanings.

Readers of Augustan literature are likely to have approached *A Modest Proposal* and other satires with more hospitable premises. The task at hand, therefore, is not to argue the *need* for alternative assumptions but to try to be explicit about what they are and involve. For the same reason, I do not propose to argue again that satire *is* "art"; such a claim can only mean, finally, that however difficult the words "satire" and "art" may be one does not consider them mutually exclusive. Rather I want to explore what the claim has actually tended to mean in discussions of satire and what it could mean for thinking about satire and its relation to other modes of literature.

A reader of satire as literature usually proceeds with two basic assumptions in hand, if not always fully in mind, that are conspicuously absent from the "Romanticism" outlined above. One is that literature and rhetoric are not automatically separate categories; that is, that a literary work may have persuasive "palpable designs" on the reader. The other is that the referentiality of a work need not be reducible to authorial or textual *self*-referentiality to count as literary; that is, that the "grievances" usually regarded (unlike "griefs") as historical topicality may be constitutive of rather than accidental to a work.

From these assumptions two general principles would seem to follow, running counter to New Critical formalism and newer critical textualism: (1) the consideration of authorial intention is an inevitable part of the response to satire, and (2) the relation of "past significance" and "present meaning" is an interpretive as well as historical question. (I will return to these terms of Robert Weimann's in a moment.) The first principle follows from granting the rhetorical function of satire, since there is no way to discuss the persuasive success of "blame" without attributing intentionality. We can speak of the "unintentional satire" of a text, but the phrase is usually a name for rhetorical failure.[6] The question of intent remains vexed. New Critical orthodoxy concerning the "intentional fallacy" survives more or less unscathed in

---

[6] Thus David Nokes, in *Raillery and Rage: A Study of Eighteenth-Century Satire* (Brighton: Harvester Press, 1987), says that the "satirical content of a work may be independent of the 'intentions' of the author," but goes on to illustrate the statement with examples of earnest bathos from political rhetoric and popular romances (pp. 27–30).

contemporary suspicions of "presence," "phonocentrism," or subjectivity as a metaphysical category.[7]

But it is difficult, perhaps impossible, to read without some idea of intent, even if one remains professionally skeptical of the idea. Jonathan Culler, for example, argues that Habermas's theory of a "universal pragmatics" depends on a notion of speakers' intentions which literary critics should find too straightforward and credulous. But even in making the case against presumptions about authors or speakers, Culler grants that the "assumption of significance" that makes reading possible is equivalent to presuming "an underlying intentionality." Just how readers posit intentionality is a complex question; were it not, disagreements would be as rare and short in criticismland as in Houyhnhnmland. The point here is simply that readers *do* posit it (as Stephen Knapp and Walter Benn Michaels have argued "theoretically"), even in the case of the briefest lyric poem.[8]

To insist upon the recognition of intentionality in satire is not to say that determinate meaning must therefore be recoverable, but rather

[7] Candace D. Lang discusses the problem of intention in recent accounts of irony most helpfully in *Irony/Humor* (Baltimore and London: Johns Hopkins University Press, 1988), esp. pp. 5–9, 37–58. Attempting to distinguish "ironic" from "humorous" texts, Lang argues that the former term should be used for works where intention and authorial control seem apparent, reserving "humorous" to describe texts that are less univocal, less determinate, and more subversive of the assumed priority of signifieds to signifiers. The distinction seems generally very promising but in some respects inapplicable to Augustan writers. For Lang, the ironist, unlike the humorist, subscribes "to the essentially Platonic notion of language as mere representation of ideas, or of writing as a necessary but potentially dangerous supplement to conceptualization" (p. 6). As my earlier chapters indicate, according to this opposition I would regard Locke as a linguistic "Platonist" but not Prior. In other words, the recognition Lang reserves for the humorist, that language has "a constitutive role in thought and therefore in the ego," is one I see at work in Augustan irony. Nonetheless, Lang's distinction may be very helpful on at least two fronts: in showing the inadequacies of some traditional "ironic" categories, such as those of Wayne Booth's *A Rhetoric of Irony*, for some twentieth-century writing, and in discouraging partisans of indeterminacy from taking signs of authorial intent as evidence of "failed" or "shallow" irony. See also the interesting collection of essays gathered by David Newton-De Molina in *On Literary Intention* (Edinburgh: Edinburgh University Press, 1976).

[8] Culler's examples include Apollinaire's one-line "Chantre" and Herrick's "Upon Julia's Clothes." In his formulation, differences in literary interpretation may arise from how critics describe the relation between "the posited speaking voice and those of the posited authorial attitude"; see *Framing the Sign: Criticism and its Institutions* (Norman: University of Oklahoma Press, 1988), 192–93. In "Against Theory" Knapp and Michaels argue that all utterances are read as intentional and that to regard a text as authorless is in fact to view it not as words but as marks merely resembling words. The essay originally appeared in *Critical Inquiry*, 8 (Summer 1982), 723–42, and is reprinted, with several responses, in W.J.T. Mitchell (ed.), *Against Theory* (Chicago: University of Chicago Press, 1985). I do not agree with their argument that intention determines and exhausts meaning – a claim made more emphatically in "Against Theory 2: Hermeneutics and Deconstruction," *Critical Inquiry*, 14 (Autumn 1987), 49–68 – but simply with the point that reading involves the continual positing of intention, whether veridical or not.

that readers tend to regard the meaning of satires as determin*able*. We may learn more, simply change our minds, and revise our interpretations. But the pressure of referentiality serves to define the satiric text "as *utterance*." Bakhtin, who thought all texts were to be read in this manner, goes on to speak of "two aspects that define the text as an utterance: its plan (intention) and the realization of this plan." But the perception of intentionality does not equal meaning; it is simply the condition for it. The relation between intention and realization is "dynamic," a "struggle," and "their divergence" is precisely the subject of much interpretive criticism.[9]

Readers of satire may or may not be quick to go "beyond" the work to try to find out more about an author's intentions, but they will probably be slow to regard such discoveries as irrelevant. The discovery of a cache of letters indicating that Swift thought the Irish in 1729 were doing too little for the prosperity of England would immediately begin to affect critical reading. Again, intention does not equal achievement in persuasive writing, but it is not separate from understanding. It would seem that one would need to consider a literary work to be innocent of rhetorical ends to regard the "disappearance of the author" as desirable – critically or politically. To read a work as a satire means in part to accept an invitation to consider its intentional occasion. The fact that this occasion is in the past (emphatically so for canonical works but recognizably so even for last week's newspaper column) brings us to the second principle asserted above, namely that past significance and present meaning must both enter into one's response to satire. For Weimann, this binocular focus is important in both the history *and* the criticism of any genre:

The dialectic of past significance and present meaning relates genesis to reception, origin to effect. The structure of literature is correlated with its function in society; a fundamental connection is made between the writing and the reading of literature as a social activity. Such a connection is a historical one; and, at the same time, it is one that involves value, in the sense that the writer and reader can potentially achieve a more profound apprehension and comprehension of the world and of themselves.[10]

The conspicuous topicality of satire compels a recognition of

---

9 "The Problem of the Text," in *Speech Genres and Other Late Essays*, trans. Vern W. McGee (Austin: University of Texas Press, 1986); the quotations are on p. 104.

10 Robert Weimann, *Structure and Society in Literary History* (Baltimore: Johns Hopkins University Press, 1984), 9; cf. 48–53 and 187. The dialectical relation of *then* and *now* is more important in Weimann's theory than any connotative difference between "significance" and "meaning." The latter terms could as easily be reversed, as they are in E.D. Hirsch, Jr.'s analogous distinction in "Objective Interpretation," *PMLA* 75 (1960), 463–79.

historical as well as strictly biographical purposiveness. However much
one may be predisposed to emphasize a satire's formal attributes, there
is no good way to overlook its referential claims or to exclude from one's
reading the question of whether it offers a plausible analysis of
historical circumstances. It is easier, perhaps, to make this point by
hypothetical example than by theoretical precision. Let us remain with
the instance of *A Modest Proposal*, since it is not only one of the most
famous satires but one that readers are not tempted to call something
else first – not a poem, novel, or drama which is secondarily a satire.
Suppose that we were to discover new documents neither by nor about
Swift personally but which instead gave convincing evidence that
Ireland was unmistakably more prosperous than England in the 1720s.
Our confidence that such evidence will not arise is implicit, as much so
in our critical as in our historical proceedings. Were it somehow to
arise, however, what reader of *A Modest Proposal* could consider it as
merely extrinsic to understanding the work?

Historical intentionality is ultimately more fundamental to satire
than authorial identity. Although we may prefer that our satires come
with known authors, anonymous satires exist in great numbers;
ahistorical or non-referential satires do not exist at all. To read a text
as rhetorical we do not need the rhetorician's name, but we do need to
know, or posit, an external context in which the persuasive attempt has
operated. This is not news, since discussions of rhetoric from Aristotle
onward have given a prominent place to the immediate audience:
listeners with choices to make. Nor is it novel to assert that satires are
historically referential. Unlike most lyric poems, satires normally come
to the reader through clouds of footnotes, sufficient to discourage
illusions of literary autonomy and historical transparency. Edward
Rosenheim's admirable brief definition of satire emphasizes topicality
as one of its three parts: "satire consists of an attack by means of a
manifest fiction upon discernible historic particulars."[11] The definition
does not solve all problems, of course, but its usefulness is generally
recognized.

We might wonder, then, why it has not had more influence on
literary criticism over the last twenty-five years. Since satiric writing, in
other words, is conspicuously rhetorical and historically referential,
and since many of the most studied Augustan works are satiric, why has
the discussion of Augustan literature not figured more importantly in
recent demystifications of literary autonomy? The most "theoretical"

---

[11] Edward W. Rosenheim, Jr., *Swift and the Satirist's Art* (Chicago and London: University of
Chicago Press, 1963), 31.

explanation might be that many influential literary theorists over the past few decades have apparently cared little about Augustan literature and have, primarily, carried on a somewhat obsessive dialogue with Romanticism. Closer to home in eighteenth-century studies, two important tendencies direct commentaries on Augustan satiric writing. One is the inclination to decide that the works or parts of works one finds most powerful are not really satires but something else. The other has been a habit of emphasizing the first or second of Rosenheim's ingredients – the attack and the fiction – to the near exclusion of the "historical particulars." Annotation emphasizes the particulars, of course, and it slackens not; but the most important reflections on satire and readings of many of the major works have had more to say about the "power" of satire as aggression controlled by artistry (fictions, plots) than about its topicality.[12]

The tendency of criticism to minimize the history in satire may be seen as historically motivated. Several of the major studies were written in the prevailing winds of New Criticism and often in the belief (justified, I think) that the question of whether satire is "art" still required an answer. In such a context, it was natural to answer it by stressing the unity or formal coherence of satiric works. More generally, it may well be that the discussion of genres or modes necessarily favors "centripetal" over "centrifugal" elements of literature, cohesion over correspondence. It remains true that in most accounts of satire, as Craig Howes notes, the "specific historical situation which gave rise to satire in the first place" (all the "material" that "cries out for footnotes") tends to become secondary to form. "A plot of satire thus almost of necessity recasts any discussion into the language of literature, the mythic."[13] Such emphases will, in any case, tend to answer real pedagogical needs. Modern or Postmodern, anyone teaching *Absalom and Achitophel* in the twentieth century is likelier to feel the need to emphasize that it has form than that it needs notes.

Pedagogical and historical needs cannot be fully distinguished, since teachers and students meet in an institutional time and space. Within the past forty or fifty years and within the institution of academic

[12] Robert C. Elliott's *The Power of Satire: Magic, Ritual, Art* (Princeton: Princeton University Press, 1960) has strongly influenced most "aggressive" thinking about satire over the last three decades. Such arguments are likely to seek a satiric universal in cultural anthropology or biological theory; a provocative instance of the latter is Alvin B. Kernan's "Aggression and Satire: Art Considered as a Form of Biological Adaptation," in Frank Brady, John Palmer, and Martin Price (eds.), *Literary Theory and Structure: Essays in Honor of William K. Wimsatt* (New Haven: Yale University Press, 1973), 115–29.

[13] Craig Howes, "Rhetorics of Attack: Bakhtin and the Aesthetics of Satire," *Genre*, 18 (1986), 215–43; the phrases are quoted from p. 216.

literary study, "rhetoric" has become a potentially respectable term in discussions of satire. But at the same time, the more positive meaning of rhetoric has narrowed to, roughly, the study of tropes. Robert Scholes seems correct in arguing that when Paul de Man calls texts "rhetorical," for example, "what he means by rhetoric is what has traditionally been meant by poetry," namely texts which are indeterminate and resistant to referential interpretation.[14] This "tropical," literary view of rhetoric is partly compatible with Aristotle, but only partly. Aristotle at one point defines rhetoric as the "faculty of observing in any given case the available means of persuasion" [1355^b]. Still, because Aristotle believes that rhetoric deals in knowledge and argument as well as in character and psychology, he views it as an "offshoot of dialectic and also ethical studies," adding at once that "ethical studies may fairly be called political..." (1356^a; cf. 1359^b).[15] Unless we think of rhetoric more traditionally, think of it as more concretely social and politically referential than has been fashionable in literary discussion, the recognition that satire is rhetorical does not by itself bring *poesis* and *polis* any closer together.

For various reasons, then, theorizing about satire has tended to suppress the constituent of most satires that first strikes most readers, historical specificity. The desire to attribute "universal significance" to the works we admire remains strong, a way of equating historical survival – as well as our own sympathies – with a universality "above" history. Ironically, this desire may operate more strongly in discussions of satire, because the critic's wish to dignify his or her subject may here be defensive as well as appropriative. And within eighteenth-century studies it has operated most visibly in the case of works where the claim may most readily be made that the subject is "timeless," that the theme is (really) "man" or the "human predicament." Let us turn, therefore, to an instance much discussed but inescapable, the critical debates concerning book IV of *Gulliver's Travels*.

[14] Scholes, *Textual Power: Literary Theory and the Teaching of English* (New Haven: Yale University Press, 1985), 77–79. Cf. Terry Eagleton's forceful argument that the opposition of "rhetoric" to "poetry" beginning in Romanticism leads to an ostensibly depoliticized notion of rhetoric in twentieth-century academic criticism, in *Walter Benjamin, or Towards a Revolutionary Criticism* (London: New Left Books, 1981), 101–11.

[15] Aristotle, *Rhetoric*, ed. W. Rhys Roberts (Oxford: Clarendon Press, 1924), pp. 5–6 (sect. 1355^b–1356^a);cf. 15–16 (sect. 1359^b); further references in the text are to this edition.

Instance in Houyhnhnmland: human history over human nature

Since critics rarely like to think of themselves as soft-headed and have, until recently at least, liked to think their analyses were "penetrating," it is not surprising that the opposition of interpretations of book IV into "hard" and "soft" schools was born privileged. James Clifford, who elaborated the distinction in 1974, identified himself with the "hard" school, and we do not find the terms invoked today by anyone arguing what Clifford sees as the "soft" position. The latter position generally involves emphasizing the distance between Gulliver and Swift, seeing Gulliver's final identification of man with Yahoo and his idolization of the Houyhnhnms as mistaken, and his ultimate isolation as – if one must choose between the poles – more ludicrous than profound. (For the softer of the "soft" readers, the Houyhnhnms are unattractive; for middling-soft readers, they are not satirized but are largely irrelevant to human life.) Recognizing that the opposition oversimplifies, Clifford nevertheless concludes by dividing the world into those who find Gulliver's final reaction to be comic or tragic. The former see in it "an unrealistic attempt to take the confusions of life more seriously than necessary." But for Clifford "and for most others of the 'hard school,' it is poignantly moving, a truly tragic realization of man's flawed condition, trapped in a situation which he cannot control."[16]

The association of tough-minded and "tragic" readings of one of the world's great satires is curious and instructive. It is not easy to see what is "hard" about an interpretation that melts Swift's laughter and indignation into melancholy, universalizing his subject (now "man's flawed condition") beyond historical responsibility (a "situation" humans "cannot control"). The effect of such thinking is to elevate the work by abstracting it from social concerns and relocating it in an arbitrarily constructed realm of personal consciousness. The operative assumption is close to Frost's and more restrictive: not only great poems but even one of our greatest satires must ultimately be more about "griefs" than "grievances."

Such a reading is not, of course, "above politics," since it redefines Swift's aggressive specificity into a politics of sensibility, the "realization" that we are "trapped." This position is presumably considered

---

[16] James L. Clifford, "Gulliver's Fourth Voyage: 'Hard' and 'Soft' Schools of Interpretation," in Larry S. Champion (ed.), *Quick Springs of Sense: Studies in the Eighteenth Century* (Athens: University of Georgia Press, 1974), 33–49; the quotation is from p. 47.

"hard" because the "we" invoked is intended to be unflinchingly inclusive and timeless. *We* will not evade the satire; *we* will rigorously confront the situation Swift defines as ours, however uncomfortable. If we historicize the "we," however, and see that it means primarily modern academic intellectuals, then we might also recognize that the "hard" position of reflective resignation is perhaps rather comfortable. "Hard" readers are sometimes given to faulting others for softening Swift's attack by limiting his targets. But satire may surely be softened as well by "universality." The premise of a more recent and aggressively "hard" interpretation – that the target of *Gulliver's Travels* "is always man's pride" – does not differ fundamentally from most of the readings criticized for being too "soft" on humanity.[17]

As my earlier remarks on Gulliver's "progress" and on Pope's Gulliver poems no doubt reveal, I find much of the "soft school" more sympathetic than the "hard." It has the advantage of keeping in view the fact that *Gulliver's Travels* is one of the great comic works, of not having to ignore Gulliver's absurdities and lies, and of not having to assume that Pope somehow missed the proper wit of Swift's end but that Swift did not notice or was too polite to object. But a "comic" reading needs to be made on other than the usual "soft" terms, as I will try to show, if it is to accommodate Swift's specificity. It is time to abandon the hard/soft opposition, not only because of its masculinist bias but because both sides tend to make the basic error of assuming that Swift's subject is solitary and ahistorical – the "human predicament," for example.[18]

I have concentrated on the "hard school" because its claims of greater rigor make its errors more conspicuous. These arise primarily, I think, from a stubborn predisposition of modernist criticism to think that (1) "tragic" writing is more "serious" than comic writing, (2) the most "serious" writing is that which most approaches "universality," and (3) "tragic truths" are above politics.[19] The incompatibility of these assumptions with Augustan practice becomes apparent when we compare Clifford's and Dryden's use of "tragic" in connection with

[17] Donald Keesey, "The Distorted Image: Swift's Yahoos and the Critics," *Papers on Language and Literature*, 15 (1979), 320–32; the phrase is on p. 323.
[18] The phrase is quoted from Steward LaCasce, but it has been in common use in commentary on book IV. In "Gulliver's Fourth Voyage: A New Look at the Critical Debate," *Satire Newsletter*, 8.1 (Fall 1970), 5–7, LaCasce wants to change the terms of the hard/soft debate but never questions that "this predicament" is Swift's subject.
[19] For a cogent attack on such idealizations of tragedy, however, see Jonathan Dollimore, *Radical Tragedy* (Chicago: University of Chicago Press, 1984), esp. ch. 16, "Beyond Essentialist Humanism."

satire. For Dryden, satire grows tragic not when it asserts that humans are in a situation "beyond control" but when it attacks great crimes and vices instead of bad manners. Juvenal wrote "tragic satire" because he attacked larger wrongs in higher places and with greater indignation than did Horace, not because his targets were any less historically particular or the wrongs any less capable of being righted.

Dryden's "tragic satire" is a high form of historical interpretation, not a transcendence of history. He would not readily understand our century's praise of satiric works for going "beyond" satire to "tragedy." Nor would Shaftesbury, though he might grasp the politics of the categorization. Shaftesbury explicitly recognizes an aspect of the tragedy which later critics seem to endorse less reflectively, its potential for affirming the political status quo: "The genius of this poetry consists in the lively representation of the disorders and misery of the great; to the end that the people and those of a lower condition may be taught the better to content themselves with privacy, enjoy their safer state, and prize the equality and justice of their guardian laws" (*Advice to an Author, Characteristics*, i. 143). Shaftesbury sees tragedy as politically benign, not as politically innocent. The specific political function of tragedy differs from that of satire; for Shaftesbury, tragedy helps preserve liberty, satire to establish it. But both are "persuasive arts," originating, like all of what we now call literature, in the rhetorical desire to "charm the public ear" and guide the "polity." Their common mother is "the goddess PERSUASION" (i. 154).

If modern "tragic" readings of satire are likely to obscure the politically rhetorical aims of Augustan satire, "comic" interpretations do not necessarily restore its historical particularity. Although critics are somewhat less given to invoking "*comic* truth" as transcendental (and thus to finding the "human predicament" at every turn), to regard a satire as "essentially" comic may quickly introduce claims of ahistorical "universality" in another manner. For comedy itself is often seen religiously or anthropologically as "essentially" festive, ritualistic, seasonal, and so on, views which emphasize "sacred" time (cyclical, formal) rather than "profane" (linear, historical) time as its base. 'Twere profanation of our joys to allow historical time into the hypothetical world of "pure comedy," and it seems to be considered at least somewhat irreverent to do so in the presence of the frankly impure comedy of satire. We should, however, take satire's familiar call to irreverence seriously.

Comedy as a category may ultimately pose a greater problem in discussions of satires because most satiric works can be appropriated to it more readily than to tragedy. The tendency of comic generic expectations to suppress specificity may be seen at work even in one of the most thoughtful studies of Swift, Rosenheim's *Swift and the Satirist's Art*. I want to consider the main features of Rosenheim's discussion for several reasons. First, it will become clear that my interpretations of some important parts of Swift's writing (notably the *Tale*'s "Digression concerning Madness" and the last book of *Gulliver's Travels*) differ from his, and I believe his work is too good as well as too influential to disagree with casually. Secondly, while Rosenheim is more explicit than most critics about "historical particulars" in satire (rightly, I believe), his account nonetheless operates at crucial points to demote particulars in the quest for "universals." In this respect it is a paradigm case. Thirdly, it seems reasonable to assume that if such a demotion occurs in a study so historically informed and committed, we need to see how and why it happens if we hope to find a different path.

"Historical particulars" enter Rosenheim's definition (which already included "attack" and "manifest fiction") to help distinguish between satire and comedy. The distinction is meant to be simple and descriptive: like satire, comedy criticizes actors and actions and does so by means of fiction; unlike satire, comedy does not assert that the actors or actions it attacks exist historically (are potentially discernible by other means). But in fact the distinction is difficult and evaluative. To understand its origin and function, we need to see its relation to two other distinctions, between satire and "rhetoric" and, within satire, between "persuasive" and "punitive" satire. Rosenheim acknowledges that the distinctions are not neat and is careful to place the second on a satiric "spectrum," where satires might be distinguished by the predominance of "instructive" or "abusive" ends. I want to concentrate on this spectrum for a moment, since it is an odd one and suggests some of the oddities that surface in other discussions of satire. To begin with, it turns out not to be a horizontal continuum but a vertical structure with "lower" and "upper" niches:

> comedy
> punitive satire
> persuasive satire
> rhetoric.

The surprising elevation of "punitive" over "persuasive" satire is useful in questioning conventional pieties about the higher pleasures of instruction and lower pleasures of indignation; but the vertical "spectrum" serves an equally conventional hierarchy. While the punitive/persuasive distinction can not work logically, since even the most "punitive" satire makes some attempt to persuade one to regard the punishment as appropriate, it works to confirm traditional "literary" values. Punitive satire is higher in this view because it approaches comedy (unmistakably part of literature); persuasive satire is lower because it approaches rhetoric (purportedly unliterary).

In light of this spectral hierarchy it is easier to see how a theorist of satire comes to discuss much of what is taken as Swift's best work as punitive rather than persuasive writing or often as something "*above*" satire entirely. The latter move is conspicuously strange in a study of "Swift's achievement as a satirist" (p. vii), but it is evident several times. For example, the third book of *Gulliver's Travels* is the "most thoroughly and genuinely satiric of the four," but it is also the "least successful" (p. 97 and note). Most of the first two books attain an "essentially comic quality" because their fiction has "a life of its own," "transcending" the "satiric attack upon particulars" (pp. 98–99). The discussion of happiness in *A Tale of a Tub* is "more than satiric" because it "transcends the particulars of either satire or comedy" to reach a "universality" that is "philosophic" (pp. 198, 204). Similarly, book iv of *Gulliver's Travels* is "neither a concentrated attack nor a comic fabrication" but a "mythical statement of a profound and terrible belief about the human condition," addressing "universal problems" that are the "province not of the satiric but of the philosophic mind" (p. 101).

These judgments are notable not only for occurring in a book devoted equally to Swift *and* satire but because they are not unusual. Historical particulars are introduced into the account only to disappear as criticism "rises." Initially a constituent of satire, historical particulars soon become something to be "transcended" – by the "satirist's art." The full hierarchy behind such comments clearly ascends from particularity to generality: from rhetoric to persuasive satire to punitive satire to comedy, to, finally, philosophic myth. In the pressure of argument, historical particulars soon begin to appear an embarrassment, to be sacrificed in order to assure ourselves that satire *is* art. Thus Michael Seidel, in a more recent study that frequently acknowledges the relation of satire to "history," means by that term an essentially Girardian narrative already well on its way to universalization. "If for a critic such as Girard history is the encoding of violence,

satire is the decoding of violence. If history requires the careful selection
of victims, satire turns history into a pattern of universal victimi-
zation."[20]

Since we seem prepared to agree that "rhetoric" is pragmatically
specific, but unprepared to grant that "literature" might be so, the
ambivalence toward particularity evident even in discussions of satire
suggests that much literary criticism may be based on a "rhetoric
anxiety." I take something like this to be what Frank Lentricchia has
in mind as the "marked effort of literary theorists ... since the later
eighteenth century, to denigrate rhetoric in order to elevate the
imaginative," or, more broadly, as "the idea of the literary as the
uncontingent, the universal, a kind of mimesis that is always pretty
much above it all." This idea, Lentricchia argues, is maintained by
opposing literature to the non-literary realm of "the historical and the
rhetorical (and therefore to the political), and it "has dominated, and
continues to dominate, the history of criticism."[21]

The Yeatsian desire to distance literature from rhetoric is still with
us, and in relation to satire it is likely to result in either of two critical
strains. One may, as Rosenheim does, draw an arbitrarily rigid line
between "facts" and "fictions" and put rhetoric on the side of fact.
The following description suggests just how wishful this distinction can
be. "The true rhetorician is assumed to proceed in a literal manner. His
evidence is presumably susceptible of objective scrutiny; his emotional
appeals are taken to rise from and be directed to authentic emotions;
his logic should withstand the rigors of logical examination" (pp.
17–18). This odd idealization of rhetoric seems at first to depress
literature – implying that fictions dwell in *in*authentic emotions – but
its real function is to save literature from rhetoric by defining literature
as essentially figurative. We pass through the bottom of the satiric
spectrum, for example, when we come to fictionless works that use the
"literal methods of true polemic" (p. 23).

A second way of "refining" the historical particularity of rhetoric
out of satire is, as suggested earlier, to announce that satire is rhetorical
but then to redefine rhetoric, implicitly or explicitly, as so far removed
from truth claims about particulars that nothing is changed by the
admission. Thus James Sutherland, for example, was able to assert that
satire is an "art of persuasion" and thus a "department of rhetoric,"
only to retreat to "poesy" a few pages later: "The answer to those who
object to the satirist because he presents them with a partial or

[20] *The Satiric Inheritance: Rabelais to Sterne* (Princeton: Princeton University Press, 1979), 21.
[21] *Criticism and Social Change* (Chicago: University of Chicago Press, 1983), 55, 90.

grotesque or distorted vision of life is surely the same sort of answer as Sidney gave to those who accused the poets of being liars: the poet 'nothing affirmes, and therefore never lyeth ... Though he recount things not true, yet because hee telleth them not for true he lyeth not.'"[22]

The problem is that satirists *do* tell many things "for true" but that we seem to have trouble taking their claims seriously. We have seen how readily approaches which begin by emphasizing referentiality or rhetorical persuasion come to elevate fiction and figure as the satirist's "art." The satirist's assertion of "truth" becomes an embarrassment unless the critic can turn the assertion itself into a shaping fiction (one of the dubious effects of an overemphasis on "persona") or insist that the satirist's real truths are not historically particular but universal. Again, Seidel's emphasis on history as repetition offers a more recent illustration of the universalizing turn: "Of course, the real satiric subject is the degenerative spirit in human nature that can never be restrictively localized because it is so universally formed." Even more recently, and in a book remarkable for its sense of historical meaning and mediation, David Nokes feels the need to insist that the "imaginative power of satire as an art... transforms local facts and incidents into universal images."[23]

There is a tendency, ironically, for "hard" readers to romanticize Gulliver by casting him as hero rather than gull. The issue is in part one of generic poles simply because isolation in tragedy is often associated with profundity and in comedy with absurdity. It is also an issue of universal and particular poles because the predisposition to seek universals in *Gulliver's Travels* leads to something like Rosenheim's association of Gulliver with Conrad's Kurtz, a visionary of "the horror," confronting truths which others have managed to overlook. For Swift, however, visionaries of horror tend to be categorical fools, figured in the person of the grave philosopher in *A Tale of a Tub* who "discovers" that anything whose inside is less attractive than its outside must be "good for nothing," or the zealous student in *Cassinus and Peter* who discovers that since Celia shits everything does. Swift's consistent position seems close to the recognition that tulips *do* grow from dung but *are* tulips.[24]

---

[22] *English Satire* (Cambridge: Cambridge University Press, 1958), 5, 20.

[23] Seidel, p. 11. Nokes, *Raillery and Rage*, p. 56; cf. p. 90 for his description of satire as a "literature of universal types."

[24] For a contrary argument, however, see Keith Fort's interesting "Satire and Gnosticism" (*Religion & Literature*, 20.2 [Summer 1988], 1–18). After noting that the conclusion of "The Lady's Dressing Room" ("...Such order from confusion sprung, / Such gaudy *tulips* raised

This is not to suggest that Swift is philosophically unconcerned. I have argued in the last chapter that his central philosophic concern is precisely the issue of misplaced or misconstrued universality, that he believes in the importance of general but not abstract ideas. His categorical fools are naive materialists who – blinded by too much light – become dogmatic and "partial" skeptics, refugees from material reality; the reality they would ignore ranges from the individual body to the material social practices that make up historical life. There are good, un-"soft" reasons to see Gulliver's so-called tragic "insight" in book IV as oversight, a Laputan abstraction in flight from matter. The framework in which to read book IV is built by everything preceding it, but two of Gulliver's statements in book II seem especially pertinent. One is his defense of the narrative of his defecatory arrangements – how, "beckoning" to his Brobdingnagian mistress "not to look or follow me, I hid myself between two Leaves of Sorrel, and there discharged the Necessities of Nature." Gulliver remarks: "I hope, the gentle Reader will excuse me for dwelling on these and the like Particulars; which, however insignificantly they may appear to grovelling vulgar Minds, yet will certainly help a Philosopher to enlarge his Thoughts and Imagination, and apply them to the Benefit of public as well as private Life..." (part II, ch. 1, last para.). This paragraph concludes in a parody of the circumstantial self-importance of travel writers, but the sober statement embedded in it I take to be Swift's claim that any philosophy which does *not* take "these and the like Particulars" of material existence into account will *not* be sufficiently "enlarged"; a theory with no place for the "Necessities of Nature" is unlikely to benefit public or private life.

The second incident in book II that should be recalled in connection with Gulliver's later rejection of humans is his encounter with a Brobdingnagian book of morality. This work, belonging to a "grave" governess, runs tritely "through all the usual Topicks of *European* moralists," lamenting the weakness of the human animal "in his own Nature" and arguing that things could not always have been so bad: in former days there were giants. Gulliver's conclusion here seems fully Swift's. "For my own Part, I could not avoid reflecting, how universally this Talent was spread of drawing Lectures in Morality, or indeed

from dung") is meant to voice orthodox Christian acceptance of the body, Fort says: "But surely there is too much self-mocking in this pious conclusion for it to cancel out the strong gnostic loathing of the flesh which permeates the rest of the poem. Swift holds onto this orthodox view of the body, but by a thread" (p. 11). Gnosticism in this sense seems to me present regularly in Swift's work but as a target rather than a position.

rather Matter of Discontent and repining, from the Quarrels we raise with Nature. And, I believe upon a strict Enquiry, those Quarrels might be shewn as ill-grounded among us, as they are among that People" (ch. 7, para. 9).

My contention here is threefold: that Gulliver in book IV errs radically by raising a quarrel with nature rather than a quarrel with history, that critics have tended to follow him, and that the error is a paradigm for misreadings of satire. Establishing the first of these may not be sufficient to gain belief for the second and third, but I will begin with it as necessary.

I have, in the first chapter, described Gulliver's mistake as a failure of metaphorical competency, that is, an inability to act on a powerful metaphor (man is like a Yahoo) without turning it into an equation (man is a Yahoo). It is instructive to understand his breakdown in book IV in terms of problems of likeness, as a failure of wit. Its nature is clearest through its aftereffects: Gulliver's bathetic retreat to his stables. Whatever one's verdict concerning the proportions of Yahooness in Mary Gulliver and the children, it is clear that Gulliver's horses are *not* Houyhnhnms and that in consorting with them Gulliver is imitating only the Houyhnhnms' incidentals. Any idea of significant imitation has by this point contracted to neurotic fetishism. But we can see the breakdown itself in Houyhnhnmland – in chapters 10 and 11, to be exact.

Toward the end of chapter 10, Gulliver accepts the Houyhnhnm expulsion order, calls himself a "miserable Yahoo," and has some hopes of returning to England where he will set about "celebrating the Praises of the renowned *Houyhnhnms*, and proposing their Virtues to the Imitation of Mankind" (para. 8). But a few pages later, the Houyhnhnms are seen as beyond imitation, except, perhaps, by the Gulliver now bound for a desert island: "For in such a Solitude as I desired, I could at least enjoy my own Thoughts, and reflect with Delight on the Virtues of those *inimitable Houyhnhnms*, without any Opportunity of degenerating into the vices and Corruptions of my own Species" (ch. 11, para. 2). It is in the brief space between this pedagogical resolution and its paradoxical cancellation that Gulliver, whose "Species" he takes for Yahoo, makes his boat of Yahoo skins, stops its chinks with "*Yahoos* Tallow," and – lest there be any doubt as to whether he finds or kills the requisite number of his new brethren – sews his sail with the tender skins of the young, "the youngest I could get" (ch. 10, paras. 12–13). In a book of so many ironies, it needs to be remembered that Gulliver becomes a murderer, by his lights, midway between his hopes of imitating the Houyhnhnms and his decision to remember them as *inimitable*, thus somehow avoiding the corruption of his own species.

Gulliver displaces what should be a quarrel with history into a useless quarrel with nature in so far as he becomes obsessed with how humans are made rather than with what humans have made. For Gulliver and for many readers, fixation on the human form leads to "stable" truths about the "race of Yahoos" or the "human predicament" – sonorous, distant, safely beyond change. But for the satirist, the issue of what humans have made is more to the point because that is the area of historical variability and responsibility for improvement. The metaphor of human as Yahoo is telling and insistent; but it is finally powerful only when its limits are kept in sight. And Swift, if not Gulliver, insists on the *otherness* of the ahistorical Yahoos even as he uses the Yahoo figure to compel attention. Without belaboring the fact that the Yahoos have no language – a difference that occasions surprisingly little comment from literary critics – let us take a simple instance of Gulliver's equation of Yahoo and human (his Yahoomanism). At the end of his discourse on European wars, Gulliver explains to his Houyhnhnm master that "a Soldier is a *Yahoo* hired to kill in cold Blood as many of his own Species, who have never offended him, as possibly he can" (ch. 5, para. 4). The term Yahoo needs to be seen as something of a catachresis here, because the operative word is the verb that moves so much modern political economy, "hired." The irreducible definition, then, is not "a Soldier is a Yahoo" but "a Soldier is a Yahoo *hired*" – as literal Yahoos cannot be.

It is not accurate to say, as some critics have, that Swift's definition reduces warfare by removing it from any cultural context that would give it meaning.[25] On the contrary, Swift puts warfare *in* a political and institutional context (language, money, contracts, nationalism, and so on) in order to analyze it as something more historically particular than, for example, man's inhumanity to man. That a human can be hired to kill others – or that a lawyer will prove that black is white or white is black as he is "paid" – may reflect on human aptitudes but it reflects on them politically. Presumably, humans could be hired to do otherwise, economic arrangements could be altered, military expenditures could be reduced. The point is not whether these are seen as probabilities but whether they are inscribed as possibilities. In order to

---

[25] See Everett Zimmerman, *Swift's Narrative Satires* (Ithaca: Cornell University Press, 1983), 151, and Martin Price, *Swift's Rhetorical Art* (New Haven: Yale University Press, 1953), 99.

be possibilities, they must be cast as historical rather than natural facts. If the historical is suppressed, subsumed as "natural," the perspective is likely to be sentimental rather than satiric, as in Sterne's reflection on soldiering in *Tristram Shandy*. Separating the "miseries of war" from the soldier's personal conduct, Uncle Toby concludes the "apologetical oration" on his vocation as follows:

For what is war? what is it, Yorick, when fought as ours has been, upon principles of *liberty*, and upon principles of *honour* – what is it, but the getting together of quiet and harmless people, with their swords in their hands, to keep the ambitious and turbulent within bounds? And heaven is my witness, brother Shandy, that the pleasure I have taken in these things – and that infinite delight, in particular, which has attended my sieges in my bowling-green, has arose within me, and I hope in the corporal too, from the consciousness we both had, that in carrying them on, we were answering the great ends of our creation.

(vol. vi, ch. 32)

The opposition is not between political writing and apolitical writing, clearly, but between exposed and suppressed politics. In Swift's text, the evil is historically specific, a piece of modern European economic and cultural history. For Sterne, it appears as nature rather than history and thus, to return to the critics, as a "grief" rather than a "grievance." I put it this way to suggest why the tendency to "universalize" satire is a problem of substance rather than mere verbal slippage. One can regard universalization as little more than critical hyperbole, a state of academic enthusiasm in which "universal" is essentially an honorific term that means "praiseworthy." But I think it has become increasingly clear, especially through feminist criticism, that "universal" is not an apolitical term, any more than is "man." Praising even so aggressively historical a mode of writing as satire for "transcending" historical specificity amounts to praising all literature as expression (essentially) above historical implication; for, to paraphrase Johnson on dramatic credulity, the person who imagines this of satire may surely imagine more.

Is it not probable that praising satire's universality is as misguided as commending great works of regionalism for not being regional, like saying, for example, that the South is only incidental to the power of Faulkner's novels? We could use, in the discussion of satire, a concept of "*temporal* regionalism." Such a concept might help make room for historical contingency. It might help us avoid the perversity of arguing, say, that the poem Pope called *One Thousand Seven Hundred and Thirty Eight* is good to the extent that it is not about the late 1730s. Finally, criticism would also be helped by regarding satire not as the exceptional case in literature but as a reasonably normative place from which to develop a theory of literature. This much, at any rate, is what I have hoped to suggest by the claim that "satire is art, only more so": namely, that all that has been said about its rhetorical basis, its referential claim, its historical occasion, and its requirement that we abandon "literary" mystifications in order to read it fully – that all of this may be true of other literary modes, if perhaps less so.

Conclusion

Because this study is an attempt to explain how and why I think several works of the late seventeenth and early eighteenth century matter collectively and currently in literary education, an excursion into pedagogical autobiography may be candid rather than self-indulgent. Increasingly over the past decade I have found myself responding to various questions about the interpretation of literature which come roughly to a single question. Typically, "the" question is posed by a genuinely troubled undergraduate, who has read or heard enough about recent critical theory to know or suspect some of the following: that thematic or existential interpretations are now often regarded as naive or nostalgic, that "ethical" or "humanist" criticism may be seen as overly exclusive of some groups and overly flattering to others, and that literary texts are considered by many to be essentially self-referential and "undecidable," as reflections of or on the problems of expression. In some form and at some point, then, he or she asks: "Are we supposed to think that literature is about life or about language?" Not liking the alternatives, but trying to honor the broad terms of the question, I have taken to replying that "literature is about life in language."

Replying rather than answering, because the reply immediately raises other questions. As noted at the beginning of the last chapter, we seem to be living in an age (or "age"?) of quotation marks, and it is likely that the late twentieth-century student will have put some into the question while asking it: "Is literature about 'life' or about language?" Readers of this book will probably have already inserted them around "literature" as well, so that it has become "Is that which we agree to call 'literature' about that which we agree to call 'life' or about language?" But of course as soon as one spells it out that way there is nothing inevitable about leaving "language" unmarked. We may be initially inclined to do so not only because it is a more specific term than "life" but also because "language" is a privileged term these days. In fact, "language" can easily operate as a personification in structuralist and post-structuralist discussions; Scholes notes, for example, that Culler describes language as establishing "arbitrary relationships between signifiers of *its own choosing* on the one hand, and signifieds of *its own choosing* on the other."[1]

The same quotation marks that come into the question would have to invade the reply, of course. "'Literature' is about 'life' in 'language.'" Unless one could satisfactorily define all three terms (and I cannot) this statement will be more slogan than solution. I will try, however, to limit two of the operative terms somewhat in order to suggest where the formulation is meant to point. First, "literature" may be regarded here as a "*functional* rather than *ontological*" term (a possibility Terry Eagleton raises before retreating to a dogmatic denial that literature exists, with or without quotation marks); in other words, what we call literature is a body of texts that are read and discussed, for institutional rather than natural reasons, in "literary" ways.[2] The second term that can be restricted is "language." There is no need here to use it metaphorically or to mean anything more than written utterances, some of which may be represented as recorded spoken utterances.

The meaning of life will have to wait for some wiser book than this in which to reveal itself. For now, "life in language" simply attempts to dissolve the immediate opposition implicit in the original question ("real" life versus language use). It points first to the fact that language is the medium of literature, that literature is "in language" as one might say photography is "in light." Beyond this obvious fact, however, "life in language" should suggest that literary works tend to use language conspicuously *and* that such works tend to call attention to the linguistic situation of characters (including narrators), who talk, listen, read, write, and in general think in words. To say that characters in literature are linguistically constituted means, first, that they are only words on a page, and this much is true of mountains or restaurants in literature; but it means also that they exist for readers only as producers and products of words. This claim need not lead to

---

[1] Robert Scholes, *Textual Power: Literary Theory and the Teaching of English* (New Haven: Yale University Press, 1985), 88; Scholes, quoting Culler's *Ferdinand de Saussure* (New York: Penguin Books, 1977), 15, has supplied the italics.

[2] Eagleton, *Literary Theory: An Introduction* (University of Minnesota Press, 1983), 9; by p. 204, however, Eagleton seems to conclude that the earlier distinction between "functional" and "ontological" status is equal to "recognizing that literature is an illusion."

disregarding inarticulate characters, but it does entail taking seriously their situation within language. If literary works do not *always* propose that "life in language" is the only life worth living, they do propose that no other is available.

If the notion of "life in language" is to do more than cheerfully evade the question of "life" *or* "language" ("Both," says the teacher, carrying a book to the window), it must allow for rethinking the terms rather than merely juggling them. As alternatives, "life" and "language" are static reifications: the former implies unchanging human hopes, fears, and so on, while the latter implies invariable problems of signification, ambiguity, misreading, and so forth. In either case, the discussion is likely to tend toward universals. "Life" suggests that all actions and attitudes are interesting as illuminating the "human condition." "Language" suggests that all utterances and gestures are to be referred back to the omnipresent "system" or "structure" of signification: texts, so to speak, are all out on *parole* from the "prison-house" of *langue*. But against these synchronic alternatives, then, "life in language" should point to an irreducibly historical range of activity, with "life" meaning people's lives (not a monolithic "condition" or "predicament") and "language" meaning a dia-chronic construction of human beings. If "language" is always fundamentally plural, an accumulation of changing historical develop-ments, variable relationships, dialogues and ideologies, so is "life."

These observations, if true, should apply more or less equally to literature of various periods. What is their particular point in relation to the linguistically constructed "life" of Augustan literature?

I began this selective map of the period by concentrating on a minor narrative mode, the character progress, that seems to be a peculiar feature of its terrain. The mode is not an aberration within the period, sharing as it does many of the more general comic, satiric, and epigrammatic tendencies of the age. It is also "of" the age in its bodily emphasis, its miniaturization – compressing long lives into twenty-line careers, for example – and its materialist insistence upon the fact of death. Whether the character progress receded *because* the novel matured remains debatable; but it is clear that its comic fatality, its playing with determinism and death, had begun by the later eighteenth century to seem as uncongenial as the earlier era's satiric scatology. Samuel Johnson is rarely a mere barometer, but one senses something more than personal anxiety in his repudiation of both Gay's "trifling" with death and Pope's and Swift's shared "delight in ideas physically impure." (See above, pp. 50, 91.) These matters were ceasing to be witty.

But its imaginative accommodation of "these matters" is much of why Augustan literature matters. Scatological imagery is not everywhere even in that portion of late seventeenth-century and early eighteenth-century writing we have been concerned with, nor does it disappear entirely from later literature. But Johnson is right in regarding its emphasis as somewhat "dated" by his time. If it is difficult to imagine the mock-epiphany that "Celia shits" orchestrated by anyone other than Swift, it is even more difficult to envision a "Swift" writing *Cassinus and Peter* in another era. The body's excretions expressed in colloquial language and in Brobdingnagian close-up are among Swift's special properties, but they are part of the same current that flows from *Mac Flecknoe*'s Pissing Alley and fecal Thames to Pope's later satires. Pope sometimes uses his subject "matter" less directly than Swift, emphasizing excrement most when pretending to be above it (as in the Virgilian imitation and notes in book II of the *Dunciad*) or by dulling the visual image to sharpen the aural imagination. When Donne's vehement characterization of a plagiarist – "...though it be knowne / The meate was mine, / Th'excrement is his owne" – cools into Pope's elegance – "Sense, past thro' him, no longer is the same, / For food digested takes another name" – the reader of course hears the now inevitable noun.[3]

A less coercive and more complexly suggestive periphrasis occurs in Pope's imitation of Horace's *Satire II. ii*, where the counsels on temperance include the couplet, "On morning wings how active springs the Mind, / That leaves the load of yesterdays behind" (lines 81–82). Although often unremarked, the final phrase seems clearly to refer to the bowels' regularity as well as to human resiliency. The lines are in themselves a compressed argument of wit, keeping together areas of experience that most later writing would insistently put asunder.

If there is something dated about such junctures there is also something historically vital. Milan Kundera's haunting meditation, in *The Unbearable Lightness of Being*, on modern "kitsch" begins from the "fact that until recently the word 'shit' appeared in print as s——." This suppression did not originate, Kundera argues, in merely moral disapproval but in the metaphysical construction of a "world in which shit is denied and everyone acts as though it did not exist. This aesthetic

---

[3] Donne, *Satyre II*, lines 29–30 in *The Satires, Epigrams and Verse Letters*, ed. W. Milgate (Oxford: Clarendon Press, 1967); Pope, *The Second Satire of Dr. John Donne... Versifyed*, lines 33–34.

ideal is called *kitsch*."[4] Kundera's essayistic interlude is not philological history, but it suggests the value of an earlier, alternative aesthetic:

"Kitsch" is a German word born in the middle of the sentimental nineteenth century, and from German it entered all Western languages. Repeated use, however, has obliterated its original metaphysical meaning: kitsch is the absolute denial of shit, in both the literal and the figurative senses of the word; kitsch excludes everything from its purview which is essentially unacceptable in human existence.

The nineteenth century's denial of defecation is essentially for Kundera a denial of mortality: "kitsch is a folding screen set up to curtain off death." Its modern extensions include the twentieth century's purges and prisons and the ghostlier prison of a wholly sanitized culture, an ideal which, if realized, would create a "world of grinning idiots" where an artist "would have nothing to say, she would die of horror within a week."

The point is not to remake the Augustans into prophets of the gulag ("a septic tank used by totalitarian kitsch to dispose of its refuse") but rather to attend at once to the period's peculiarity and pertinence. "Life" as we know it may be everywhere and always constituted in language; but the available language, like available light, is not the same in all places. Otherwise, of course, there would be no reason to leave home.

In the last chapter I argued that a reluctance to give much weight to historical particularity leads to neglect or distortion of much Augustan literature and especially of satiric writing. Anxious to keep literature "pure" of politics and rhetoric, critics often rush to find "universal" rather than historical meanings, repeating as they do so Gulliver's tendency to raise "quarrels with nature" instead of quarrels with history. I want now to try to put this problem in more historically particular but philosophical terms by returning briefly to Berkeley's criticism of "abstraction," discussed in chapter four. Berkeley, it will be recalled, attacked the "doctrine of abstraction" as the founding error both of confused ethics, where belief in virtues or vices detached from particular persons and actions has "rendered morality difficult," and of mechanistic materialism, where it has underwritten the idea of "corporeal substance" independent of perception. More specifically,

---

[4] Milan Kundera, *The Unbearable Lightness of Being*, trans. Michael Henry Heim (New York: Harper and Row, 1984), 248; the quotations immediately following are from pp. 248, 252, 253.

he attacked Locke's account of abstract ideas as contradictory, resting on a false view of how the imagination works and on a misunderstanding of how humans generalize through language. Speakers do not, he argues, generalize by using a word to designate an inconceivable abstraction but by using it to combine "several particular ideas, any one of which it indifferently suggests to the mind." Berkeley insists that his analysis does not deny the existence of general ideas but only of "*abstract* general ideas."

The distinction between general and abstract ideas, invoked earlier to comment on Swift's characterization of the difference between Brobdingnagian and Laputan philosophy, may also be useful in thinking about problems in the interpretation of satire. The relevant analogy is between Berkeley's "abstraction" and the critic's "universality." *General* ideas will be useful, even unavoidable, in studying satire; *universal* ideas are neither inevitable nor helpful. There is no reason to deny that works we continue to talk about are ones we can reformulate in general terms, that, prose and poetry alike, they are "news that stays news." The point is that the terms of the reformulation are general *historical* terms, not universal ones unrelated to historical contingency, continuity, or commentary.

The search for universals in literature – whether in the ethical categories of "life" and the "human condition" or in the formalist categories of "language" and "textuality" – seems often to involve not only an abstraction from historical communities in the overtly political sense but also from communities of historically situated readers.[5] While I believe that denial of historical community generally leads to critical entanglement, I want simply to propose here that it does so very conspicuously in criticism of Augustan literature, where the social relationships of writers and readers are themselves conspicuous. Johnson's discomfort with the wit of Gay and Pope, for example, seems closely connected to a longing for the "stability of truth," for propositions not dependent upon rhetorical variables. This is not to ignore Johnson's own rhetorical power or his many appeals to popular approval in his criticism. But in thinking about Johnson's distance from the wit of the early eighteenth-century writers it may be instructive to recall his dismissal of Pope's definition of wit in favor of a more

[5] Robert Weimann describes the synchronic emphasis of structuralism as having culminated in "that triple abstraction from the 'external linguistic' reality: an abstraction from (1) both the speakers and the contexts or situations of speaking, from (2) the subject matter or object of discourse, and finally from (3) the history of language"; see *Structure and Society in Literary History* (Baltimore: Johns Hopkins University Press, 1984), 146–47.

"philosophical" consideration of wit, "abstracted from its effect upon the hearer." From the early years of the century, Berkeley might ask (rhetorically) whether a "nicer strain of abstraction" were possible, since "for anyone to pretend to a notion of entity or existence, *abstracted* from *spirit* and *idea*, from perceiving and being perceived, is, I suspect, a downright repugnance and trifling with words."[6] Whatever problems one might see elsewhere in the philosophy of Berkeley's *Principles* and his works on vision, in respect to writing it seems to be Berkeley rather than Johnson who kicks the stone on behalf of common sense. With its insistent appeal to "sensible objects," "particular ideas," and their perceivers, Augustan literature is inconceivable, then and now, apart from people who hear its trees falling. Insofar as much of our contemporary critical perspective has remained neo-Romantic, the author of *The New Theory of Vision* might help students of the Augustan period toward a new vision of theory.

The connection between current neo-Romanticism and the desire to find universals in textuality can be seen in de Man's influential account of irony, "The Rhetoric of Temporality."[7] De Man is actually describing Romantic irony *as opposed to* earlier eighteenth-century practice, although he is never quite as explicit about that distinction as he is in the discussion of allegory (the other half of the same essay), where Romantic allegory is seen as related only oppositionally to the "sensualistic analogism" of "the baroque and the rococo." Much as genuine allegory is seen as "more intimate" and "less formal" in its "unveiling of an authentically temporal destiny" than the "exterior" associationism preceding it, so genuine (Romantic) ironic language "splits the subject into an empirical self that exists in a state of inauthenticity and a self that exists only in the form of a language that asserts the knowledge of this inauthenticity."

Before indicating how the mystifying "universals" of de Man's account do not accommodate Augustan writing, I want to acknowledge the suggestiveness of his analysis of ironic language and its applicability to some – notably, the most nearly "tragic – parts of important

[6] *A Treatise concerning the Principles of Human Knowledge*, paras. 5 and 81, quoted from *The Works of George Berkeley*, vol. ii, ed. A.A. Luce and T.E. Jessop (London: Thomas Nelson and Sons, 1949).

[7] "The Rhetoric of Temporality," since collected in de Man's *Blindness and Insight* (1971; rev. edn. Minneapolis: University of Minnesota Press, 1983), first appeared in Charles Singleton (ed.), *Interpretation* (Baltimore: Johns Hopkins University Press, 1969), 173–209, from which I quote; the references in the remainder of the para. are from Singleton, pp. 188–90 and 197.

eighteenth-century works. De Man's "absolute irony" may be misnamed, but his description of it could enrich criticism of *A Tale of a Tub* and the *Dunciad*:

absolute irony is a consciousness of madness, itself the end of all consciousness; it is a consciousness of non-consciousness, a reflection of madness from the inside of madness itself. But this reflection is made possible only by the double structure of ironic language: the ironist invents a form of himself that is "mad" but that does not know its own madness; he then proceeds to reflect on his madness thus objectified.

This description is undoubtedly a more probing psychology of irony than traditional "inversion" theories (blame by praise, for example). Despite its subtle windings, however, the quest for an "absolute" point toward which all irony tends is ultimately ahistorical.

De Man's theory is ahistorical in two ways. These are related to each other and both are related to why the theory obscures more than it can clarify in the broader current of Augustan irony that is not primarily concerned with the authenticity or inauthenticity of the isolated mind, a current that of course includes much of the *Dunciad* and *A Tale of a Tub* as well. De Man's theory is ahistorical in denying the importance of historical criticism made *through* irony (attacks on historical referents) and in denying the possibility of historical criticism *of* irony. These denials come together in de Man's explanation of why he constructed a history of allegory (the Romantics' strenuous "renunciation" of the preceding generations in order to "rediscover" the true allegorical tradition of the Renaissance) but why he finds it inappropriate to discuss irony historically: "in the case of irony one has to start out from the structure of the trope itself, taking one's cue from texts that are demystified and, to a large extent, themselves ironical. For that matter, the target of their irony is very often the *claim to speak about human matters as if they were facts of history*" (my italics). Probably this is a *re*mystification even of Romantic irony; certainly it does not character-ize Augustan irony. Gulliver's error and, as I have been arguing, the error which critics of Swift often repeat is precisely the opposite: the claim to speak about historical matters as if they were universally "human." And again, whether the abstract universal is seized under the banner of Life (the "human predicament") or Language (here the putative "structure of the trope itself") does not much matter. It is hard to see how as a general principle the belief that in "irony we are dealing not with the history of an error but with a problem that exists within the self" would leave any room in literature for historical particulars *or* generalities. De Man's "Rhetoric of Temporality" turns out to be neither rhetorical in a recognizable political sense nor temporal in a historical sense beyond the self's repetitions.

In at least one respect de Man is well in the mainstream of modern definitions of irony, which tend to distinguish it from satire on the grounds that irony is less "militant" than satire, less an attack on "external" circumstances, more diffusely self-reflexive. This opposition, too, seems to grow out of Romantic values and theory – as anxiety is fear without an object so irony is criticism without an objectified other – but it remains useful nonetheless. We do need a relatively simple way of differentiating a mode of writing that depicts a condition "there" as remediable from one that depicts a condition "here" as inescapable. According to this distinction, Brecht satirizes, Beckett ironizes. The opposition has, however, the defect as well as the merit of simplicity; it tends to cast irony as a primarily linguistic affair and satire as primarily a matter of attitude. De Man speaks of "ironic language" as one would not attempt to speak of "satiric language." But since so much of what could reasonably be called ironic in Augustan literature occurs in works that are satiric – which is to say that we are not likely to think of its irony as essentially concerned with dilemmas of subjectivity – viewing satire and irony oppositionally may simply frustrate historical understanding.[8]

A more inclusive way of thinking about irony would need to continue to put irony "in language" but at the same time allow for the "external" referentiality normally associated with satire. To do both of these things one needs consistently to conceive of language as socially temporal – a public process as well as public property – and as fundamentally dialogic. One would then be looking not for the "structure of the trope itself" but for a relationship of utterances that makes irony possible. Such an approach is suggested by the "pragmatic-rhetorical" theory of Dan Sperber and Deirdre Wilson, who conclude that irony is in fact not a trope at all. In "Irony and the Use-Mention Distinction" (1981) and later in *Relevance: Communication and Cognition* (1986), the authors describe irony in effect as a kind of tacit quotation. According to this view the speaker who says "What a lovely day for a picnic!" while getting drenched in a rainstorm is being ironic not because she says the opposite of what she means but because her remark is an "echoic" utterance. It echoes a statement made

[8] W.B. Carnochan speaks of the "almost convertible relationship between Augustan satire and Augustan irony"; see *Lemuel Gulliver's Mirror for Man* (Berkeley and Los Angeles: University of California Press, 1968), 167.

earlier (in simple "use") to the effect that it would be a good day for a picnic. In cases of "mention" one expresses a belief "about" an utterance rather than "by means of it."[9]

This distinction is neater in logic than in literature, but the general characterization of irony as a kind of "echoic allusion" (*Relevance*, p. 239) is immediately helpful, I think, because it accommodates the intuitive perception that there is something "behind" irony – rather than necessarily "under" it – and that the something is the language used previously by others. Unlike metaphor, for example, which can be thought of as a monologic trope, irony presupposes an ongoing dialogue. "Metaphor plays on the relationship between the propositional form of an utterance and the speaker's thought; irony plays on the relationship between the speaker's thought and a thought of someone other than the speaker" (*Relevance*, p. 243). More particularly, thinking of irony as a form of allusion allows us to grant (with Geoffrey Hartmann, for example) that in literature the words "call attention to themselves as words" without implying that they therefore stop being literary when they call attention to anything else. The words emphasize "themselves" precisely because they are in dialogue with words prior to the text.

This pragmatic reorientation, which entails more attention to speakers consciously situated in communities, in turn is useful in reading Augustan literature because the period's most characteristic irony consists in the recognition that priority is impossible, that as a writer one stands in a long literary history and as a person in a crowd of competing voices.[10] We can speak theologically and say that allusion is the readiest way of acknowledging the Fall, so long as we do not presume that the Fall was felt to be continuous. (It is not true that even at their most "Ancient" Pope or Swift thought that 1730 was necessarily "worse" than 1710, which in turn was worse than 1690, and so on, *ad Augustum*). A strong meaning of the Fall is simply that one is not Adam nor was meant to be, that one therefore cannot pretend to

---

[9] *Relevance: Communication and Cognition* (Cambridge, MA: Harvard University Press, 1986), 239; "Irony and the Use-Mention Distinction," in Peter Cole (ed.), *Radical Pragmatics* (New York: Academic Press, 1981), 302.

[10] Julia Kristeva suggests that irony characteristically includes a relation to precedent: "For Rabelais, Swift, Lautremont, and Joyce are ironic only when we posit them (or when they posit themselves) as subjects tapping a meaning that is always already old, always already out of date, as funny as it is ephemeral." See *Desire in Language: A Semiotic Approach to Literature and Art* (New York: Columbia University Press, 1980), 109. In the case of Augustan authors I would stress that "they posit themselves" as ironic latecomers through allusion.

use a language, of the sort Locke imagined for Judgment, innocent of allusion. In more secular terms, the use of allusion that Locke associated with Wit can be seen as a recognition that language is always (already) intertextual. This recognition is underscored in Augustan literature by the prevalence of characters who fail to recognize that others have preceded them. Typical "exposures" of such characters occur when they allude without knowing it, echoing Milton in mock-heroics, or mouthing "choicest commonplaces," as in the character progresses with which we began. At such moments, Augustan texts argue that both writers and agents often have only two alternatives, to use their wit through allusion or to allude unwittingly.

The difficulty of dissociating satire from irony and irony from allusion in Augustan literature emphasizes the usefulness of the vague but inclusive term "wit." I have returned to that word more regularly than to any other in this book because the Augustans employed it so often and because it is elastic enough to include anything from manifest learning and intelligence to quickness in speech, a play of visual and stylistic perspectives, and a display of artificiality. In the works considered here all of these meanings involve recognitions I have referred to as materialist: recognitions of the materiality of the body as existing in physical space and biological time, of the materiality of the relation of writers and readers in a context of shared particularity, and everywhere of the materiality of language as the composition of human beings within the socially temporal and spatial world called history.

The last of these materialist recognitions is in a sense first as well, because "wit written" in Augustan writing begins and ends with an acceptance of artifice, of the making of language into common property – shared "propriety" – and the construction of works that show how and where they were made. I have described wit earlier, and very approximately, as verbal formulations that give pleasure by striking readers as at once "natural" and "artificial; I have tried, too, to relate this double effect to the paradoxical ideal of art concealing art, since in Augustan practice that ideal also means art calling attention to art. Parading one's artifice can of course strike merely as preciosity or, to use the period's term for it, "foppery." Typically, however, Augustan writers seem to see greater dangers of affectation in presenting one's production, or oneself, as a force of nature. For all the praise of "easy and natural" writing, naturalness in literature is seen as institution-alized labor, the product of "Art, not Chance" (in the construction Pope liked enough to use twice), "As those move easiest who have learn'd to dance" (*Essay on Criticism*, lines 362–63; Horatian *Epistle II. ii*, lines 178–79).

The arguments of and about wit in the late seventeenth and early eighteenth century do not reduce all wit to allusion, but they do imply its centrality. Through quotations, echoes, invocations of clichés, historical symmetries, and stylistic impersonations they emphasize that literary works are parts of a continual dialogue and are made out of available material. In our time, when "writerly" texts (Barthes's *scriptible* versus *lisible* works) that call attention to their own constructedness are felt to be more critical and less mystifying than "readerly" texts that pose as natural representations, there should be much to learn from authors who, to echo Matthew Prior, do but compose in language and are amused when others pretend to create.

Index